Changing Higher Education for a Changing World

Bloomsbury Higher Education Research

Series editor: Simon Marginson

Bloomsbury's Higher Education Research Series provides the evidence-based academic output of the world's leading research centre on higher education, the ESRC/HEFCE Centre for Global Higher Education (CGHE) in the UK. CGHE, with its central office at the University of Oxford, is a research partnership of 15 British and international universities, financed by £8.1 million in funding (2015-2023) from the UK Economic and Social Research Council, partner universities and other sources. The core focus of CGHE's research work and of the Bloomsbury Higher Education Research Series is higher education, especially *the future of higher education in the changing global landscape.*

National higher education systems take in 40 per cent of all young people worldwide and are engines of technological and social innovation. Beyond North America and Europe higher education and science are growing very rapidly in Asia, Africa and Latin America. Monographs in the series highlight local, national and international aspects of higher education, aiming for worldwide readership. Topics range from teaching and learning and technologies; to research and science; national system design; the public role of universities; access, equity and social stratification; governance and management; and the cross-border mobility of people, institutions, ideas and knowledge.

Much of CGHE's the work is global and comparative in scale, drawing lessons from higher education in many different countries and authors based in the UK, United States, Australia, Ireland, China, Hong Kong, Japan, South Africa and much of Europe, including the postdoctoral and doctoral scholars who will be tomorrow's research leaders in this field. The Bloomsbury Higher Education Research Series is at the cutting edge of world research on higher education.

Changing Higher Education for a Changing World

Edited by
Claire Callender, William Locke
and Simon Marginson

BLOOMSBURY ACADEMIC
LONDON • NEW YORK • OXFORD • NEW DELHI • SYDNEY

BLOOMSBURY ACADEMIC
Bloomsbury Publishing Plc
50 Bedford Square, London, WC1B 3DP, UK
1385 Broadway, New York, NY 10018, USA
29 Earlsfort Terrace, Dublin 2, Ireland

BLOOMSBURY, BLOOMSBURY ACADEMIC and the Diana logo are trademarks of Bloomsbury Publishing Plc

First published in Great Britain 2020
This paperback edition published in 2022

Series design by Adriana Brioso
Cover image © Setthasith Wansuksri/EyeEm/Getty Images

A catalogue record for this book is available from the British Library.

A catalog record for this book is available from the Library of Congress.

Library of Congress Control Number: 2020940638

ISBN: HB: 978-1-3501-0841-7
PB: 978-1-3501-9694-0
ePDF: 978-1-3501-0842-4
eBook: 978-1-3501-0843-1

Series: Bloomsbury Higher Education Research

Typeset by Deanta Global Publishing Services, Chennai, India

Contents

Illustrations

Figures

Tables

Contributors

Paul Ashwin is Professor of Higher Education in the Department of Educational Research at Lancaster University, UK, coordinating editor for the international journal *Higher Education*, and co-editor of the Bloomsbury book series *Understanding Student Experiences of Higher Education*. His research focuses on teaching, learning and curriculum practices in higher education and how these practices are shaped by higher education policies.

Vikki Boliver is Professor of Sociology at Durham University, UK. Her primary research focus is on social class and ethnic inequalities of access to elite forms of higher education.

Claire Callender is Professor of Higher Education Policy at UCL Institute of Education, University College London, UK, where she is Deputy Director of the ESRC/OFSRE Centre for Global Higher Education and Professor of Higher Education Studies at Birkbeck, University of London, UK. Her research focuses primarily on undergraduate student funding and associated issues.

Jennifer M. Case is Professor and Head of the Department of Engineering Education at Virginia Polytechnic Institute and State University (Virginia Tech), USA, and she was previously Professor in the Department of Chemical Engineering at the University of Cape Town, South Africa. Her work is especially focused on the student experience of learning, teaching and curriculum.

Bruce Chapman holds the Sir Roland Wilson Chair of Economics in the College of Business and Economics at the Australian National University, Australia. He has published on a range of issues including income-contingent loans, the application of income-contingent financing as an instrument of social and economic reform, long-term unemployment, the meaning of job flows data, the economics of crime, the economics of cricket, fertility, marital separation and government as risk manager.

KC Deane is a doctoral candidate at the Center for the Study of Higher and Postsecondary Education at the University of Michigan, USA. Her research focuses on higher education in the United States, specifically state-led efforts to improve outcomes at public two- and four-year colleges, state and federal funding for higher education, and federal student loan repayment.

Lorraine Dearden is Professor of Economics and Social Statistics at University College London, UK, and Research Fellow at the Institute for Fiscal Studies, where she has focused on higher education finance in the UK for the last fifteen years. Her research covers a wide range of issues, including the impact of education and training on labour market outcomes and company performance; evaluation of education and labour market policies; conditional cash transfers for school students; the evaluation of childcare, home learning environment and early years policies on children's and parents' outcomes; the determinants and impact of early childhood adversity; ethnic inequality and discrimination; the determinants of the demand for different types of schooling; intergenerational income and education mobility; and programme evaluation issues and methods.

Stephen L. DesJardins is Marvin W. Peterson Collegiate Professor of Education, School of Education, and Professor in the Gerald R. Ford School of Public Policy at the University of Michigan, USA. His research interests include student transitions from high school to college, what happens to students once they enrol in college, the economics of postsecondary education, and applying new statistical techniques to the study of these issues.

Dung Doan is Research Fellow at the Research School of Economics at the Australian National University, Australia, and a Research Associate with the Centre for Global Higher Education. Her current research focuses on improving the measurement of repayment burdens of student loans and designing income-contingent loans in Korea, the United States and Vietnam; previously she worked on poverty, spatial inequality and child malnutrition in the South Asia region.

Ariane de Gayardon is a research associate in the ESRC/OFSRE Centre for Global Higher Education at the UCL Institute of Education, University College London, UK, and Associate Editor of the *Journal of Studies in International Education*. Her research focuses on international higher education financing and its consequences for access and equity.

Stephen Gorard is Professor of Education and Public Policy in the School of Education at Durham University, UK. His work concerns the robust evaluation of education as a lifelong process, focused on issues of equity and effectiveness.

Francis Green is Professor of Work and Education Economics in UCL Institute of Education, University College London, UK, where he works in the ESRC/OFSRE Centre for Global Higher Education and at the LLAKES Centre. His research focuses on education, skills, the graduate labour market and the quality of work.

Golo Henseke is a Senior Research Fellow at the UCL Institute of Education, University College London, UK, working as an applied economist at the ESRC/OFSRE Centre for Global Higher Education and the Centre for Research on Learning and Life Chances. His research focuses on issues surrounding skills utilization, skills development and their intersection with job quality.

Stephen A. Hunt is a research associate in the ESRC/OFSRE Centre for Global Higher Education. His current research focuses on alternative providers of higher education; he has also conducted investigations of risk perception, trust and risk communication.

Eileen Kennedy is a senior research associate at UCL Knowledge Lab, University College London, UK, where her research focuses on the potential of scaled up online learning to transform higher education.

Janja Komljenovic is a Lecturer in Higher Education at Lancaster University, UK. She is interested in the diversity and complexity of markets in and around universities, including the variety of actors that have entered the sector, their strategies, ways of working, and consequences for higher education and societies at large.

Diana Laurillard is Professor of Learning with Digital Technologies at UCL Knowledge Lab, UK, where she leads research on digital design tools for teachers and scaling up online learning.

Nian C. Liu is Professor and Dean of the Graduate School of Education at Shanghai Jiao Tong University, China. His research interests include world-class universities and research universities, university evaluation and academic ranking, and globalization and internationalization of higher education.

William Locke is Professor and Director of the Melbourne Centre for the Study of Higher Education at the University of Melbourne, Australia, and Joint Editor of the journal *Policy Reviews in Higher Education*. His research interests include the governance and management of higher education institutions; the changing academic profession; higher education policy and policy-making; the influence of marketization and rankings systems on higher education institutions and systems.

Jan McArthur is Senior Lecturer in Education and Social Justice in the Department of Educational Research at Lancaster University, UK. Her research focuses on the achievement of greater social justice within and through higher education, spanning the purposes of higher education down to the daily practices of teaching, learning and assessment.

Simon Marginson is Professor of Higher Education at the University of Oxford, UK, Director of the ESRC/OFSRE Centre for Global Higher Education, Editor-in-Chief of the journal *Higher Education*, a lead researcher with the Institute of Education at the Higher School of Economics in Moscow and a professorial fellow of the University of Melbourne. His work is mostly focused on international and global aspects of higher education, the contributions of higher education, and higher education and social equality.

Vassiliki Papatsiba is Senior Lecturer and Director of the Centre for the Study of Higher Education in the School of Education at the University of Sheffield, UK. Her research focuses on internationalization in higher education and European academic mobility; international research collaboration, academic agendas of knowledge generation and public policies; and universities, their international and local networks.

Nadia Siddiqu is Associate Professor in the School of Education at Durham University, UK. Her research explores issues of equity in education with a particular focus on the evaluation of school-based learning interventions.

Lin Tian is a PhD candidate in the Center for World-Class Universities (CWCU) at Shanghai Jiao Tong University, China. Her research interests include functions of world-class universities and internationalization of higher education.

Xin Xu is an ESRC Postdoctoral Research Fellow in the ESRC/OFSRE Centre for Global Higher Education, Department of Education at the University of Oxford, UK. Her research mainly focuses on higher education policy, research on research, and international and comparative education.

Preface

This book is about higher education and the future development of that ever-growing sector of human activity, in the UK and across the world. It gathers together selected outcomes from the UK Economic and Social Research Council (ESRC)-supported Centre for Global Higher Education (CGHE) mostly reflecting work done in the 2017–19 period. CGHE is a partnership of six UK and nine international universities funded to carry out sixteen individual research projects on global, national and local higher education. CGHE's research on higher education and related topics – the sub-disciplinary field is usually titled 'higher education studies' – draws on a range of social science disciplines, primarily economics, sociology, political science and policy studies, anthropology, and learning theory in psychology. CGHE is one of the largest research centres in the world working on higher education as its topic area, and within this field it houses the most extensive programme of fundamental research with a longer-term horizon.

CGHE's full title is the 'ESRC/OFSRE Centre for Global Higher Education'. OFS refers to the UK Office for Students and RE to Research England. The predecessor body of the OFS and RE, the Higher Education Funding Council for England (HEFCE), played a key role in founding CGHE by financing part of the ESRC's grant for the work of the Centre.

The Centre began its funded research in November 2015 with a research programme covering most of the main issues and emerging trends in higher education (which in large part refers to degree-level programmes) in the UK and abroad: the growth and widening of participation in higher education; sustainable financing of higher education and tuition loans systems; student learning; digital applications to learning; graduate labour markets, new private sector providers; the public good role of higher education; university-industry links, higher education governance; the academic profession; international students and migration policy. The chapters in this book cover most of these issues and represent some of our mid-range findings (there are more findings and more books to come). Our distinctive approach has been to move beyond the nation-bound or region-bound character of most of the research that is done on higher education topics to pursue these issues on the local, national and global planes at the same time, and in association with a widely distributed international research network.

An important part of the Centre's agenda is building research impact, including advice to government and committees of the parliament in the UK, work with national and international organizations focused on higher and international education, and extensive engagement in public discussion. We have generated more than fifty published CGHE Working Papers, numerous CGHE Policy Briefings and CGHE Research Findings bulletins for broad dissemination. Impact-related work is by no means confined to the UK. The Centre's international researchers are active in their own national policy spaces and many members of the research team contribute in countries other than their own, especially in East Asia – a dynamic zone not only in relation to higher education and science themselves but also for research on higher education.

CGHE's starting set of issues all remain important to the future of higher education. At the same time, much has changed since November 2015. We have seen the June 2016 Brexit referendum in the UK, three prime ministers and five ministers for higher education in that country; a surge of populist politics in Europe and other parts of the world; the Trump presidency in the United States; the beginning of a protracted global struggle by the United States to 'contain' China; accelerating climate emergencies and unprecedented attacks on climate scientists; and growing tensions over migration in many countries that are affect all forms of mobility including academic travel and international students. As we finalised this book the COVID-19 pandemic hit. National and global politics are more unstable than they were in 2015 – just how much more unstable we will discover in the coming years. Higher education and research are staid by comparison but inevitably affected by a volatile political environment, which can lead either to neglect (in the UK many policy issues have been on hold since 2016) or to capricious political interventions to win votes or create scapegoats. In December 2018, in Hungary the Orbán government forced the Central European University to relocate from Budapest to Vienna in Austria.

Inevitably, our research and policy-related work have been nudged along by the changing setting. We have responded to new issues and trends as they have emerged in areas as tuition finance, graduate labour markets, international students, education and development, and academic freedom across the world. This has been possible because our research project list and research team cover a broad range of content areas and research expertise. Just before the main work of CGHE started in late 2015 we added a project on student/graduate pathways in South Africa. In early 2017 we added an ESRC project on Brexit and UK higher education, funded separately from the main Centre grant as part of the

ESRC's Brexit Priority Grant programme, led by UK in a Changing Europe. This entailed case studies and interviews concerning the consequences of Brexit, and institutional responses to it, in twelve higher education institutions in the four UK nations. The first data-based outcomes from the Brexit-related research are reported in Chapter 5 of this book.

If newly planning the Centre for Global Higher Education today we might be discussing possible project work on global research cooperation, which has grown by leaps and bounds, and a comparison of national research assessment processes; tertiary system design including relations between degree-level and sub-degree education and between universities, further education colleges and private higher education colleges; the interface between research universities and their regions/local communities in increasingly unequal societies; academic freedom in different nations; and perhaps the debates about science and about public truth. We will take up some of these issues after the first funding period ends in November 2020, as the ESRC has agreed to fund a Transition Centre CGHE until October 2023.

CGHE's full team of academic researchers in the UK as of November 2019 is as follows: at the University of Oxford Simon Marginson (CGHE Director) and Alis Oancea; at University College London (UCL) Institute of Education Claire Callender (CGHE Deputy Director), Vincent Carpentier, Francis Green, Diana Laurillard, Mike Shattock and Celia Whitchurch; at Lancaster University Paul Ashwin, Jana Komljenovic and Jan McArthur; at Sheffield University Vassiliki Papatsiba; at University of Bath Jurgen Enders; at Durham University Vikki Boliver. Claire Callender holds a joint appointment at UCL Institute of Education and Birkbeck, University of London. William Locke was a deputy director of CGHE at the UCL Institute of Education prior to moving to the University of Melbourne and Simon Marginson also previously worked at UCL Institute of Education. Gareth Parry, Peter Scott and James Wilsdon all previously served on CGHE's Research Management Committee.

The designated international researchers are Futao Huang at Hiroshima University in Japan, Nian Cai Liu at Shanghai Jiao Tong University in China, Ka Ho Mok at Lingnan University in Hong Kong, Bruce Chapman at the Australian National University, Jenni Case at Virginia Tech in the United States and formerly at the University of Cape Town in South Africa, Stephen DesJardins at the University of Michigan, Ellen Hazelkorn at Technological University Dublin in Ireland and Robert Tijssen at Leiden University in the Netherlands. CGHE is also well served by its past and present postdoc researchers, in UK and abroad, eight of whom figure as sole or joint authors in this book.

None of this would have been possible without the initial and ongoing support provided by the ESRC, including the care and attention of Joy Todd, Rebecca Griggs and Maria Sigala. The main 2015–2020 ESRC award supporting CGHE is ES/M010082/1, The Future of HE – Centre for Engaged Global Higher Education. Research discussed in this book was also supported under ES/R000166/1 (see Chapter 5) and ES/N009894/1 and NRF UID 98365 (see Chapter 15).

We are delighted to be working with Bloomsbury in the publication of the Bloomsbury Higher Education Research Series which was established to disseminate the work of the Centre. This is the second book in the series: the first, *The Governance of British Higher Education* by Mike Shattock and Aniko Horvath, based on case study work in the four UK nations, was released in October 2019. We gratefully thank Alison Baker, Maria Giovanna Brauzzi and Kim Brown at Bloomsbury for their professionalism, their cheerfulness and kindness and in the case of this book, their patience. We also thank the reviewers who helped us to tune the manuscript.

We are also grateful to Katharine Buckle and Ellie Gaspar who were Administrators of CGHE while the book was being put together and Anna Phillips and Trevor Treharne who were CGHE Communications Officers during that time. A highly professional, proactive and responsive communications function has been indispensable to CGHE's work. We also express our sincere gratitude to David Sweeney at Research England, Chris Millward at the Office for Students, Bob Burgess, chair of CGHE's Advisory Board, Nicola Brewer UCL's Vice-Provost (International) and the other members of the Advisory Board.

We also thank each other, and Claire and William thank Simon who has carried the larger burden in the putting together of this book.

Claire Callender, William Locke and Simon Marginson
London, Melbourne and Oxford
15 November 2019

Part I

Introduction

1

Higher Education in Fast Moving Times

Larger, Steeper, More Global and More Contested

Simon Marginson, Claire Callender and William Locke

Introduction

The rise and rise of higher education to a central role in modern life is a story yet to be fully told. Developments in artificial intelligence and biotechnology grab our attention. Discoveries of dinosaurs, archaeological sites, black holes and wandering asteroids are news. Anything and everything American presidents say on Twitter is important. The slower transformation of higher educated societies mostly slips under the radar.

Yet in historical terms the pace of change is not slow. Since 1990 the proportion of young people across the world entering some form of tertiary education has jumped from 14 to 38 per cent, almost two persons in every five, taking all countries – rich, middle income and poor – into the calculation (see Figure 1.1). The participation rate was rising at 1 per cent a year, making it 40 per cent in 2019. Most of these students enrol in the degree programmes often designated 'higher education' (UNESCO 2019).

The Growth of Tertiary and Higher Education

At the present pace of growth, by 2030 or soon after *half of all young people everywhere will enter tertiary education*, with half of those gaining a first degree.

According to the UNESCO Institute of Statistics data the gross enrolment ratio in tertiary education is growing rapidly in every region in the world except those where it is already close to universal levels. It exceeds 50 per cent of the age group in Asia-Pacific and Latin America and is around 80 per cent or higher in North America, Western Europe and Eastern Europe/Russia. In China between 1990

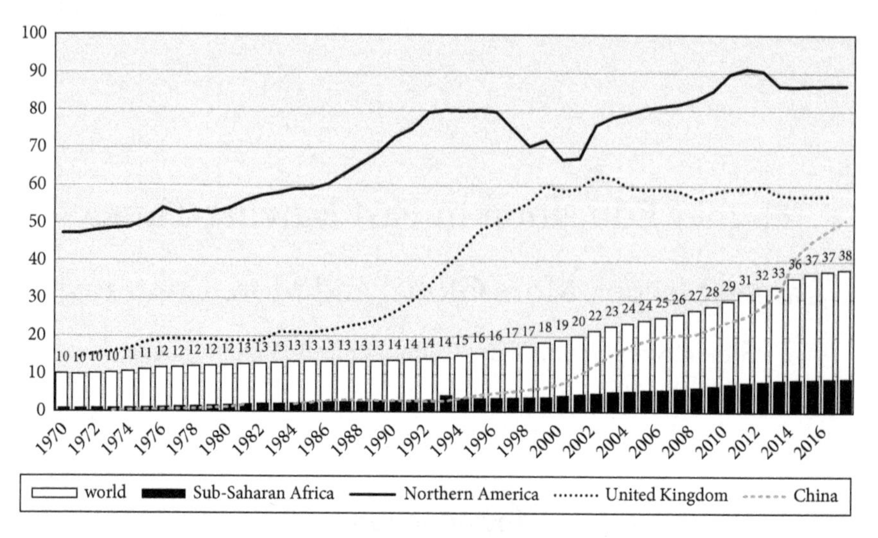

Figure 1.1 Gross enrolment ratio for tertiary education, World, United States, United Kingdom, China and Sub-Saharan Africa: 1970–2017.
Source: UNESCO 2019.

and 2017 the ratio increased from 3 to 51 per cent; in India it increased from 6 to 28 per cent. Though participation is still low in Sub-Saharan Africa (Figure 1.1) and parts of South Asia, enrolments are now climbing in those regions. In one-fifth of countries, with low incomes, tertiary enrolments are yet to take off. All other countries are moving towards high participation (UNESCO 2019).

'Tertiary education' in the UNESCO database includes all degree courses of three years or more plus two-year full-time equivalent courses at degree and sub-degree levels. About 80 per cent of the world's tertiary education students are pursuing degrees. The understanding of 'higher education' varies by country but includes almost all degree courses. In some countries, including the United States, the definition of 'higher education' is extended to two-year college courses as well. In this book 'higher education' (which is the main focus of the chapters) refers to universities, institutes and colleges that are primarily focused on degree-level educational provision. Some but not all of these higher education institutions also conduct funded research.

The primary driver of growth of tertiary/higher education is not government. Nor is it the economy. Rapid educational growth is occurring in countries with a wide configuration of GDP growth rates. It is occurring in economies that are primarily commodity traders, in manufacturing economies and in services economies. The only economies where it is not happening are those that are still primarily agricultural. Urbanization and the growth of tertiary enrolments are correlated. Between 1970 and 2018 the proportion of the world's people who live in cities rose from 37 to 55 per cent (World Bank 2019). Cities supply tertiary/higher education on the basis of economies of scale, provide jobs for graduates and also concentrate social demand for entry. The primary driver of the growth of tertiary/higher education is accumulating social demand for opportunities. The data record across the world shows that once participation becomes a norm for middle-class families, and then all families, it keeps on growing until it reaches near universal levels (Cantwell, Marginson and Smolentseva 2018). This happens while in expanding education systems the average private earnings attached to degrees are in decline. It can happen even when the income advantages enjoyed by graduates compared to non-graduates, the graduate premium, is falling.

A key reason for this powerful growth dynamic is that higher education offers not just better salaries or employment rates. It also confers a recognized social distinction that has currency within and between countries. It offers esteem, satisfaction, personal agency and self-respect. Governments must respond to social demand on this scale, though they may transfer part of the cost of expansion to students and families (Chapter 6). Some governments control the number of places and thereby regulate the pace of expansion, but in the long run this power is limited. Governments only ever increase participation rates. They never decrease them.

Much is concealed by aggregate data on the growth of educational participation. The nature and quality of tertiary/higher education vary greatly within and between countries. Nevertheless, we are seeing an astonishing leap in not just education but educability. The old expectation that only a small part of the population is capable of advanced levels of education has been decisively swept away. Correspondingly, the joint responsibilities of higher education systems and institutions have expanded and will go on expanding.

Higher education matters, increasingly, in every society that provides it. Higher education provides conditions and resources for the self-formation of students and leaves a lifelong mark on graduates. The knowledges in which students become immersed shape not only skills but also values and sensibilities. New research continually emerging in universities extends the boundaries of the possible. Apart from the massification of higher education, we see the increasing number of research-intensive universities, the growth of scientific output and the explosive growth of cross-border research collaborations (Chapter 3). Science grows along with education.

It all places ever-growing pressure on resources and infrastructure – will countries have the buildings, facilities, equipment and trained staff that they need in larger higher education systems? – and underlines problems of financial sustainability (Chapter 6). More significant than the effects in higher education are the larger social effects. The future of high-participation higher education feeds directly into the future of human society. What happens to collective productivity when half of the world's workforces have tertiary training and the more advanced skills in technology that go with that? What happens when many more people have the advanced capabilities in social relations, communications, analysis, problem solving, managing more complex information and dealing with government and organizations that are associated with tertiary study? When people have the confidence and capacity, on a much larger scale, to render states more transparent and accountable, what does this mean for political systems? When many more people are experienced and capable in geographical mobility, cross-cultural relations and bridging social gaps (skills that university websites present as graduate attributes) does this reduce the potential for populist capture of politics based on blood-and-soil nativism, anti-migration and the 'othering' of people who are different?

There is also the question of social justice in increasingly unequal societies (Piketty 2014). The distribution of opportunities in higher education determines which members of society can access the forms of agency fostered by it. With half or more of the population in many countries holding degrees and diplomas, the divide between the graduate and the early school leaver becomes more crucial in shaping (and limiting) lives. The stratified structure of higher education itself is also crucial. It can create a ranked hierarchy within the graduate population. The discipline and the status of the institution matter. Systems of higher education are more or less just, in the sense of egalitarian. There are few locations where society can intervene to make itself more just. Education, open to structural change, is one of those locations. Everywhere the intractable problem of social equity in higher education demands to be addressed.

Globalization

As this suggests, the growth of tertiary and higher education does not take place in a vacuum. Institutional education helps to shape its social, economic, political and cultural setting – and reciprocally, is shaped by that broader setting. In the four years since the ESRC/OFSRE Centre for Global Higher Education (CGHE) began its research programme there have been notable shifts in the external landscape.

CGHE was established in 2015 amid awareness of the transformative potential of globalization, meaning connectedness and integration on a global or world-regional scale (Conrad 2016). Across the world higher education institutions, especially research universities, are among the most internationally active and globalized of social institutions. A quarter of all published research papers have authors from more than one country. At the same time global rankings frame the world as a competitive hierarchy of universities, in which university leaders advance their position by forming partnerships and consortia, and running programmes and sometimes, bricks-and-mortar campuses, in other countries. More than five million students cross-national borders each year to enrol in foreign degree and diploma programmes. At last count, prior to COVID-19, international students were increasing at 6 per cent a year (OECD 2018: 224; Chapter 4). Europe has been especially important for British higher education institutions (Chapter 5). Almost every university, it seems, proclaims its 'internationalization' strategy on its website.

At the same time, global communications and information-processing technologies have underpinned the rapid growth and diversification of modes of delivery at a distance – and greatly facilitated both on-site communications and information storage, retrieval and sharing in higher education and research. We have moved closer to the idea of the world as a single knowledge bank or library and higher education as a unified network of institutions that understand each other. This has transformed many aspects of the sector and made everyone more globally aware. Though electronic delivery has not replaced the face-to-face classroom and its personalized relationships, in some countries, for example in Sub-Saharan Africa, Brazil and South Asia, it is primary in the expansion of access.

However, while global integration and convergence continue to shape the world, especially in cultural matters and in worldwide scientific networks, in certain other domains global integration appears to have come to a halt or is in retreat – and in some (though not all) countries the reception of global people flows has become less positive. This has created new issues and problems, especially for research universities.

The Economy

Between the foundation of the internet in 1990 and the 2008 recession, global trade boomed in a more deregulated financial environment in which tariffs and the cost of communications, data transfer and transport were all progressively reduced. An increasing share of production was carried by globalized supply chains in which raw materials, components and managerial know-how from different parts of the world were joined together in finished products. Between 1990 and 2011 the share of foreign value added in a country's exports rose from 20 to almost 30 per cent (*The Economist* 2019).

Some aspects of global economic integration have now slowed or reversed. This change predates the Trump presidency and the new Cold War that is now developing between the United States and China, with its tariff barriers and conflicts over technology. Looking at trends in political economy, the partial unravelling of 1990s/2000s globalization dates from the 2008 recession. Between 2007 and 2016 cross-border capital flows dropped from 5 per cent of global GDP to less than 2 per cent (*The Economist* 2019). Between 1986 and 2008 total global trade grew at twice the pace of global GDP; but since 2008 global trade in goods has scarcely kept pace with GDP, and the G-20 countries have implemented more than 6,600 protectionist measures (Lund and Tyson 2018: 130–3). Supply chains, subject to fragmented national regulation, are becoming more costly and are shortening. The profitability of American and European multinationals has declined, compared to nation-centred companies, except in the tech sector (*The Economist* 2017).

Economic globalization is now primarily driven by automation and digital technology. International parcel volume rose from 50 to 176 million between 2007 and 2017 while cross-border bandwidth grew from 11 to 704 terrabits per second. However, the America-China tussle over 5-G may lead to a bifurcation in the roll-out of the technology, a costly 'splinternet of things' that would disrupt e-commerce (*The Economist* 2019).

The Politics

Dan Rodrik (2017) argues that in the absence of government intervention designed to promote equalization of incomes, open global economic competition must have diminishing returns for labour. The gain in economic efficiency from each reduction in trade barriers shrinks while the number of losers created by liberalization – for example, unskilled workers displaced by the offshoring of production – increases (p. 27). In the United States, import competition has driven down the labour share of income. High inequality is tolerated providing there is belief in social mobility, but offshore production is seen as unfair competition. Financial globalization also has negative distributional impacts:

> Capital-account liberalisation leads to statistically significant and long-lasting declines in the labor share of income and corresponding increases in the Gini coefficient of income inequality and in the shares of top 1, 5, and 10 percent

> of income. … Financial globalisation appears to have complemented trade in exerting downwards pressure on the labour share of income. (Rodrik 2017: 18–19)

Economic globalization still had upsides for emerging countries like China, but the decline in global inequality has been 'accompanied by an increase in domestic inequality and cleavages' in the United States (Rodrik 2017: 21). Popular movements use differing narratives of left and right to explain the negative distributional outcomes. The political left creates an 'income/social class cleavage'. The populist right has created 'an ethno-national cultural cleavage' (p. 24) in which non-white migrants and urban cultural cosmopolitans are seen as the beneficiaries of globalization who secured their gains unfairly at the expense of displaced white Americans. Hence 'even when the underlying shock is fundamentally economic the political manifestations can be cultural and nativist' (p. 25). At the same time, in Europe the ethno-national cultural cleavage turns on the apparent threat of migrants and refugees to closed welfare state economies (p. 24).

In addition, populist resistance to globalization has been fuelled by the emergence of the trade and technology Cold War between the United States and China and the inflammatory rhetoric associated with the conflict. The Trump decision to break cooperation with China appears to have bipartisan support in the United States. As US–China collaboration in science and higher education has been especially close and fruitful since China's opening up began in 1978, and as the Chinese presence in American science has become identified as a battleground, it is hard to see how higher education can avoid fall-out from the Cold War.

Implications for Higher Education

The global situation has two implications for higher education. First, with migration now a central political fault line in many countries, all forms of cross-mobility in higher education are potentially problematized, including cross-border academic recruitment, short-term academic visits and international student mobility. While these problems are by no means universal there are growing signs that global geopolitical conflict and national anti-migration politics are affecting higher education in some countries:

- Jenny Lee and John Haupt note the now frequent claims in the United States about a 'China threat' in science and research. It is alleged that China is engaged in academic espionage, that (a few? some? all?) scholars and students from China are 'spies' who routinely 'steal' intellectual property.

Normal collaborative relations in research, that until recently appeared innocent and were sought by all parties – relations that have not changed in essence – have become reinterpreted in these highly negative terms (Lee and Haupt 2019).

- Numerous scientists in the United States, most of Chinese descent and some with citizenship or ongoing residence in the United States, have been investigated for alleged security breaches for sharing information about National Institute of Health funding applications outside the United States, and even for not naming an affiliation to a Chinese university (though multiple institutional affiliation is common across the academic world). Some of those investigated have lost their positions (Lee and Haupt 2019).
- The duration of American visas for Chinese graduate students in high-tech fields have been shortened from five years to one year (Lee and Haupt 2019).
- In the UK, although there is no evidence of significant popular opposition to incoming international students, policy and regulation maintained the intake of students in a flatline position between 2010–11 and 2017–18, and at different times government ministers have foreshadowed substantial reductions in the total number of students (Chapter 4).
- In the UK there are recurring blockages to academic visas for visitors from countries, for example in Sub-Saharan Africa, whose nationals are deemed by the Home Office to have a relatively high probability of overstay (Hill 2019).
- In the Netherlands the government has sharply reduced the budget of the Dutch Organization promoting internationalization in education, Nuffic (de Wit 2019).
- In Denmark there is opposition to the provision of higher education through the medium of global English, and such Masters level programmes will be phased out. While there are strong reasons for sustaining the national language as a medium of learning, a reduction in bilingual provision may reduce mobility into the countries concerned.

Blocking cross-border flows of academic faculty and students does nothing to redress inequality. Anti-mobility politics is a form of scapegoating in which at bottom, foreigners are being blamed for local exclusions, impoverishment and injustice. This is both absurd and dangerous. Governments and universities committed to open flows of faculty and students will need to closely monitor these patterns. Ongoing research is needed.

Second, the natural associations of higher education institutions with urban cultural elites and global cosmopolitan connections have the potential to isolate those institutions amid a nativist revolt. In the UK this spectre was suggested by the Brexit referendum in 2016, in which Remain-voting university communities in the North and Midlands of England sat within impoverished Leave-voting regions. The argument could be made: 'Why is our university spending its time on international research that doesn't benefit us? Why is it educating foreign students when our students can't get in?'

Growing Inequality

Here higher education runs up against the overhanging problem of growing economic and social inequality in most countries. Higher education acting alone cannot solve this and other sectors are often more important, such as wage and salary determination, taxation and government social programmes. Growing inequality is not inevitable. When global economic competition is unchecked, market forces must generate greater economic inequality over time, but national states can intervene via tax-and-spend redistribution to modify those market forces, as the Nordic countries do. Neoliberal economic policy at national level, which has let the markets rip, has been as important as globalization in shifting income in favour of the top 1 per cent and the top 0.01 per cent.

However, stratified higher education does play a part in unequal societies. This is one of the frameworks through which stratified labour markets are reproduced and inequality is legitimated. Again, the problem of social equity in higher education demands to be addressed. Top universities are mostly captured by affluent families. In higher education the best antidotes to inequality are to extend the boundaries of participation to take in more of the social groups previously excluded from higher education opportunities, to lift second- and third-tier institutions so that there is less at stake in institutional stratification, and to reform social entry into high-demand elite universities. All these solutions require concerted political will and take time to achieve.

In the absence of these changes, growing inequality poses immediate and difficult challenges for institutions. They face different imperatives, depending on their locality. The challenges facing global universities in global cities differ from those in regions.

Global Cities and Their Opposite

In all countries globalization has increased the economic and social weight of the networked global city – the concentration of economic capital, jobs, skills and talents, social capital, education, knowledge and cultural resources in leading cities networked into a single system at world level (Rossi 2017). The aggrandizement of global cities is fostered more by the networked global economy/society than by factors at the national level. The centralizing and networking logics of globalization work in tandem across economics, communications, transport, science and services. These logics create universal systems, everyone is affected by the same global forces, but at the same time they favour globally effective agents, and concentrations of those agents, and push down those people who are less globally active and effective.

The part fragmentation of economic globalization may slow the rise of the global city but is unlikely to reverse it. Global cities suck everything into themselves. While global cities like London, Frankfurt, Shanghai and Singapore rise and rise, economic capital and social value is emptied out of the medium-sized towns, villages and rural hinterlands. There are exceptions to the mega-city pattern – for example smaller wealthy satellites of the global cities like Oxford or Bristol in the UK – but the great geospatial change since about 1970 has been the weakening of most established urban centres (the relative decline of non-urban rural areas goes back further, to the beginning of industrialization).

Europe and North America are full of regional cities that were once leaders of manufacturing or public services but are now struggling. As the regional cities decline their capacity to sustain their own hinterlands in economic, social and cultural terms also declines. The further one moves from the hub of the regional cities, the lesser the level of global and national connectivity, the lower the level of economic prosperity, and the lesser the potential for social and geographical mobility. People become place-bound.

Again taking the UK as the example, using the EU's Classification of Territorial Units for Statistics (NUTS), in 2016, twenty-eight of the UK's forty NUTS2 regions were below the level of average income per capita in the EU. (Average EU income includes Southern and Eastern Europe: it is not a high figure.) Meanwhile inner West London, in the global city, had 611 per cent of the EU average income per head, more than twice as rich as the second wealthiest concentration in Europe, Luxembourg (257 per cent). The rest of London was not as wealthy at this but most of London was above most of the UK (Eurostat 2018).

The lowest income regions in UK, classified as 'less developed' by the EU, were West Wales and the valleys (68 per cent of average EU per capita income), Cornwall (69 per cent), and Lincolnshire, South Yorkshire, Tees Valley and Durham (all 72 per cent). In these regions the issues for higher education are very different to those in London.

Strategies in the Face of Inequality

To be effective high research-intensive universities in global cities or their satellite urban areas must be players in worldwide networks and contribute to the innovation economy. They also train high paid graduates for finance and technology sectors. These universities appear culpable in the political economy of growing inequality, in which networked big cities have the momentum, and, while by no means everyone in global cities is advantaged, globally networked persons tend to rise above others.

Yet the culpability of global universities for inequality should be kept in proportion. First, not everything global is socially regressive. International research collaboration produces common goods. Mobility funding and scholarships that help poorer students to go abroad spread the empowerment that mobility brings. Second, global universities can and often do foster understanding of inequality and its costs, through their programmes in teaching and research. Third, it is hard to see how individual global universities could decouple from global cities or global satellite cities with their concentrations of economic and social capital, without losing the cutting edge of their research role, losing influence and support and losing reputation. This decoupling would not diminish social inequality.

The one domain where global universities *can* address inequality is in student selection. Here the record is mixed. There are clear negative and positive cases. Though the negative cases tend to outweigh the positives ones, the leading campuses of the University of California (UC), at Berkeley and Los Angeles, are encouraging examples. The UC is a high-demand university with a large cohort of academically brilliant school students from which to choose, some from poorer districts and poorer families. UC admissions ensure that a large minority of students at Berkeley and UCLA are from Pell grant (low income) families, with many coming from homes where the parents have no tertiary education. This broadens social mobility in California (Marginson 2016).

For regional research universities the problems and solutions are different. Like global universities in global cities, regional universities have research ambitions; and in countries like the UK where international student fees are essential to their income, they must recruit some of their students from offshore. But they do so in a different context. In a growing number of regional UK research universities, such as Nottingham, Lincoln, Keele/Stoke and Sheffield, the polarization in the Brexit referendum has triggered a new focus on programmes linked to local communities. Nottingham focuses on bringing its international connectedness into conjunction with its local outreach. Some institutions want to be locally and globally effective at the same time; others are talking in either/or terms. In these stirrings a new politics of higher education and inequality is emerging.

Contents of the Book

These topics and many others are taken up in the chapters that follow.

In Chapter 2 William Locke takes issue with one-idea claims about the 'inevitable' pathways (or disappearance) of higher education. He argues for multiple and situated understandings of the future of higher education, and suggests that the futurologists ought to listen more to academic and professional staff.

The three chapters on 'Global factors in higher education' reflect on the uneasy tectonics where the national and the global planes of action meet. In Chapter 3 Simon Marginson discusses the fast-growing global research system, which is often determining vis-à-vis national research and where the rise of East Asia is changing the global balance of power. In Chapter 4 Marginson examines incoming student mobility (education export) in the UK, a textbook case where the logics of global mobility and trade are confounded by national migration resistance. In Chapter 5, Marginson, Vassilki Papatsiba and Xin Xu trace UK higher education's engagement with Europe and report the emotions expressed by 127 interviewees during research on the consequences of Brexit.

The section of the book on 'Financing and Widening Participation' takes national higher education systems as its frame of reference but touches on common factors relevant in many countries. In Chapter 6, Bruce Chapman, Lorraine Dearden and Dung Doan discuss the worldwide spread of income-contingent loan systems of tuition financing and their advantages over time-based repayment loans. Chapter 7 by Claire Callender, KC Deane, Ariane de Gayardon and Stephen L. DesJardins reviews the literature on student loans and their effects on student and graduate behaviours. In Chapter 8 Vikki Boliver, Stephen Gorard and Nadia Siddiqu discuss the obstacles facing UK students from less advantaged backgrounds. They recommend contextualized admission policies that use indicators of disadvantage, and high-quality second-chance education including university courses with open admission policies.

The section on 'Teaching and Learning' is led by Paul Ashwin's Chapter 9 on principles of national system-wide approaches to furthering teaching excellence.

It emphasizes that meaningful measures of educational processes and outcomes can only be developed through collaborative conversations between academics, students and others involved in educational processes. Jan McArthur's Chapter 10 is concerned with the power of assessment processes to shape knowledge-based student learning, including learning about social justice in disciplinary frameworks. In Chapter 11, Diana Laurillard and Eileen Kennedy discuss the global potential of massive open online courses (MOOCs) to widen access to professional education and orchestrate exchange and development of knowledge in professional communities.

In Chapter 12 in 'Graduates and Work' Francis Green and Golo Henseke highlight both graduate underemployment – in tuition-based systems some graduate face a future of no net returns to their degrees – and growing demands for high-skilled work. The balance between supply of, and demand for, high skills varies considerably by country.

The section on 'Institutions and Markets' considers trends in the marketization of higher education in two different ways. Chapter 13 by Janja Komeljenovic examines four devices used in making higher education markets: the 'students as consumer' reform in the UK; the LinkedIn platform and its network; MOOCS; and international student recruitment agencies. Market friendly devices 'frame a particular kind of future, which seems to be increasingly competitive, digital, quantified and relational'. In Chapter 14 Stephen Hunt and Vikki Boliver discuss whether subsidized private colleges in the UK will succeed in breaking into the higher education mainstream.

The final section is on the 'Public and Social Benefit' of higher education. In Chapter 15, Paul Ashwin and Jennifer M. Case draw from their project on student/graduate pathways in South Africa to argue that there needs to be more extensive and detailed public debate about the nature of the public good role that higher education is intended to play in South African society. Chapter 16 by Lin Tian and Nian C. Liu reports on interviews in government and two universities in China on expectations of the role of higher education in generating public and common good. In Chapter 17, Simon Marginson reviews those key concepts, and higher education as a 'public sphere', and sketches a comprehensive framework for researching all of the contributions of higher education.

Limits and Future Work

These chapters by no means exhaust the list of the research centre projects, nor the issues in higher education at this time.

For example, there is no chapter specifically focused on student experience and student agency, though Chapters 4, 7, 9, 10 and 12 (among others) touch on key student issues. There is no chapter specifically on higher education governance, the topic of a separate book in this Bloomsbury series by Michael Shattock and Aniko Horvath. Nor are there chapters on higher education management or staffing, though each of these themes appears in many of the chapters on other topics. The outcomes of CGHE projects on the career outcomes experienced by East Asian international graduates, collaboration between university and industry researchers in the UK, and the long-term patterns of educational participation and financing in England and France have been published separately (https://www.researchcghe.org/publications/) and are not included here. Future books will expand on these areas and other issues.

In its first four years CGHE has pursued research projects in relation to some regions of the world but not others. As well as the UK and Europe we have focused closely on East Asia, given the dynamism of the region (three of our affiliated researchers are from China, Hong Kong SAR and Japan), we have linked to North America and South Africa and have begun to engage in Russia, India and Latin America. In the next four years it is planned to develop research in other parts of Sub-Saharan Africa, Central Asia and the Caucuses. Inevitably CGHE's work is shaped and, in some respects, limited by the UK-specific location and vision of most of our researchers. Nevertheless, research networks have an expansionary logic and as the connections grow and different empirical sites become better known to each other, the centre is developing a stronger overview of higher education as a whole. In doing so it hopes to live up to the 'Global' in its title.

A global perspective combines awareness of the world as an interdependent system, with understanding of the differing positions and perspectives that constitute it. The old idea of 'unity in diversity', which is foundational to Western thought, Chinese civilization and many indigenous cultures, is as good a summation as any of global higher education.

References

Cantwell, B., Marginson, S. and Smolentseva, A. (eds) (2018), *High Participation Systems of Higher Education*, Oxford: Oxford University Press.

Conrad, S. (2016), *What is Global History?*, Princeton: Princeton University Press.

De Wit, H. (2019), 'Dutch Cuts to Internationalisation Send Wrong Message', *Inside Higher Ed*, 22 July. https://www.insidehighered.com/blogs/world-view/dutch-cuts-internationalization-send-wrong-message

The Economist (2017), 'The Retreat of the Global Company', 28 January.

The Economist (2019), 'A Slow ~Unravelling', 13 July.

Eurostat (2018), 'Regional Gross Domestic Product (PPS per Inhabitant in % of the EU28 Average) by NUTS 2 Regions'. http://ec.europa.eu/eurostat/tgm/table.do?tab=table&init=1&language=en&pcode=tgs00006&plugin=1

Hill, A. (2019), 'UNESCO Chair Blasts 'Discriminatory' UK Visitor Visa System', *The Guardian*, 24 June.

Lee, J. and Haupt, J. (2019), 'Winners and Losers in US-China Scientific-Research Collaboration', *Higher Education* [TBA].

Lund, S. and Tyson, L. (2018), 'Digital Technology and the Future of Trade', *Foreign Affairs*, 97 (3): 130–40.

Marginson, S. (2016), *The Dream Is Over: The Crisis of Clark Kerr's California Idea of Higher Education*, Berkeley: University of California Press.

Organisation for Economic Cooperation and Development, OECD (2018), *Education at a Glance, 2018*, Paris: OECD.

Piketty, T. (2014), *Capital in the Twenty-First Century* (A. Goldhammer, Trans.), Cambridge, MA: Belknap Harvard University Press.

Rodrik, D. (2017), *Populism and the Economics of Globalization*, John F. Kennedy School of Government, Harvard University. https://drodrik.scholar.harvard.edu/files/dani-rodrik/files/populism_and_the_economics_of_globalization.pdf Accessed 76 October 2017

Rossi, U. (2017), *Cities in Global Capitalism*, Cambridge: Polity.

United National Educational Social and Cultural Organisation (UNESCO) (2019), 'UNESCO Institute of Statistics Data'. http://data.uis.unesco.org/#

World Bank (2019), 'Data on Urban Share of Population'. https://data.worldbank.org/indicator/SP.URB.TOTL.IN.ZS?view=chart

2

Visions of Higher Education Futures

The Shape of Things to Come?

William Locke

Introduction

Many higher education futurologists in the English-speaking world – including management consultants, 'thought leaders' and journalists – tend to present a series of cataclysmic scenarios, in which various factors combine to challenge and 'disrupt' traditional academic conventions, business models and working practices in public universities. These scenarios usually feature some combination of the following: the transformation of graduate employment, raised student expectations, a technology revolution including the widespread use of online learning and data analytics, expansion and public financing constraints, policy turbulence and growing global competition, particularly from private for-profit universities and colleges and from emerging nations. They predict the future will bring rapid and continuous change, challenge and uncertainty for those who manage and work in universities who, in response, will need to fundamentally transform themselves in order to adapt to these new conditions and demands (PWC/AHEIA 2016). A few develop future scenarios for higher education or models of universities that would thrive, survive or nose dive in such circumstances (ACE 2013; Barber, Donnelly and Rizvi 2013; Ernst & Young 2018). Some commentators speculate that these transformations may come to threaten the very foundations of higher education, its economic value and its role in society (Ernst & Young 2012).

These futurologists conclude that the conservativism, 'silo mentality' and the slow pace of change in public universities will have to be overcome and, in some areas, the 'legacy' architecture of higher education dismantled (PA Consulting/HEFCE 2010; PWC/AHEIA 2016). One key component of this architecture is staff – the higher education 'workforce'. Most versions conclude that the academic workforce of the future will need to be more 'agile' and 'flexible', become 'professionalized' and subject to greater 'specialization' (e.g. PWC/AHEIA 2016). One version even predicts that academics will largely become freelance workers operating across several higher education institutions (HEIs) and businesses (Ernst and Young 2018).

In most cases, these efforts in futurology draw on interviews and surveys of university heads, 'thought leaders', senior policy-makers and key stakeholders, such as business leaders and graduate employers. They very rarely seek the views of staff or students working and studying in HEIs, let alone consult the existing research on developments and trends within their national higher education systems, or even internationally. They almost exclusively cite previous management consultancy reports, policy documents and newspaper articles. Consequently, they recycle myths and folklore that do not stand up to empirical scrutiny. Nevertheless, they are important because they replay the views and perspectives – and fears – of these sector leaders back to them in a self-perpetuating dialogue and discourse about cataclysmic change and the need for radical transformation. Some explicitly ask the heads of institutions whether their university has the capability to address the challenges presented and, if so, to consider how it will do this (for example, Ernst & Young 2012, 2018). Clearly, when management consultant firms do this, they are positioning themselves to advise these same HEIs on how to respond to the supposed challenges in both the short and longer term, in a deliberate attempt to generate business for their firms. So, this futurology circulates among influential networks and begins to inform current strategy making within institutions and policy-making at state, national and global levels. This is why such futurology should not simply be dismissed as speculative marketing but evaluated as a discourse with influence and material impact on HEIs' behaviour and decision-making.

This chapter will critically evaluate the claims of these futurologists in the light of recent research evidence of academic staffing trends emerging in mature higher education systems in English-speaking countries. It will also examine the impact of this increasingly dominant policy and management discourse – of extrinsic disruption and the need for institutional responsiveness and transformation – as it influences current working relationships and staffing policies within HEIs. An example of this influence was provided by a university Human Resources director (Russell Group University, Southern England) interviewed for the Centre for Global Higher Education (CGHE) research study on The Future Higher Education Workforce, who could have been summarizing from one of the futurologist reports:

> Universities largely, over time, have grown incrementally and it's [assumed] we'll continue to grow on the same basis incrementally into the future and [colleagues are] not really understanding that the future potentially is going to be very different to anything we've seen in the past ... there's a tsunami coming and ... these waves of change are coming, [but] because we can't see them doesn't necessarily mean they aren't coming. [You have to take] the opportunities to engage and respond in a proactive way, rather than waiting for the wave to hit you and then, you know, you're just reacting to something.

In particular, this chapter will highlight the marginalization of the experiences and perspectives of academics and other staff in these discourses and the limited and selective use of evidence in supporting their conclusions. Finally, it will argue that these narratives seriously underestimate, ignore and undermine the role that universities could – and do – have in challenging many of these 'disruptive' ideas and developments, in pointing out that they are not inevitable or unopposable, and in suggesting alternative futures for higher education and those who work in it.

The Main Drivers of the Future

Most cataclysmic futurology starts with a caricature of existing models of public higher education and its organizational forms. Universities are said to be traditional, 'twentieth-century' institutions that are academic- or producer-oriented rather than student- and customer-focused (Ernst & Young 2018). They are comprehensive teaching and research organizations supported by an extensive asset base and a large, predominantly in-house and 'cumbersome back office' (Ernst & Young 2012: 4, see also Economist Intelligence Unit 2014). In some systems, particularly Australia, they have become too similar, competing in the same markets and seeking the same forms of reputation and prestige (Ernst & Young 2018). Dominated by an ageing academic workforce that is resistant to change and averse to taking risks, it is argued, they are wedded to 'outmoded' and costly collective bargaining agreements (PA Consulting/HEFCE 2010; PWC/AHEIA 2016; Lee Hecht Harrison 2016). Several extrinsic drivers are then predicted to combine to challenge traditional higher education and, particularly, 'incumbent' public universities, including the transformation of graduate work, students' changing characteristics and expectations, reduced government funding and deregulation, increased use of technology, and growing competition from for-profit universities and colleges. Each of these drivers will be summarized briefly, as they serve to inform the kinds of scenarios that the futurologists build when developing their discourses about the challenges and prospects for higher education and how these should influence current discussions and strategy making in universities.

The Transformation of Graduate Work

There is a widespread view from the surveys that inform these reports that, in the medium to long term, many existing jobs in the general labour market will disappear because of the increased use of robotics and the application of artificial intelligence. Many respondents assume that some of these jobs will be replaced by new graduate positions, often managing and developing this automation and expanding it into new areas (PWC/AHEIA 2016). In the short term, it is expected that the professional relevance of the higher education curriculum will need to be enhanced, in particular, to develop the entrepreneurial skills and inventiveness needed for future economic growth, job creation and innovation (Economist Intelligence Unit 2014; Lee Hecht Harrison 2016).

Students' Changing Characteristics and Expectations

In the territories covered by the reports, expansion in the number of students is expected to continue, including international students as well as larger proportions of their domestic populations. However, a gap is thought to have already opened-up between the expectations and learning styles of current digitally literate students and the conventional pedagogical approaches of most university degrees (ACE 2014b; Lee Hecht Harrison 2016). This gap is strongly expected to increase unless universities catch up and begin to anticipate the needs and desires of more discerning generations of learners, given the increasing costs of study. It is expected these students will ask searching questions about value for money; whether they will need a traditional higher education qualification; whether and how to seek accreditation of prior learning; what curriculum content they will need; where, when and how they will study during their working lives; and which forms of assessment will reflect the types of credentials they will need. At the very least, it is claimed, they will be expecting a much more 'customer-focused and convenient offering' (PWC/AHEIA 2016: 12).

Reduced Government Funding and Deregulation

The recent expansion of higher education, at least in English-speaking countries, has been accompanied by reduced government funding per student and increased tuition fees, sometimes backed by loans. This 'quasi-privatization' of higher education has been accompanied by the introduction of market mechanisms (e.g. unrestrained student numbers or tuition fees, course-comparison information for applicants and easier entry into the market for private colleges and universities) to intensify competition between higher education providers for students. The assumption – of futurologists and some policy-makers alike – is that this competition will drive up quality and increase institutions' focus on students as the latter become more selective consumers. Greater competition between universities induces increased uncertainty about income streams which, in turn, leads to efforts to reduce costs, eliminate cross-subsidies, investigate additional sources of revenue and explore partnerships with other providers (including private education businesses) and even mergers (Economist Intelligence Unit 2014; Forbes 2018). Ultimately though, according to the futurologists, these developments should lead to universities reviewing their activities, rethinking their business models, reframing their 'value proposition' and 'reimagining' themselves as organizations (Deloitte 2013, 2014).

Increased Use of Technology

The reduction of costs is often seen as one of the major potential benefits of the adoption of technology across the whole range of a university's operations, despite evidence suggesting a tendency in higher education for it to be used to improve quality, even leading to increased costs in some cases (Archibald and Feldman 2010). However, this is only part of the story for the futurologists. In the delivery of education, this includes the blending of educational technologies with traditional classroom-based methods and moving courses entirely online in order to open up new markets for distance learning (Ernst & Young 2012; Gallagher and Garrett 2013). Also, aspects of student assessment and feedback are expected to be automated and elements of curricular content replaced by open educational resources. Increasingly, data is expected to be gathered on a range of student activities – such as module choice, attendance, library and facility use, movement around campus and on-site purchases – and analytical and predictive tools are being deployed to investigate patterns and associations to inform interventions (Deloitte 2014; Contact North 2016). The implications of online and automated learning for traditional universities are seen as far-reaching, including the reallocation of classroom space, the redesign of future facilities and the reduction in the overall size of university estate. Somehow, this is also expected to reduce the need for academic staff – who might be redeployed, for example, to focus on higher level programmes (PWC/AHEIA 2016) – and professional staff, much of whose work it is assumed could be automated.

Growing Competition from For-Profit Colleges and Universities

The entry and expansion of private providers in the higher education market is seen as a major driver for change and innovation among existing public universities (PWC/AHEIA 2016; Ernst & Young 2018). Focusing on teaching – and vocational subjects in particular – they are seen as not having the overheads required to undertake research or to offer a comprehensive curriculum, including expensive laboratory-based or clinical subjects. They can target specific groups of students within niche areas; offer customized options of fully online, blended or classroom-only instruction; and tailor their physical estate accordingly. Many are experimenting with year-round timetabling and operations, multiple programme entry points and maximizing the usage of their buildings and facilities. They limit the provision of non-educational facilities and student activities (accommodation, leisure and sporting facilities, for example) to further minimize costs.

A Leap of Faith

While each of these external drivers is claimed to be significant in itself, according to the futurologists, it is their combination which makes them irresistible: changing student characteristics will be a catalyst for the adoption of new technologies; reduced government funding will force HEIs to partner more closely with industry; growing competition will drive institutions to reduce costs and increases their responsiveness to student consumers; and online and distance education will accelerate the 'unbundling' of programmes and the functions of course design, curriculum content, teaching delivery and student assessment. It is this mutual reinforcement that heralds a crisis that is claimed to render the 'legacy' models of the university redundant (Ernst & Young 2012). Higher education is supposedly at a crossroads (ACE 2014a) and radical transformation is inevitable. The core characteristics of the traditional model tend to be regarded as obstacles or forms of resistance to inevitable change, and as potential causes of the failure of particular 'incumbent' institutions to survive.

However, the futurologists rarely provide clear and rational connections between, on the one hand, their analyses of the drivers and trends that are selected as challenging the traditional models of higher education and, on the other, the models or solutions they propose and the outcomes they predict. These efforts largely comprise a leap of faith, with little or no reference to trends or current successful innovations and are rarely convincing as potential options for existing universities, however forward-thinking they may be.

While little of this will be surprising coming from management consultancy firms, 'thought-leaders' and journalists who have bought into the ideology and the agenda, its importance lies in the fact that it partly draws on the contributions of some institutional and sector leaders and replays these back to them through a particularly narrow funnel. In doing so, this discourse reinforces some of the dominant assumptions and folklore about such things as industrial relations in higher education, 'silo-mentalities', linear academic careers and academics' attitudes towards business. While claiming to stimulate discussion and debate, it turns these into seductive but selective narratives about future developments in higher education that are aimed at creating an agenda for transforming current thinking and practices and existing endeavours.

The Implications for Academic Roles, Work and Careers

Not all of the future scenarios explicitly address the implications for academic faculty, although there is a shared assumption that the nature of academic roles, work and careers will be radically transformed as a result of the predicted changes. Common to most versions is the unbundling of academic roles to match the unbundling of university functions (PWC/AHEIA 2016). It is assumed that academic faculty will have to spend more time on teaching, curriculum design and assessment to reflect higher education's expected greater focus on students, learning and credentialing. Accordingly, they will have to target particular groups of students and their requirements for skills and knowledge, and devise programmes around the needs of those students rather than the exigencies and constraints of the discipline. This will include working more closely with graduate employers in order to understand the changing work environments. It will also mean the interchange of professionals and industry practitioners with academic staff. Greater collaboration between universities and industry will also require faculty to develop their business acumen as they attempt to commercialize their research and pedagogy and meet the new skills needs (PWC/AHEIA 2016; Ernst & Young 2018).

Only one of the reports covered here focuses primarily on the workforce issues raised by its vision of the future: a PWC report commissioned by the Australian Higher Education Industrial Association (AHEIA). The AHEIA is the employer association for the higher education sector in Australia, and it identified the key themes for the study carried out by PWC: environmental impact factors, the changing nature of work, changing business models, student expectations and future workforce needs (PWC/AHEIA 2016: 6). The aim of the report, it claims, is to start a national discussion about how to establish and maintain 'a future-ready workforce in the university sector' and to explore 'how universities might future proof the way in which their staff workforces are structured, engaged and developed' (PWC/AHEIA 2016: 5). The report commences by quoting a vice chancellor: 'Is the traditional idea of an academic career the wrong idea?' (PWC/AHEIA 2016: 4). While echoing other reports in urging greater responsiveness to student markets and to business, it claims that university performance management and promotion processes inhibit this by focusing on research, research metrics and university rankings. 'This deters academic staff from gaining industry experience, reducing the permeability between university and industry, and results in an immobile workforce' (PWC/AHEIA 2016: 16). The report states that the university leaders they spoke to are seeking a 'workforce with skills that are transferable across boundaries' such as those between disciplines and sub-disciplines and between universities and industry (PWC/AHEIA 2016: 22).

According to PWC, their 'research' identified three future workforce attributes that all universities ought to have (PWC/AHEIA 2016: 14): agility and flexibility, professionalization and specialization. The workforce attribute 'agility' appears to be conceived as the ability of an organization or individual to adapt quickly to changes in the operating environment, such as shifts in sources of income and variations in the demand for services. Also, flexibility is only applied one way, by the higher education institution in varying the composition of the workforce, which is expected to adjust to changing academic markets. According to the report, this can only be achieved by universities reducing their reliance on full-time permanent, 'tenured' or 'tenure track' faculty who undertake a combination of teaching, research and service, and expanding the proportion of part-time teaching-focused academics and practitioners from industry on fixed-term contracts.

Professionalization is conceived in the PWC report as 'a lever to ensure the sustained relevance of capability and skill set of the university workforce. ... This encompasses both continuous development of skills to deliver in current roles ... as well as the acquisition of new domain expertise' (PWC/AHEIA 2016: 14). In this sense, it is a prerequisite for agility and flexibility, but is a highly individualized notion of professionalism that focuses on instant skills and know-how that can be provided by training on demand rather than knowledge and expertise that is developed through long-term research and scholarship.

Finally, specialization is 'moving away from the 40/40/20 academic workload allocation model, and changing the "one size fits all" expectation regarding research participation' (PWC/AHEIA 2016: 14). The increased focus on 'teaching and learning andragogy' and the development of 'practitioner academics' is combined with new specializations for 'para-academics' in digital technology, learning design and analytics to enhance learning outcomes. In effect, if research and scholarship are no longer the basis of higher education, then the disciplinary knowledge and expertise of individual academics can be replaced by technique and performance. Academic work is reduced to that which delivers the university's strategic goals and, especially, to gaining competitive advantage in the various markets in which it operates. Academic (and other) staff are converted from a profession into a workforce that must be agile and flexible and subject to professionalization and specialization, even though these 'attributes' are often in tension with each other.

What is absent from this and other accounts of the future of academia is evidence of the perspectives and experiences of academics themselves, and an accurate account of their current roles, work activities and career trajectories. The PWC/AHEIA and other reports ignore the existing research findings and reported experiences of the diverse range of university employees involved in academic work. Critically, they exclude any significant account of the successful, effective and innovative practices that can be found in universities, which might act as a guide to future options and opportunities.

The Existing Research Evidence about Trends in Academic Work, Roles and Careers

The futurologists ignore much of the existing research evidence about academic work, roles and careers (Mauri 2016). They assume that the academic profession is still largely homogenous and that the vast majority of academics are in permanent positions, undertaking both teaching and research. Yet, there is a burgeoning research literature on the diversification of the academic 'profession', the wide range of entrants (including from other professions), the different career paths they take and, indeed, the erosion of the linear academic career (e.g. Finkelstein, Conley and Schuster 2016; Kwiek 2019). The initial findings of the CGHE research project on The Future Higher Education Workforce appear to confirm this, in the UK context at least (Whitchurch, Locke and Marini 2019). Also, part-time, fixed-term, contingent, teaching-only and non-tenure track faculty have grown significantly in the UK, Australia and United States in recent years. In the UK, those academics in teaching-only and research-only roles have made up the majority since 2014 (Locke et al. 2016). In Australia, the majority of those teaching in universities are casual or on fixed-term contracts (Long 2018). In all US HEIs, 73 per cent of teaching positions are off the tenure track (AAUP 2018).

The majority in these precarious positions are women and early career academics earning much less than their full-time, permanent and tenured colleagues, and with limited prospects for career progression (Locke et al. 2016). Furthermore, these categories of academic staff are far less likely to have access to the kinds of opportunities for continuing professional development that might be necessary to meet future challenges (Finkelstein, Conley and Schuster 2016; Locke et al. 2016; Probert 2013). Indeed, there are clear drawbacks in having a largely insecure workforce, with reduced commitment to the institution, less involvement in academic decision-making and fewer resources to support students and pursue research and scholarship. Research in the United States and elsewhere is beginning to show how greater reliance on 'contingent' faculty can actually have detrimental impacts on student applications and enrolments, student-faculty ratios, the quality of learning and teaching, graduation rates and, ultimately, institutions' net revenues (Hearn, Burns and Riffe 2018. See also May et al. 2011 for the Australian context).

For the futurologists, the supposed advantage of contingent academic labour is to provide the institution with flexibility to respond to market volatility. However, this flexibility is not applied the other way – to the employment conditions for staff and the ways that universities engage academics in work that matches their talents and achieves the institutional mission and strategic goals. Evidence is emerging, again in the United States, that flexible employment policies for individual staff foster improved inclusion of diverse faculty; increased efficiency, greater organizational commitment and productivity; and enhanced perceptions of a fair work environment (O'Meara 2015). It seems likely that this more balanced approach to flexibility will achieve the forms of professionalism, and long-term commitment to developing expertise in research, scholarship, teaching, exchanging knowledge with business and engaging with the public required of academics now, and in the future. This is not the 'professionalisation' of academia, conceived as a process that is imposed from above on a new 'flexible' workforce, it is a collective endeavour that emerges from within, and is undertaken by, a profession (Locke 2014). The need for a more delicate balance in optimizing individual aspirations and institutional missions in higher education is also emerging from the Centre's higher education workforce research (Whitchurch, Locke and Marini 2019).

Conclusion: Re-imagining the Future of Higher Education and Those Who Work in It

The accounts of the future of higher education and those who work in it considered in this chapter are intended to have an impact on current thinking and lead activity in specific directions and for particular ideological ends. Understanding this can help us begin to re-imagine the future in different ways, in more diverse directions and for multiple, explicit purposes. In contrast to these accounts, we can start with an accurate analysis of the present, based on the best current research evidence and analysis of trends in the recent, mid- and long-term past. This might include rigorous analysis of existing examples of effective and successful practice that could offer embryonic illustrations of developments for the future. The European Union-sponsored 'Universities of the Future' programme (Universities of the Future 2019) and the University of Lincoln's 21st Century Lab – Thinking Ahead (University of Lincoln 2019) are two examples. These evidence-based and iterative approaches can ensure that we evaluate the full range of factors, including the sociocultural, political and environmental (and even quasi-legal) factors as well as the economic and technological. When examining the economic, technological and other drivers, we can avoid reductionist approaches that privilege particular activities and deterministic assumptions that prioritize specific outcomes. We can adopt pluralist approaches which draw on the different perspectives of students, staff and other stakeholders – including those from outside higher education with relevant perspectives – as well as leaders and policy-makers.

Our investigations into the future of higher education can recognize the diverse range of providers of higher education, including teaching-oriented, research-intensive and specialist universities, research institutes, non-university HEIs, tertiary institutions, two- and four-year colleges, not-for-profit private and for-profit private providers and those new organizational and networked arrangements that are only just being conceived. They can include hybrid forms of higher education that blend new ideas and technologies with existing forms and practices in innovative and creative ways, without necessarily discarding traditional methods altogether. They can reflect developments in the internationalization of higher education in the context of wider geopolitical realignments and explore its future from a global perspective, while recognizing the importance of regional, national and local contexts. Perhaps most important of all, our analyses can acknowledge the active role that universities and the scholars they house – often in collaboration with others – play in initiating and directing many of the intellectual, social, technological and environmental innovations that will shape the future, not just of higher education but of societies in general.

References

AAUP (2018), *Data Snapshot: Contingent Faculty in US Higher Ed*, American Association of University Professors, Washington DC, https://www.aaup.org/sites/default/files/10112018%20Data%20Snapshot%20Tenure.pdf (last accessed January 2019).

ACE (2013), *Signals and Shifts in the Postsecondary Landscape*, American Council on Education, Center for Education Attainment and Innovation, Presidential Innovation Lab White Paper Series, Washington DC, http://www.acenet.edu/news-room/Documents/Signals-and-Shifts-in-the-Postsecondary-Landscape.pdf (last accessed August 2018).

ACE (2014a), *Beyond the Inflection Point – Reimagining Business Models for Higher Education*, American Council on Education, Center for Education Attainment and Innovation, Presidential Innovation Lab White Paper Series, Washington DC, http://www.acenet.edu/news-room/Documents/Beyond-the-Inflection-Point-Reimagining-Business-Models-for-Higher-Education.pdf (last accessed August 2018).

ACE (2014b), *The Students of the Future, American Council on Education*, Center for Education Attainment and Innovation, Presidential Innovation Lab White Paper Series, Washington DC, http://www.acenet.edu/news-room/Documents/The-Students-of-the-Future.pdf (last accessed August 2018).

Archibald, R. and Feldman, D. (2010), *Why Does College Cost So Much?*, New York: Oxford University Press.

Barber, M., Donnelly, K. and Rizvi, S. (2013), *An Avalanche Is Coming – Higher Education and the Revolution Ahead*, London: Institute for Public Policy Research, https://www.ippr.org/publications/an-avalanche-is-coming-higher-education-and-the-revolution-ahead (last accessed August 2018).

Contact North (2016), A 2016 *Look at the Future of Online Learning*, https://teachonline.ca/sites/default/files/tools-trends/downloads/2016_look_at_online_learning.pdf (last accessed August 2018).

Deloitte (2013), *Higher Education Is Evolving – As the Business Model Changes, the Governance Model Must Too*, Burlington, ON: Deloitte LLP, https://www2.deloitte.com/ca/en/pages/human-capital/articles/higher-education-is-evolving.html (last accessed August 2018).

Deloitte (2014), *Reimagining Higher Education: How Colleges, Universities, Businesses, and Governments Can Prepare for a New Age of Lifelong Learning*, A GovLab Report by Lindsay Sledge and Tiffany Dovey Fishman, Deloitte University Press, https://www2.deloitte.com/insights/us/en/industry/public-sector/reimagining-higher-education.html (last accessed August 2018).

Economist Intelligence Unit (2014), *Higher Education in the 21st Century – Meeting Real-World Demands*, L. Barack, London and New York: The Economist and Academic Partnerships.

Ernst & Young (2012), *University of the Future – A Thousand Year Old Industry on the Cusp of Profound Change*, Sydney: Ernst & Young, https://web.archive.org/web/20121119092916/http://www.ey.com/Publication/vwLUAssets/University_of_the_future/%24FILE/University_of_the_future_2012.pdf (last accessed August 2018).

Ernst & Young (2018), *Can the Universities of Today Lead Learning for Tomorrow?* The University of the Future, Sydney: Ernst & Young, http://www.ey.com/au/en/industries/government---public-sector/uof_university-of-the-future (last accessed July 2018).

Finkelstein, M. J., Conley, V. M. and Schuster, J. H. (2016) *The Faculty Factor: Reassessing the American Academy in a Turbulent Era*, Baltimore, MD: Johns Hopkins University Press.

Forbes (2018), *The Changing Business Model For Colleges And Universities*, L. Lapovsky, 6 February 2018, https://www.forbes.com/sites/lucielapovsky/2018/02/06/the-changing-business-model-for-colleges-and-universities/#2b7835545ed5 (last accessed August 2018).

Gallagher, S. and Garrett, G. (2013), *Disruptive Education: Technology Enabled Universities*, The United States Studies Centre at The University of Sydney / UNSW, https://assets.ussc.edu.au/view/25/f3/26/2d/c0/a7/a5/18/fa/b4/cd/e5/d2/d2/85/e6/original/959a3d253927020b0ed1a1bd671e65306f29b4f4/130801_DisruptiveEducation_GallagherGarrett.pdf (last accessed August 2018).

Hearn, J. C., Burns, R. A. and Riffe, K. A. (2018), *Academic Workforce Flexibility and Strategic Outcomes in Four-Year Colleges and Universities, Trends and Issues*, May, New York: TIAA Institute (Teachers Insurance and Annuity Association of America), https://www.tiaainstitute.org/sites/default/files/presentations/2018-05/TIAA%20Institute_Hearn_Academic%20Workforce%20Flexibility_T%26I_May%202018.pdf (last accessed July 2018).

Kwiek, M. (2019), *Changing European Academics: A Comparative Study of Social Stratification, Work Patterns and Research Productivity*, New York: Routledge.

Lee Hecht Harrison (2016), *The University for the Future: Evolutions, Revolutions and Transformations* (Rod Gutierrez, Ed.), Sydney: Lee Hecht Harrison, https://www.aheia.edu.au/cms_uploads/docs/lhh-university-for-the-future.pdf (last accessed July 2018).

Locke, W. (2014), *Shifting Academic Careers and Their Implications for Enhancing Professionalism in Teaching and Supporting Learning* (York: Higher Education Academy), https://www.heacademy.ac.uk/node/10079 (last accessed January 2019).

Locke, W., Whitchurch, C., Smith, H. and Mazenod, A. (2016), *Shifting Landscapes: Meeting the Staff Development Needs of the Changing Academic Workforce*, York: Higher Education Academy, https://www.heacademy.ac.uk/sites/default/files/shifting_landscapes_1.pdf (last accessed September 2018).

Long, C (2018), 'Casualisation of University Workforce Is a National Disgrace', *The Sydney Morning Herald*, 3 August 2018, https://www.smh.com.au/education/casualisation-of-university-workforce-is-a-national-disgrace-20180803-p4zvcm.html (last accessed January 2019).

Mauri, C. J. (2016), *Higher Education Workforce of the Future*, revisited. https://sociyology.wordpress.com/2016/11/30/higher-education-workforce-of-the-future-revisited/ (last accessed July 2018).

May, R., Strachan, G., Broadbent, K. and Peetz, D. (2011), 'The Casual Approach to University Teaching; Time for a Re-think?', in K. Krause, M. Buckridge, C. Grimmer and S. Purbrick-Illek (eds), *Research and Development in Higher Education: Reshaping Higher Education*, 34, 188–97. Gold Coast, Australia, 4–7 July 2011, http://www.herdsa.org.au/wp-content/uploads/conference/2011/papers/HERDSA_2011_May.PDF (last accessed August 2014).

O'Meara, K. A. (2015), *Flexible Workplace Agreements: Enabling Higher Education's Strategic Advantage*, New York: TIAA Institute (Teachers Insurance and Annuity Association of America): https://www.tiaainstitute.org/sites/default/files/presentations/2017-02/flexible_workplace_agreements.pdf (last accessed July 2018).

PA Consulting/HEFCE (2010), *The Future Workforce for Higher Education: A Report to HEFCE* by PA Consulting Group, Bristol: Higher Education Funding Council for England, http://www.hefce.ac.uk/pubs/rereports/year/2010/heprovisionukworkforce/ (last accessed July 2018 Check again after September 2018).

Probert, B. (2013), *Teaching-Focused Academic Appointments in Australian Universities: Recognition, Specialisation, or Stratification?*, Office for Learning and Teaching, Government of Australia, http://apo.org.au/research/teaching-focused-academic-appointments-australian-universities-recognition-specialisation (accessed 29 August 2014).

PWC/AHEIA (2016), *Australian Higher Education Workforce of the Future*, PricewaterhouseCoopers and the Australian Higher Education Industrial Association, http://www.aheia.edu.au/news/higher-education-workforce-of-the-future-167 (last accessed July 2018).

Universities of the Future (2019), 'European Union-Funded Knowledge Alliance Project', https://universitiesofthefuture.eu (last accessed November 2019).

University of Lincoln (2019), 21st Century Lab – Thinking Ahead, https://www.lincoln.ac.uk/home/researchatlincoln/21stcenturylab/ (last accessed November 2019).

Whitchurch, C., Locke, W. and Marini, G. (2019), *A Delicate Balance: Optimising Individual Aspirations and Institutional Missions in Higher Education*, Centre for Global Higher Education (CGHE) Project 3.2 Working Paper.

Part II

Global Factors in Higher Education

3

The World Research System

Expansion, Diversification, Network and Hierarchy

Simon Marginson

Research in Universities

This chapter focuses on patterns in global research science, especially in universities. ('Science' includes research in social science and the professional disciplines.) Since the internet began in 1990 universities across the world, for the first time in history, have been joined in a single interactive network of knowledge production and cooperation – a global library of English-language science and a one-world mind. Though higher education houses only part of all R&D – 23.7 per cent in the United Kingdom in 2017, 13.0 per cent in the United States, just 7.2 per cent in China (OECD 2019) – universities lead the production and distribution of codified knowledge and researcher training. Nearly all science journals are edited in universities. Most of their contributors work in universities.

Science is a complex intermesh of (a) researchers and discipline-based or cross-disciplinary research groups; (b) sites such as universities, institutes, corporations and government laboratories; (c) national research systems; and (d) the global research system. Linkages between researchers in the same intellectual discipline criss-cross the world directly. Universities and governments also matter: they fund and sponsor research and provide essential infrastructure. Yet national research systems have become embedded in global science and evolve partly in response to it. Nations build their research capacity so as to access the global pool of knowledge, the main source of research-based innovations.

Though global science cannot be observed directly it is visible in the proxy form of published research. There are two primary original sources of data on research papers and citations, both largely focused on English-language journals. These data sources are managed by Clavirate Analytics (Web of Science) and Elsevier (Scopus). One or the other is at the base of all the main global university rankings and research rankings (ARWU 2019; THE 2019; QS 2019; Leiden University 2019). Further data on R&D funding and researcher numbers are provided by the Organisation for Economic Cooperation and Development (OECD), and the United Nations Educational, Scientific and Cultural Organisation (UNESCO 2019).

In these data sets there are four standout patterns in global science: First, rapid growth in investment in research and in publications. Second, expansion of research-active countries. Third, growth in the proportion of papers co-authored from more than one country. Fourth, diversification of the leading science countries. This chapter expands on these patterns, interpretations of the patterns and their transformative impact.

The limitations of these sources must be acknowledged. Non-English-language journals are largely excluded from Clavirate Analytics and Elsevier. While US or UK science papers on parochial local themes enter the global literature, papers on universal themes in Spanish, Arabic or Chinese mostly do not. Books in all languages are also under-represented. Like the dark matter that makes up much of the universe but cannot be seen, alongside the global science discussed in this chapter, there is a large mass of invisible national-local science.

Worldwide Growth of Research

Table 3.1 shows that between 1995 and 2017 spending on R&D in higher education multiplied by 5.3 times in South Korea and 15.2 in China as each built fully fledged research sectors, and more than doubled in the United States and Canada (OECD 2019). This expanding financial capacity triggered major growth in researchers, PhDs and published science.

Between 1990 and 2011 published authors increased from 1.87 to 4.66 million (Wagner, Park and Leydesdorff 2015: 4). Between 2003 and 2016 the global output of published papers rose from 1.2 to 2.3 million. The Leiden University (2019) research ranking, using Clavirate Analytics, lists output in four-year segments. Between 2006–9 and 2014–17, the number of universities that published at least 10,000 science papers more than doubled, rising from 26 to 61, and in China from 1 to 16. Between 2000 and 2014 the number of

Table 3.1 Spending on R&D in Higher Education (Constant 2010 US dollars, PPP), Eight Countries with Highest such Spending: Five-Year Intervals 1990–2015, and Most Recent Year 2017

	($s billion)						
	1990	**1995**	**2000**	**2005**	**2010**	**2015**	**2017**
US	25.56	30.23	37.78	51.68	60.37	59.29	63.06
China	1.16	2.09	3.50	9.45	18.05	26.42	31.83
Germany	8.21	10.35	11.28	12.08	15.81	17.55	19.01
Japan	12.20	15.09	17.75	19.01	18.09	18.97	18.63
France	5.55	6.68	8.09	8.66	10.97	12.25	11.52
Canada	3.74	4.14	5.95	8.63	9.21	10.14	10.38
UK	4.52	5.20	6.45	8.90	10.15	10.59	10.25
South Korea	n.a.	1.34	2.40	3.21	4.63	6.69	7.15

n.a. indicates data not available. PPP = Purchasing Power Parity data to enable cross-country comparability.

Data listed as China 1990 are for 1991.

Source: Author, drawing from data in OECD (2019).

doctoral graduates increased by 11.2 per annum in China, 5.3 per cent in South Korea and 4.7 per cent in the UK. China and India are now the second and fifth largest annual producers of doctoral graduates (NSB 2018: Tables A2–38 and A2–39).

Diversification of Research Countries

New science nations gain access to the common pool of knowledge by sharing in its production. The network analysis of global science by Wagner, Park and Leydesdorff (2015) shows that the core group of closely engaged research systems greatly expanded after 1990. Many 'developing' (emerging) countries now have their own science systems. Data on the growth of research papers also show the expansion and diversification of research. Table 3.2 provides the annual rate of growth of science papers between 2006 and 2016 in nations producing more than 5,000 papers in 2016 where the growth rate exceeded the world level of 3.9 per cent (NSB 2018: Tables 5–27). Most of these nations housed emerging research systems. Some had a GDP per capita well below the world average, such as Indonesia and India. Like research in general, high-quality research universities are now more widely distributed. There were thirty national systems that included universities producing more than one hundred papers ranked in the top 5 per cent of their field by citation rate in 2006–9. Seven years later in 2014–17, that number of systems had risen to thirty-eight (Leiden University 2019).

Table 3.2 Annual Rate of Growth in Published Science Papers between 2006 and 2016, Nations above the World Average Growth Rate of 3.9% and Producing More Than 5,000 Papers in 2016

System	Papers in 2006	Papers in 2016	Annual growth (%)
Indonesia	619	7,729	28.7
Malaysia	3,230	20,332	20.2
Saudi Arabia	1,898	9,232	17.1
Colombia	1,368	6,121	16.2
Iran	10,073	40,974	15.1
Pakistan	2,809	9,181	12.6
Romania	3,523	10,194	11.2
India	38,590	110,320	11.1
Tunisia	1,980	5,266	10.3
Egypt	3,958	10,807	10.6
China	189,760	426,165	8.4
Thailand	4,270	9,582	8.4
Chile	3,122	6,746	8.0
South Africa	5,636	11,881	7.7
Slovakia	2,644	5,359	7.3
Russia	29,369	59,134	7.2
Portugal	7,136	13,773	6.8
Brazil	28,160	53,607	6.6
Serbia	2,843	5,052	6.6
Czech Republic	8,839	15,963	6.1
South Korea	36,747	63,063	5.5
Denmark	8,536	13,471	4.7
Poland	21,267	32,978	4.5
Mexico	9,322	14,529	4.5
Argentina	5,600	8,648	4.4
Australia	33,100	51,068	4.4
Norway	7,093	10,726	4.2
WORLD	**1,567,422**	**2,295,608**	**3.9**

Data for Serbia are from 2007 to 2016. In joint papers national authorship is allocated on a weighted basis.

Source: Author, drawing on data from NSB (2018), Table 5-27.

Cross-Border Research Collaboration

In 1970, internationally co-authored papers constituted only 1.9 per cent of articles indexed in Web of Science (Olechnicka, Ploszaj and Celinska-Janowicz 2019: 78). Between 2006 and 2016 the proportion of papers in Scopus that were internationally co-authored rose from 16.7 to 21.7 per cent (NSB 2018: Table A5–42). Wagner, Park and Leydesdorff (2015) argue that international research collaboration within open science, like all networks (Castells 2000), contains an inbuilt tendency to growth in both collaboration rate and shared output.

Some international connections are relatively thick in terms of the total volume of co-authored papers. In 2016 US and UK researchers together published 25,858 papers (NSB 2018: Tables A5–43), almost one-third of all internationally collaborative papers from the UK. Some connections between countries exhibit thickness in another sense, the propensity to collaborate, when compared with the pattern of collaborations overall.

Where there are formal programmes for collaboration, where equipment is cost shared (e.g. telescopes, synchrotrons), or where subject matter is intrinsically global (e.g. climate change, water management, epidemic disease) then collaboration increases. In 2016, 54 per cent of all papers in astronomy were internationally co-authored and collaboration exceeded 20 per cent in geosciences, biological sciences, mathematics, physics and chemistry. In social sciences the collaboration rate was 15 per cent (NSB 2018: 122).

There are marked variations between countries as Table 3.3 shows. Collaboration is lower in large national systems with many potential national co-authors (e.g. China) and increases slower, or falls (e.g. India and Iran), in fast-growing systems with multiplying national co-authors (NSB 2018: Table A5–42). Given the size factor, 37 per cent collaboration in the very large US research system is high, and signifies its leadership role in science. Collaboration is very high in Europe, where research funding often requires cross-country teams (NSB 2018: 122), especially in small- to medium-sized countries.

Collaboration is concentrated in networked global cities (Olechnicka, Ploszaj and Celinska-Janowicz 2019: 86) and global satellites like Boston and Oxford. Leading research universities are engines of networked cooperation, with high rates of co-authorship compared to other universities in the same systems. Harvard published 37,562 collaborative international papers in 2014–17, half of all papers involving Harvard researchers (Table 3.4). There is a noticeable increase in all collaboration rates in the eight-year span of the table (Leiden University 2019).

Clumping within Global Science

Historic ties, geographical proximity, linguistic commonality (regional languages such as Spanish or Arabic), economic interests and political ties all play a role in fostering high-intensity collaboration. Intensity is measured by rate of international co-authorship in science papers between countries in a pair,

Table 3.3 Proportion of All Science Papers That Were Internationally Co-authored, Selected Countries: 2003 and 2016

	2003 (%)	2016 (%)
TEN LARGEST RESEARCH SYSTEMS		
United Kingdom	36.9	57.1
France	39.6	54.8
Germany	39.4	51.0
Italy	33.1	47.3
United States	23.3	37.0
Japan	18.9	27.9
South Korea	25.1	27.0
Russia	26.9	25.1
China	15.3	20.3
India	18.1	17.4
STRONG SMALLER RESEARCH SYSTEMS		
Switzerland	54.5	69.2
Denmark	47.7	63.3
Singapore	35.0	62.8
Netherlands	44.7	61.8
Finland	41.2	60.4
RECENTLY EMERGED SYSTEMS		
Saudi Arabia	34.5	76.8
Chile	52.7	61.7
Brazil	27.2	32.5
Iran	24.2	20.8

Large research systems identified by total paper output in 2016.

Source: Author, drawing on data from NSB (2018), Table A5–42.

relative to their co-authorship with all countries. A rate of 1.00 indicates that intensity of collaboration is the expected level given the overall patterns in the two countries (the number is the same for both countries); 0.50 indicates slow propensity; 1.50 indicates high propensity.

English-speaking countries often, but not always, collaborate at above average rates: 3.38 between neighbours Australia and New Zealand in 2016, but 0.77 between United States and United Kingdom, which each have many other connections. The UK collaborated 1.33 with South Africa and 1.35 with New Zealand. There is intense collaboration within Spanish-speaking Latin America, such as 8.31 between Chile and Argentina, though the volume of co-authored papers between each and the United States is much higher. There is close regional collaboration among Nordic nations Denmark, Finland, Norway and Sweden, which share geographical location, historic ties and social systems. The

Table 3.4 Leading Twenty Universities in the Production of Internationally Co-authored Papers: 2014–17

University		All published papers (2014–17)	Papers in top 5% by citation (2014–17)	Proportion international (2006–7)(%)	Proportion international (2014–17)(%)	International co-authored (2014–17)
Harvard U	USA	33,188	4,242	36.0	50.4	37,562
U Oxford	UK	14,698	1,571	54.5	67.4	24,006
U Toronto	Canada	22,149	1,653	43.6	55.4	23,555
U College London	UK	14,256	1,382	50.3	64.2	22,554
U Cambridge	UK	13,154	1,324	50.6	67.9	20,968
Imperial College London	UK	11,584	1,137	53.7	67.8	19,404
Sorbonne U	France	8,604	552	53.9	65.7	19,360
Johns Hopkins U	USA	16,902	1,424	33.3	43.2	16,828
U Copenhagen	Denmark	12,277	780	55.4	64.5	16,728
National U Singapore	Singapore	11,929	890	46.0	65.1	16,381
Katholieke U Leuven	Belgium	10,636	774	56.1	68.5	16,271
Stanford U	USA	15,543	2,044	31.7	44.7	15,874
U British Columbia	Canada	12,594	909	46.8	58.7	15,669
U Melbourne	Australia	12,307	815	41.0	54.6	15,266
U Sydney	Australia	12,242	809	42.8	56.1	15,114
U Sao Paulo	Brazil	16,846	465	31.2	44.3	14,757
MIT	USA	10,358	1,549	38.0	55.1	14,601
ETH Zurich	Switzerland	9,152	912	59.0	69.3	14,551
Karolinska Institute	Sweden	8,152	573	56.5	68.1	14,340
U Michigan	USA	18,203	1,469	27.0	37.8	14,160

'All published papers' is weighted by share of authorship. 'Internationally co-authored' includes all papers in which the university's authors participate regardless of share of authorship. 'Papers in top 5%' refer to the number of a university's publications that, compared with other publications in the same field and in the same year, belong to the top 5% most frequently cited, including all citations up to the end of 2018.

Source: Author, using data from Leiden University (2019), derived from Clarivate Analytics.

six possible permutations generated indexes of 3.16 to 4.54. There were 9,865 Nordic collaborative papers in total, which was 60 per cent of the number of joint Nordic-US papers (NSB 2018: Tables A5–43 and A5–44).

High-intensity pairings of neighbours in Europe in 2016 included Poland-Czech Republic (5.47), Turkey-Greece (4.11), Spain-Portugal (3.43), Netherlands-Belgium (3.09), Finland-Russia (2.83), Austria-Germany (2.63), Austria-Switzerland (2.51) and UK-Ireland (2.16), though all European countries are integrated neighbours in science. Some had indexes above 1.00 in 2016 with *every* other European country and few outside Europe. UK collaboration exceeded 1.00 with all European systems except the Czech Republic and Russia (NSB 2018: Table A5–43).

US science collaborated with neighbours Canada at 1.13 and Mexico at 1.04 in 2016. There were special ties with Israel (1.33) and with South Korea (1.23) and Taiwan (1.04), where US universities maintain a strong role in doctoral training. The United States is also an important partner in many countries where pairings are below 1.00. In 2016, US authors shared 29 per cent of all cross-border papers in Germany, 25 per cent in France, 30 per cent in Netherlands, 32 per cent in India, 33 per cent in Japan and 48 per cent in Korea. Researchers in China had an intensive relationship with Singapore (2.03), Taiwan (1.73) and growing links to Pakistan (1.23). Collaboration with Japan declined from 1.51 in 2006 to 1.09 in 2016. China sustained a strong link with Australia (1.15, 9246 papers) and the United States (1.19) (NSB 2018: Tables A5-43 and A5-44).

In 2016, there were 43,968 joint China-American papers, compared to 5406 papers in 2006. This is much the thickest nation-to-nation linkage in global science in terms of volume. In 2016, 23 per cent of all US international co-publishing was with China, while 46 per cent of all China's co-publishing was with the United States (NSB 2018: Tables 5–26, A5–43, A5–44). The nation states of the United States and China are engaged in global rivalry (Bush and Hass 2019). Yet, their relations in science, sustained by all of bottom-up disciplinary networks, university–university collaboration and national policies, constitute a great zone of cooperation.

Cross-Border Doctoral Students

Another form of international collaboration, often leading to co-authored publications and career-long ties, is doctoral student mobility. In 2016, 26 per cent of doctoral students in OECD nations had crossed borders (OECD 2018: 327). 'Mobile students gain tacit knowledge that is often shared through direct personal interactions and that enables their home country to integrate

Table 3.5 Proportion (%) of research degree students and doctoral students** that were international*, selected OECD countries: 2007–16

Country	2007 (%)	2008 (%)	2009 (%)	2010 (%)	2011 (%)	2012 (%)	2013 (%)	2014 (%)	2015 (%)	2016 (%)
High Internationalization (40% or more in 2016)										
Switzerland	45	46	47	48	50	51	52	53	54	55
United Kingdom	42	42	43	42	41	41	41	42	43	43
United States	24	28	28	28	28	29	32	35	38	40
France	38*	40*	41*	42*	42*	42*	40	40	40	40
Moderate Internationalization (15–40% in 2016)										
Australia	21	23	26	29	31	32	33	34	34	34
Denmark	7	5	11	21	23	24	30	30	32	34
Portugal	10*	7	7	8	9	10	15	16	21	26
Japan	16	16	16	17	19	19	19	19	18	18
Lower Internationalization (less than 15% in 2016)										
Slovenia	7	7	10	7	8	10	8	8	9	10
South Korea	6*	7*	7*	7*	8*	7*	8*	8*	9*	9*
Germany	n.a.	n.a.	n.a.	n.a.	6	7	7	7	9	9
Hungary	7	7	6	6	6	6	7	8	7	12

* Proportion of students that were foreign, not incoming mobile international students. Not all countries collect data on the latter, though those doing so increased in 2007–16. Foreign student proportions are generally higher, all else equal.

** Advanced research programme students until 2012, then doctoral students. In some countries the former category included a small number of research Masters students so all else being equal the percentage falls slightly after 2012.

Slovenia became a full OECD member country in 2009. n.a. = data not available.

Source: Successive annual volumes of OECD *Education at a Glance* (OECD 2018).

into global knowledge networks' (OECD 2017: 287). In the United States and United Kingdom, over 40 per cent of doctoral students were international while less than 15 per cent were international in Korea and Germany. Doctoral internationalization was increasing sharply only in Denmark, United States, Portugal, Australia and Switzerland (Table 3.5) (OECD 2018 and previous years).

Between 1995 and 2015, 68,379 students from China received US doctorates, 32,737 from India, 20,626 from Korea and 13,001 from Taiwan (NSB 2018: Tables A2–14 and A2–15)

Diversification of Research Power

The pluralization of global science has seen also a pluralization of strong systems. A feature of the last twenty-five years has been the rise of East Asia. Universities in China, Korea and Singapore have followed Japan, which established national science in the previous generation. Figure 3.1 shows that from 2003 to 2016 the number of papers multiplied by 2.72 in Korea and 4.92 in China. China's annual output exceeded the United States in 2016 (NSB 2018: Table A5–27).

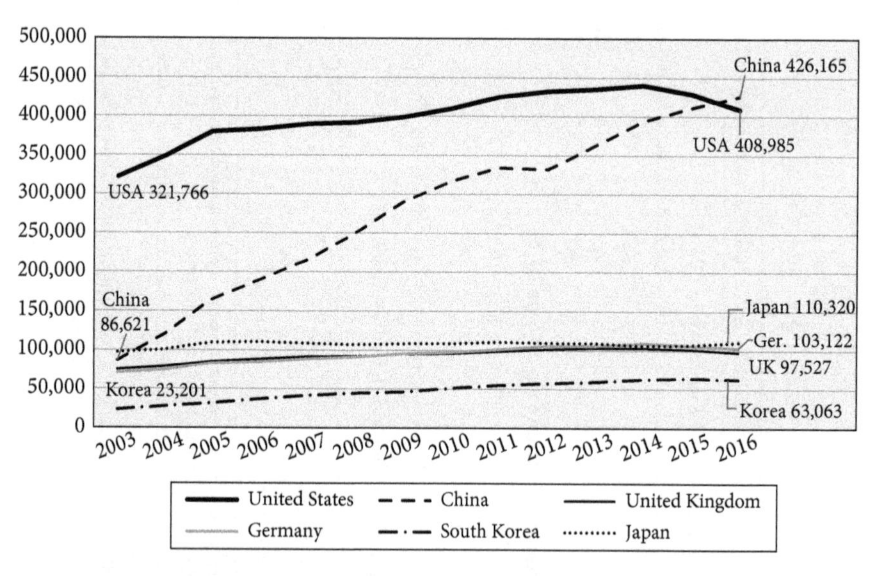

Figure 3.1 Annual number of published science papers, United States, China, Germany, United Kingdom, Japan, South Korea: 2003–16.

These are six of the eight largest producers of science papers ; the others are France and Italy. The selection shows the contrasting trajectories of the US, UK, Germany and the East Asian systems.

Source: Prepared by author drawing on data from NSB (2018), Table A5-27. Original data from Scopus. Paper numbers for 2015 and 2016 appear incomplete. It is likely in future compilations papers for those years will increase, for all countries.

Xie and Freeman (2018) find that papers authored in China rose from 4 per cent of the Scopus count in 2000 to 18 per cent in 2016. When researchers with Chinese names working outside China are added, including collaborative papers with weighted allocations, China's share rises to 23 per cent. This becomes 35 per cent of science when it includes all papers with at least one Chinese address or name without weighting, and 45 per cent when science papers in the 4,216 Chinese language journals (2017) are added. Xie and Freeman (2018: 9) conclude that China has 'a huge role in developing the knowledge-based economy'.

The rise of the East Asia rests on investment, international benchmarking and talent recruitment (Wang, Wang and Liu 2011). Along with the expansion of quantity, quality as measured by citation rates has improved, albeit from modest levels. Between 1996 and 2014 the average citation rate of papers by Chinese authors rose from 0.46 to 0.96 compared to the world average of 1.00. In South Korea average citations rose from 0.79 to 1.06, and in Singapore from 1.00 to 1.83. In 2014, 3.02 per cent of all Singapore-authored papers were in the top 1 per cent by citation rate (NSB 2018: Tables A5–50 and A5–51).

The leading universities in East Asia perform more strongly in comparative terms than do their national systems overall, an outcome of policies designed to fast-forward the development of 'World-Class Universities' (Salmi 2009). Between 2006–09 and 2014–17 papers in the top 5 per cent of their field by citation rate grew by at least *13 per cent per annum* in the top-ten Chinese universities and Singapore's Nanyang TU. In 2014–17 Tsinghua in China produced 1,270 such papers, just below 1,324 at Cambridge (Leiden University 2019).

There is still a performance gap overall. In 2014–17, 6.9 per cent of Tsinghua's papers were in the top 5 per cent of their field compared to 10.1 per cent at Cambridge and 15.0 per cent at MIT. However, in the STEM discipline cluster, the priority of East Asian governments – physics, chemistry, engineering, mathematics, computing and related fields – China and Singapore have closed the gap. Table 3.6 lists the top universities in 2014–17 on the basis of top 5 per cent papers. China was well ahead of the United States in mathematics and complex computing and in all STEM disciplines taken together, Tsinghua was number one. When the measure is switched to top 1 per cent papers, Tsinghua with forty-five papers was number two after Harbin (forty-six) in mathematics and computing. MIT had thirty-eight. In physical sciences and engineering Tsinghua had 155 papers, third behind MIT (187) and Stanford (172) but ahead of Harvard on 149 (Leiden University 2019).

East Asia is weaker in comparative terms in biomedicine and the life sciences. In 2014–17 Harvard had 2935 top 5 per cent papers in biomedicine and health

Table 3.6 Leading Universities in (1) Physical Sciences and Engineering, and (2) Mathematics and Complex Computing, Published Papers in Top 5% of Field by Citation Rate, World: 2013–16

University	System	(1) physical sciences & engineering 2013-16	University	System	(2) maths & complex computing 2013–16
Tsinghua U	CHINA	776	Tsinghua U	CHINA	236
Massachusetts IT	USA	691	Harbin IT	CHINA	182
Stanford U	USA	598	Zhejiang U	CHINA	155
U California, Berkeley	USA	580	Huazhong U S&T	CHINA	153
Harvard U	USA	552	U Electronic S&T	CHINA	143
Zhejiang U	CHINA	509	Xidian U	CHINA	142
Nanyang TU	SINGAPORE	503	Beihang U	CHINA	141
U Science & Technol.	CHINA	452	Massachusetts IT	USA	138
U Cambridge	UK	449	Nanyang TU	SINGAPORE	137
Shanghai Jiao Tong U	CHINA	398	NU Singapore	SINGAPORE	137
ETH Zurich	SWITZERLAND	394	Shanghai Jiao Tong U	CHINA	130
Peking U	CHINA	389	City U Hong Kong	HK SAR	124
Imperial Col., London	UK	388	South East U	CHINA	123
NU Singapore	SINGAPORE	384	Stanford U	USA	119
Xi'an Jiatong U	CHINA	379	Xi'an Jiatong U	CHINA	101

Technol. = Technology.

Source: Author, drawing from Leiden University (2018) data.

sciences and Toronto 1071. The leading Chinese university, Shanghai Jiao Tong, had 336. US researchers lead overwhelmingly in all disciplinary fields outside STEM. Of the first fifty universities in terms of top 5 per cent papers in all fields, twenty-eight are located in the United States (Leiden University 2019).

Global Role of US Research

'The contemporary global scientific network is woven around the US' (Olechnicka, Ploszaj and Celinska-Janowicz 2019: 92). US Americans 'appear as directly linked to most countries and indirectly linked to all countries in the global network' (Wagner, Park and Leydesdorff 2015: 7). US-based authors shared 39 per cent of all co-published articles in 2016 (NSB 2018: Table A5–42). The UK plays a smaller role. Oxford, Cambridge, UCL and Imperial are among the top eighteen universities in the number of top 5 per cent papers and four of the six largest in the number of collaborative papers.

US and UK universities especially, and others in Europe and East Asia, help to build capacity in emerging systems through research training and collaborative projects. Emerging systems go on to freely develop relations with everyone in global science. The United States and United Kingdom are not gatekeepers. 'The networks are dense but not highly centralised' (Wagner, Whetsell and Leydesdoff 2017: 1641). This does not mean that all countries and researchers have equal weight. Networked cooperation is not necessarily symmetrical, reciprocal or egalitarian. Some pairings indicate a dominant–subordinate relationship, or isomorphic relations in which one party copies or adapts the creative work of another.

One way to define connections is to examine the directionality of citation behaviour, the extent to which researchers in country *A* cite those in country *B*, and vice versa. The world average is 1.00; 2.00 indicates very intensive citation.

Scopus citation data indicate high priority and near reciprocity in citation relations between France, Germany and UK. Patterns involving US research are different. Figure 3.2 demonstrates the extent to which US researchers cite researchers from other nations, and conversely, researchers from other nations cite US Americans. US researchers are cited by others much more than vice versa. Researchers in only the two English-speaking countries are cited by US researchers above 1.00, Canada and UK (NSB 2018: Table 5–28). However, US researchers cite each other at an exceptionally high 2.93. This might show that American researchers are culturally biased, or that good science is mostly in the United States, or both together. It might also suggest that knowledge generated

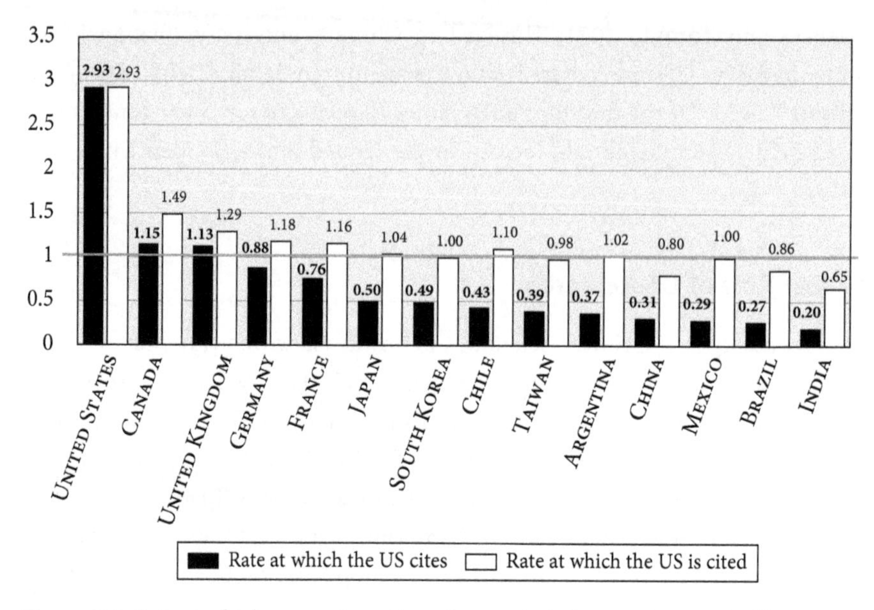

Figure 3.2 Rate at which papers by authors from selected countries are cited by papers with authors from United States, compared to the rate authors from these countries cite US authors: 2014 (1.00 = world average citation rate. 0.50 is very low citation rate, 2.00 is very high citation rate).

The expected value of citation is 1.00 (blue line). In each case, authors from the other nation cite US authors at a higher rate than US authors cite them.

Source: Author, using data from NSB (2018), Table 5–28.

by new and rising science powers is more likely to be cited in the rest of the world than in the United States.

Interpretations

In published work there are four alternate imaginings of global science: (1) a national arms race in which governments invest in innovation in competition with each other; (2) a global market of world-class Universities (WCUs), the idea in global ranking (e.g. THE 2019); (3) an interactive and expanding network (Castells 2000; Wagner, Park and Leydesdorff 2015); and (4) a centre–periphery hierarchy (e.g. Olechnicka, Ploszaj and Celinska-Janowicz 2019). Each has influenced social science thinking. The first two ideas are potent in policy and public discussion, though of the four imaginings they are the least grounded in reality.

The arms race idea breaks down because in most countries, national industry is more likely to source innovations from foreign than national science, nationally generated ideas might help industry abroad more than at home, and science is increasingly collaborative on a global basis. The idea of a global market of WCUs likewise fails the test of realism because of the dynamism of global research collaboration and because both collaboration and competition are primarily bottom-up. In science institutional (WCU) agency is less determining than researcher agency.

Network models come closer to the dynamics of science. They are compatible with the tendency of science to spread freely on the basis of self-organization and explain the hyper-expansion of collaboration with linkages in all directions. They grasp the open and 'flat' aspects of science, and the global system as distinct from national systems, including the potential for determination at the global level. However, they are less effective in grasping the hierarchical and non-reciprocal aspects of science, as shown in the asymmetric pattern of citations to/from the United States.

In world systems analyses the core science countries in North America and Europe disseminate knowledge so as to maintain unequal relations of power and have a vested interest in keeping the periphery weak. Centre–periphery analysis identifies the leading role of the United States but is unable to provide a strong explanation for the rapid growth and spread of science, for the openness and fecundity of networked collaboration and for the rise of a strong new centre in China.

Arguably, world science combines network and hierarchy. Both sets of dynamics are in play and each has an ongoing potential to modify the other. Nevertheless, it is important to recognize that science is more open than most social systems are. There are severe inequalities of resources and know-how. Commercial interests and military agendas partition off parts of research. The agendas of world science are largely patterned by powerful, sometimes dominant, national cases. Yet the evolution of the global science system is towards more rather than less openness and inclusion over time. Scientific networks connect researchers directly with each other in unmediated fashion. Science is less controlled than are most human activities by nation states and by economic capital.

Conclusion

Like all forms of global integration (Conrad 2016), the global research system is not a universal container. Its reach is incomplete. Though science has become global it continues to be national and local. Relations between global, national and local science are complex. Wagner, Whetsell and Leydesdorff (2017: 1634) argue that science spreads via 'preferential attachment', not just in 'big science' large-scale projects but in one-to-one and small group cooperation. Researchers in the same or related disciplines want to work with each other. They fulfil their individual and collective agency by creating knowledge. All national governments provide essential conditions for science. Nevertheless, in more than half of all countries, global science is now more determining of national patterns than vice versa (Wagner, Park and Leydesdorff 2015).

The global science system is resilient and dynamic. Since 2010, the globalization of trade, investment and production have faltered (see Chapter 1). In some countries, migration resistance retards cross-border people movement, including international student mobility into the UK. However, knowledge flows freely, and science and its connections continue to grow and spread in all directions. Though global systems have a limited role in human affairs, especially in politics, which for the most part remains nationally bordered, those global systems are more potent in research and universities. Global science is broadening the potentials of global society.

References

Academic Ranking of World Universities, ARWU (2018), Shanghai: Shanghai Jiao Tong University Graduate School of Education. http://www.shanghairanking.com/index.html

Bush, R. and Hass, R. (2019), 'The China Debate Is Here to Stay', Brookings. https://www.brookings.edu/blog/order-from-chaos/2019/03/04/the-china-debate-is-here-to-stay/

Castells, M. (2000), *Rise of the Network Society*. 2nd edn, Oxford: Blackwell.

Conrad, S. (2016), *What Is Global History?*, Princeton: Princeton University Press.

Leiden University (2019), *CWTS Leiden Ranking 2019*, Leiden: Leiden University Centre for Science and Technology Studies, www.leidenranking.com

National Science Board, NSB (2018), *Science and Engineering Indicators 2018*. https://www.nsf.gov/statistics/2018/nsb20181/assets/nsb20181.pdf

Olechnicka, A., Ploszaj, A. and Celinska-Janowicz, D. (2019), *The Geography of Scientific Collaboration*, Oxford: Routledge.

Organization for Economic Cooperation and Development, OECD (2017), *Education at a Glance, 2017*, Paris: OECD.

Organisation for Economic Cooperation and Development, OECD (2018), *Education at a Glance, 2018*, Paris: OECD.

Organization for Economic Cooperation and Development, OECD (2019), *Science and Technology Indicators*. https://stats.oecd.org/Index.aspx?DataSetCode=MSTI_PUB

QS (2019), *World University Rankings*. https://www.qs.com/rankings/

Salmi, J. (2009), *The Challenge of Establishing World-Class Universities*, Washington: World Bank.

Times Higher Education (2019), *World University Rankings*. https://www.timeshighereducation.com/world-university-rankings

United Nations Educational, Social and Cultural Organization (UNESCO) (2019), UNESCO Institute for Statistics Data on Education. http://data.uis.unesco.org/

Wagner, C., Park, H. and Leydesdorff, L. (2015), 'The Continuing Growth of Global Cooperation Networks in Research: A Conundrum for National Governments', *PLoS ONE*, 10 (7): e0131816. doi:10.1371/journal.pone.0131816.

Wagner, C., Whetsell, T. and Leydesdorff, L. (2017), 'Growth of International Collaboration in Science: Revisiting Six Specialities', *Scienceometrics*, 110: 1633–52.

Wang, Q. H., Wang, Q. and Liu, N. (2011), 'Building World-Class Universities in China: Shanghai Jiao Tong University', in P. Altbach and J. Salmi (eds), *The Road to Academic Excellence: The Making of World-Class Research Universities*, 33–62, Washington: World Bank.

Xie, Q. and Freeman, R. (2018), 'Bigger than You Thought: China's Contribution to Scientific Publications', NBER Working Paper No. 24829. http://www.nber.org/papers/w24829

4

International Students in UK

Global Mobility Versus National Migration Politics

Simon Marginson

Introduction

The politics of migration are naturally unstable. There is an irreducible tension between human desires to move anywhere in the world on the basis of free movement and prior national occupancy of specific territories. This tension is fundamental to all societies. It means that apparently fixed national policies on people mobility can always break down.

On the one hand, migration is as old as humanity, and no community, no nation, controls the same land forever. People everywhere are chronically curious (Cunliffe 2015), and the grass is always greener somewhere else. A border is an invitation to cross. Tourists bridle when they are told that a fascinating precinct in a foreign country is off limits. Yet, the same tourists often see mobility differently when they return home. No one wants their patch invaded against their will. Not all international visitors are always equally welcome.

In countries like UK where entry is in demand and residence is rationed, the politics of migration fluctuate along this fault line between the norm of global mobility and the reflex of national protection. The fluctuation of opinion typically becomes manifest in medium-term swings (often of five- to ten-year duration) between two differing attitudes towards inward people movement, which can be called 'openness' and 'closure'. In a globally integrated world some inward people movement is inevitable. Nevertheless, in the last decade the UK, like much of Europe, has been in the throes of 'closure'. It has been a time of migration resistance. A survey conducted immediately after the June 2016 Brexit referendum found that among the majority who voted to 'Leave' the European Union (EU), 80 per cent regarded migration and 81 per cent regarded multiculturalism as 'forces for ill' (HEC 2018: 45).

Parties on the political right have made sizeable gains by playing on fears of labour competition, the threat of terrorism and blood-and-soil nativism. The fears have been potent in UK regions with low numbers of migrants but high poverty and underemployment. Migration resistance was a primary influence in the UK's exit from the EU. Cross-border international education in the UK – the inward movement of students into British universities and colleges, which being temporary, like tourism, both is and is not a form of migration, and is sometimes but not always a precursor of a desire to stay longer – has been caught up willy-nilly in all this.

Successive policies, statements and regulatory changes have borne down on onshore international education. After rapid growth in the first decade of the twenty-first century, international students flatlined in the seven counts up to 2017–18 (HESA 2019). With world student mobility increasing at 6 per cent a year (OECD 2018: 226) the UK was unique among English-speaking countries in this long absence of substantial growth (Figure 4.1).

This makes no sense. Because the UK runs international education as an income generating export business it is naturally expansionary, and because of the prestige of UK universities growth is always in prospect. National policy that

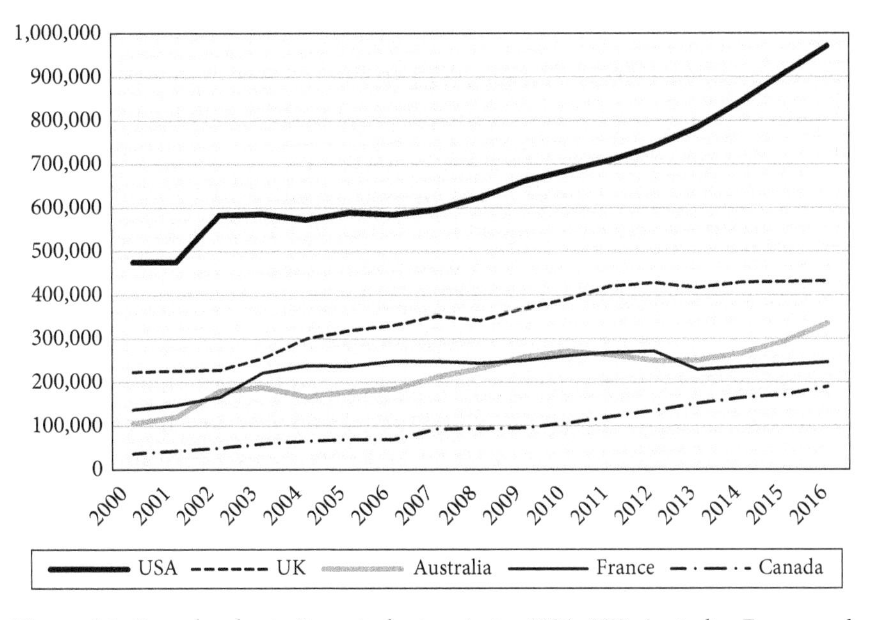

Figure 4.1 Cross-border tertiary students entering USA, UK, Australia, France and Canada, students in programmes of at least one year in length: 2000–16.

Includes only students enrolled in the country of education for a year or more. Data for Germany not available.

Source: UNESCO 2019.

unambiguously encouraged education export made the UK the second largest provider after the United States (though this status is now at risk). The sector appears to be win-win all round: for international students who want to study and research in UK (if they or their families can afford to pay the fees), for those domestic students (a minority) who enjoy cross-cultural learning, for the UK science system that draws on international doctoral students, for a nation that wants soft power, for the institutions paid to service the students and for cities and regions where international education quickens economic activity. For example, the 2015–16 cohort of international students is expected to generate £20.3 billion (UUK 2019) over the course of their studies and Oxford Economics estimates that in 2014–15 international education created 206,000 UK jobs (UUK 2017).

International education is about much more than making money. It expands people, enriches higher education and fosters worldwide community. There are internal tensions between the goals of profit, soft power and cosmopolitan education. Nevertheless, UK higher education institutions have managed to keep all the contrary objectives in sight.

However, since 2010 these internal tensions in international education have been overshadowed by an existential crisis triggered by the unstable UK politics of migration. For international students are strangers who can be made into a bogey – and in the UK, holding down international students is the easiest way to limit the reported intake of migrants. Further, pushing post-study work visas out of reach of most graduates is another way to cut migration, though it weakens the UK in global competition for talent.

One current CGHE research project focuses on contradictions between cross-border student mobility and migration policy in Japan, China, France and the UK. In addition, Simon Marginson served as co-chair of the ten-month Higher Education Commission (HEC) Inquiry into education export in 2017–18. The HEC is a semi-government body in Westminster consisting of parliamentarians and university leaders that focuses on higher education-related policy matters. In six public sessions the HEC, consisting of parliamentarians and educational leaders, gathered evidence on issues in UK international education. This chapter draws on both sets of evidence but primarily the HEC Inquiry. It starts with the global market in education, and in the UK, before considering recent problems of this sector amid UK migration politics.

The chapter will discuss international education as it looks from UK onshore higher education where most UK export revenues are generated. The chapter replicates the national boundedness typical of most research on international education. It does not explore transnational education (TNE) – cross-border education provided by UK institutions either online or in locations outside the UK. The UK enrols the largest number of TNE students in any nation, with 693,695 in 2017–18 (HESA 2019). TNE generated 9 per cent of total export revenue in 2015 (HEC 2018: 25). The chapter does not look at international education from the viewpoint of 'the other', that of international students themselves. If it did it would highlight different issues and concerns, including student agency and rights (see Montgomery 2010; Marginson 2012; Marginson 2014).

The Global Student Market

International student mobility, on the one hand, is a freedom accessible primarily to students from families with discretionary income. Though some countries such as Germany charge no fees, the majority of places are provided on the basis of cost recovery or profit-generation. Middle-class students also dominate competition for scholarships allocated on academic merit. The global student market plays out in a world in which economic activity and wealth are increasingly concentrated in global cities (Sassen 2001), widening the gulf between those with global agency and those locally bound. To disgruntled low-income locals in the English-speaking and European worlds, it can seem that mobile students from emerging economies have more opportunities than the locals have themselves. At times this has been associated with waves of racist violence against international students (e.g. in Western Melbourne, see Marginson, Nyland, Sawir and Forbes-Mewett 2010: 207–8).

On the other hand, global mobility is not only associated with inequalities. It is also an outcome of and contributor to global equalization at country level, whereby the gap has diminished between, on the one hand, incomes in the English-speaking world, Western Europe and Japan, and, on the other hand, incomes in the rising middle countries. The expanding global middle class (Kharas and Hamel 2018) fuels global student mobility.

Drivers of International Mobility

For students and their families, studying abroad provides opportunities to gain foreign credentials useful at home and abroad, to improve global language and to learn more about themselves and life (Marginson 2014). Countries provide places for a range of reasons, including export revenues, economic stimulus, global influence and soft power, and the potential for cross-cultural education of domestic students. Many countries are also aware that 'highly educated mobile students are likely to integrate into domestic labour markets, contributing to knowledge creation, innovation and economic performance' (OECD 2018: 218) though whether a nation succeeds in the global competition for talent depends partly on the accessibility of its labour markets as well as its higher education.

Like research, the global student market is also a competition for prestige between countries and between individual universities. 'The ability to attract international students has become a criterion for assessing the performance and quality of institutions' (OECD 2018: 223). This is reinforced by those global university rankings that include as an indicator the proportion of students who are international (QS 2019; THE 2019).

Structure of the Global Market

Figure 4.2, using the UNESCO data on cross-border and foreign students, shows that while the English-speaking countries are the largest bloc in the global student market, exporters in Europe, East and Southeast Asia, and the Middle East, also

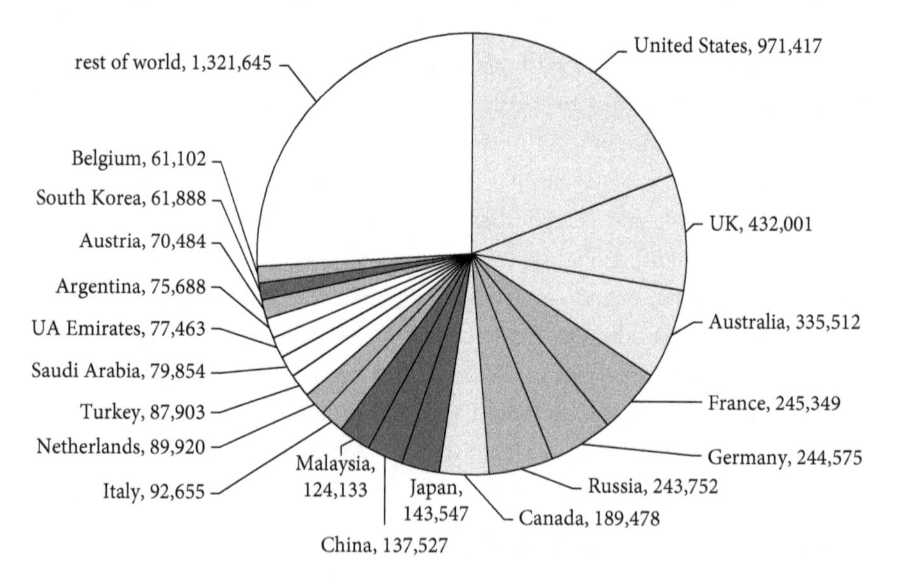

Figure 4.2 Cross-border or foreign* tertiary students in main receiving ('export') countries: 2016.

English-speaking countries in light grey, other European countries in medium grey, East and Southeast Asian countries in black. Includes only students enrolled in the country of education for a year or more.

Source: UNESCO 2019; OECD 2018: 228.

matter. The English language is the primary medium of cross-border education, being used in some programmes in Western Europe, the Middle East and East Asia as well as the English-speaking countries. The United States, with its array of higher education institutions and large and varied graduate labour markets is the most important single attractor of foreign students. The United States, United Kingdom and Australia house the three largest international student populations. Australia moved past France and Germany after 2010 (Figure 4.3). Nevertheless, the centre–periphery model of world systems theory often used in analysing the global student market (e.g. Barnett, Lee, Jiang and Park 2016: 549) is no more helpful in relation to student flows than it is in relation to the global science system (see Chapter 3 of this book).

For example, there is much regional student mobility between China, Japan, Malaysia, South Korea, Taiwan, Thailand and the Philippines. The first four countries export on a large scale; and when data for shorter stays are included, China's volume of incoming students is much larger. UNESCO includes only students who cross-borders for one year or more. Cross-border movement of students within Europe, encouraged by the Erasmus programme, and free labour movement and migration within the EU, constitutes a quarter of student mobility into OECD countries. Russia has a major regional role in educating students from the post-Soviet zone, especially from Central Asia. Like global science the global student market is multi-polar. It is also hierarchical. In some destination countries, more sought after than others, prospective student demand exceeds the supply of available places.

As this suggests, global student flows are shaped by relational factors in the market. For example, some countries have higher status universities or more potent business sectors. Global student flows are also articulated through variable national and local factors – for example, visa policies, the effects of fluctuations in national currency on relative tuition prices or the extent to which countries offer merit-based international student entry into doctoral programmes. The role of international education varies by discipline and level of tertiary education and also differs by country and over time. In 2016, though international students constituted 6 per cent of all OECD country enrolments they were 26 per cent of all doctoral students. However, doctoral research varies by country in the extent to which enrolment is internationalized: 40 per cent or more in the United States, United Kingdom, New Zealand, Switzerland, France, Netherlands, Belgium and Luxembourg and under 10 per cent in Germany, South Korea, Chile, Mexico, Poland, the Slovak Republic, Greece and Israel (OECD 2018: 228).

International Education in UK

Within the global market the UK approach to international education is distinctive in several ways. First, volume. Higher Education Statistical Agency (HESA) data show that UK higher education enrolled 458,490 non-UK students in 2017–18: 19.6 per cent of enrolled students, a high proportion in world terms. International students are a larger part of postgraduate research (41.5 per cent in 2017–18) than undergraduate programmes (14.4 per cent) or postgraduate taught programmes (34.4 per cent).

Second, the European component (see Chapter 5). Prior to Brexit the UK provided more places for international students from Europe than did any other country, taking in almost twice as many EU students as each of Germany and the United States (what will happen after Brexit is unclear). In 2017–18, 139,150 (5.9 per cent) of UK students were from other EU countries, and 319,340 (13.6 per cent) were from all other parts of the world. Just over half the UK's international students are from Asia. Asia plays a larger proportional role in other English-speaking countries. Nevertheless, as Figure 4.3 shows China is by far the most important source country in UK with 33.4 per cent of non-EU enrolments in 2017–18. Figure 4.3 also shows that while students from China, Hong Kong

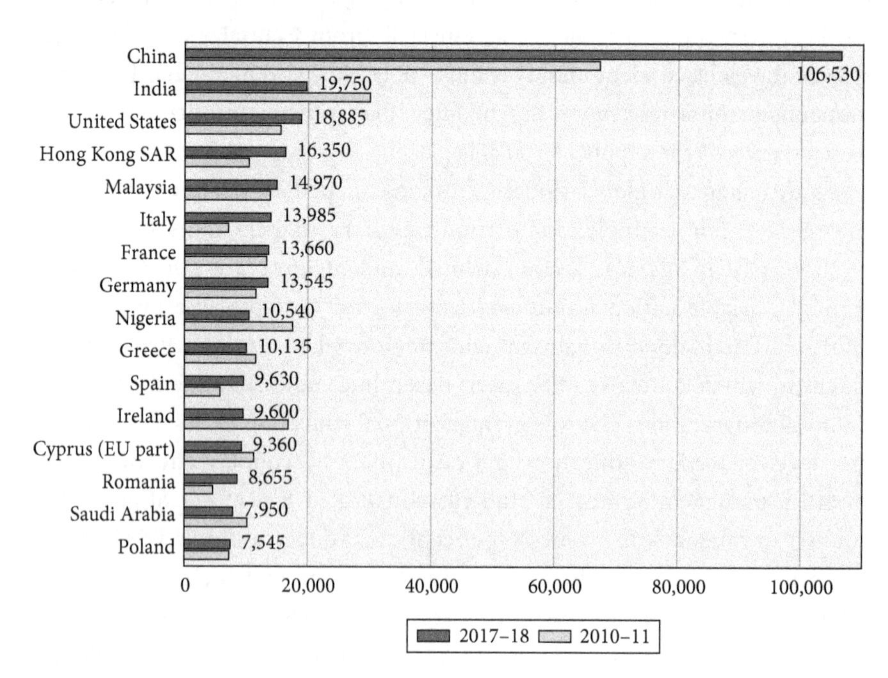

Figure 4.3 Principal source countries for international students in the UK: 2010-11 and 2017–18.

Source: HESA 2019.

SAR, Malaysia and United States had increased since the UK part of the global market began to level off in 2010–11, there were declines in India, Saudi Arabia and Nigeria. If numbers from China had not grown by almost 40,000 non-EU enrolments would have fallen sharply. Among EU countries students from Italy, Spain, Germany and Romania increased while those from Greece, Ireland and Cyprus declined (HESA 2019).

Third, as in Australia, New Zealand, Canada, Malaysia and Masters programmes in many countries but unlike Germany and parts of United States, the UK approach to international education is a largely a profit-making one. The exceptions are European students (prior to Brexit), foreign aid-based scholarships and postgraduate research. In 2017–18 EU students in those UK countries where tuition fees were changed were subject to the same tuition loan regime as domestic students, repaying their loans only when their incomes reached a threshold level. The much larger group of non-EU students paid fees, set by UK institutions, in the year of study. Prices were higher in prestigious institutions, reflecting their position within the market. Since full international student fees were introduced by the Thatcher government in 1980, they have grown in importance. This component of income is most readily adjusted upwards, and it can be used to finance capital works, facilities and services, and research capacity. In 2017–18, non-EU international student fee income constituted £5.2 billion, 13.6 per cent of all income of UK higher education institutions. The disciplinary contribution to this income was uneven. In 2017–18, over a quarter of all international students were enrolled in business studies, half at the postgraduate stage. The next largest discipline cluster was engineering and technology (HESA 2019).

Fourth, though the global market is normally modelled in terms of supply and demand the UK part is more supply-driven than demand-driven. Global prestige means that lower tier UK universities and non-university colleges are competitive, though they need to market themselves, and leading research universities can choose their extent of internationalization – providing that when they request expansion the UK Home Office says 'yes'. The Home Office has final control through its power to determine student visas. Given that the national total is shaped more by institutional targets and migration policy than by the preferences of prospective students, a flatline enrolment trend indicates that supply, not demand, is constrained. Nevertheless, active choices by students and families tend to fit available opportunities; if supply is held back for long enough this can drive down applications, as may have happened in UK in relation to Indian students.

Fifth, international students, and economic dependence on international education, are both concentrated in major cities and distributed across the UK institutions and regions. While the 2015–16 cohort of international students was expected to generate £4.64 billion in economic activity in London the estimates for other regions in England ranged from £2.44 billion in the Southeast and £1.95 billion in the West Midlands to £0.98 billion in the North East. Economic activity in Scotland was estimated at £1.94 billion, Wales £0.90 billion and Northern Ireland £0.17 billion (UUK 2019).

Table 4.1 lists concentrations of more than 5,000 international students in 2017–18. Though they are mostly found in large prestigious research universities, international education is more broadly spread. Among nine institutions in Wales, international students were 25.0 per cent of all students at Cardiff University, 22.4 per cent at Bangor, 17.9 per cent at Swansea, 17.5 per cent at Glyndwr, 17.0 per cent at Aberystwyth, 13.1 per cent at South Wales, 12.6 per cent at Cardiff Metropolitan and 5.3 per cent at Wales Trinity St David. These are lower percentages than in Table 4.1 but nevertheless mean that a significant number of international students, two-thirds of whom pay full fees essential to university revenues, lived, studied and worked in different local areas in Wales.

Postgraduate Research

In 2017–18, much of the UK's scientific capacity rested on the 31,775 research students from non-EU countries, 28.5 per cent of postgraduate research students and 4,570 (13.1 per cent) non-UK EU research students. There were 6,325 from China, 2,785 from each of Italy and Saudi Arabia, 2,690 from the United States and 2,350 from Germany. International doctoral students were a majority of postgraduate research students in mathematics, computer sciences and engineering, architecture, business studies and law. They tended to be a larger proportion of doctoral students in the leading research universities, constituting a majority at LSE, Oxford, Cambridge, Imperial, St Andrews and Edinburgh (HESA 2019). (The contribution of doctoral researchers from EU countries is further discussed in Chapter 5.)

Education Export Policy Versus Migration Policy

Why then has the UK's large and strong international education sector found itself in difficulties? The Blair Labour government's 1999 Prime Minister's Initiative provided a coherent policy for international education that focused on both growth in student numbers and the diversification of student source countries. The last years of Labour until the change of government in 2010 were marred by scandal concerning bogus colleges which triggered closer surveillance, but policy did not change significantly until the Conservative Party-led coalition took power.

Table 4.1 UK Higher Education Institutions Enrolling over 5,000 International Students: 2017–18

Institution	Full fee-paying (non-EU) international students	EU citizen students (non-UK)	All international students	All international students as a proportion of total students (%)
U College London	13,060	4,930	17,990	45.0
U Manchester	10,965	2,785	13,750	34.3
U Edinburgh	8,300	3,725	12,025	36.6
Coventry U	8,040	3,245	11,285	33.1
Kings College London	7,095	4,080	11,175	34.6
Imperial College	6,485	3,075	9,560	52.0
U of the Arts, London	6,715	2,460	9,175	48.4
U Warwick	6,490	2,500	8,990	35.0
U Sheffield	7,470	1,495	8,965	30.2
U Glasgow	5,640	3,175	8,815	29.7
U Birmingham	6,655	1,555	8,210	23.5
U Oxford	5,570	2,640	8,210	33.0
U Leeds	6,575	1,510	8,085	23.5
Cardiff U	6,420	1,505	7,925	25.0
U Liverpool	7,015	945	7,960	27.6
London School of Economics	5,825	2,060	7,885	67.9
U Nottingham	6,015	1,585	7,600	23.0
City U London	5,925	2,080	7,375	37.3
U Southampton	5,370	1,820	7,190	29.2
U Cambridge	4,415	2,635	7,050	34.4
Newcastle U	5,410	1,375	6,785	25.6
Queen Mary U London	4,765	1,935	6,700	33.4
U Westminster	4,090	2,285	6,375	33.1
U Exeter	4,520	1,490	6,010	25.0
U Bristol	4,605	1,270	5,875	23.6
U Sussex	4,260	1,320	5,580	31.3
U Bath	3,485	1,745	5,230	29.8
U Durham	4,075	1,100	5,175	28.2

Source: HESA 2019.

'A Really Hostile Environment'

Under the Coalition from 2010 and then a solely Conservative government from 2015, official promotion of international education continued, but was undermined by the government's response to migration resistance in the electorate. Education export policy found itself blocked by migration policy.

Between 2010 and 2018, the Conservative Party repeatedly promised to cut net migration from 300,000 to less than 100,000. It was impossible to reduce business and family-related migration sufficiently to meet this target. However, the real role of the target was not instrumental but symbolic. Coupled with a 2012 statement by the then home secretary Theresa May that she wanted 'to create, here in Britain, a really hostile environment for illegal migrants' (HEC 2018: 49), the target aligned the Party with migration resistance, while also providing a discursive framework in which all Home Office administered migration came under active suspicion, including international education.

There were 5,700 changes to immigration regulations between 2010 and 2018, many affecting international education (HEC 2018). Though a 2016 poll found that less than a quarter of the electorate saw international students as migrants (HEC 2018: 47), and international students contribute little to net migration because most of them leave on completion of their studies, and despite pressure from higher education institutions, the government kept international students within the migration count. It thereby retained the option securing an on-paper reduction in migrant arrivals by cutting international students. The 2016 Conservative Party conference foreshadowed a reduction in the student intake of a third or more and in the 2017 election campaign the Party promised 'tougher visa requirements for students' (HEC 2018: 21). While in the outcome the intake was not reduced, the government gained kudos from talking tough, and the 'really hostile environment' facilitated an accumulation of measures which together bore down on the flow of cross-border students so as to hold it year by year in flatline position.

These measures included steeper English-language tests; more intrusive scrutiny of students at entry ('credibility interviews') and regular surveillance of non-EU students during study; higher income requirements prior to the commencement of study and a new £150 annual health surcharge later increased to £300. Visa processing was slowed and visa and health costs became uncompetitive, as Table 4.2 shows. The administration of student surveillance was passed back to provider institutions at a reported cost to them of £40 million per annum (UUK et al. 2019: 5). Landlords were required to check on the immigration status of their tenants. There was stricter licensing of institutions that inhibited moves into new student source countries and differentiated elite providers from others. Some institutions experienced sudden falls in fee income: Bedfordshire University lost a net £72 million between 2011–12 and 2015–16 (HEC 2018: 49).

Evidence at the HEC Inquiry suggested that in the more 'hostile environment', the level of excess demand, and hence the favoured position of UK higher

Table 4.2 Comparative Costs of Student Visa and Health Cover, Six Countries: 2019

Country	Cost of student visa only (£s)	Total visa and health charges for three persons (student + dependent adult and child) (£s)
United Kingdom	348	£1,044 + £2,700 Health Surcharge
Australia	314	£626 + variable health insurance
New Zealand	150	£488 + variable health insurance
United States	126	£654 + variable health insurance
Canada	90	£273 + variable health insurance
France	89	£413 + £1,737 health insurance

Source: UUK et al. 2019.

education within the global market, may have been eroded. The potential for slippage is compounded by the pluralization of the global market: students who decide not to go to UK now have a broader range of country options. The number of students entering foundation colleges and parallel pathways into UK higher education had fallen by a third. The 2017 International Student Survey, the world's largest survey of pre-enrolled students, found that because of the EU referendum and perceptions of a more negative regulatory setting for students entering UK, 36 per cent were less likely to study in the UK (HEC 2018: 41).

In 2018, calculations on the basis of the comparative UNESCO student data for 2016 and trends in the English-speaking countries in 2017 and 2018 suggested that the number of onshore international students in UK was likely to be passed by Australia in 2019 or 2020. With international education growing strongly in Australia and flatlined in UK, in 2016 Australia passed the UK in the number of students from countries other than Europe. The UK position in Europe was expected to deteriorate after Brexit.

Barriers to Global Talent

The most important change engendered by the 'hostile environment', affecting both student demand for UK education and the volume of applications for skilled migration, was the April 2012 abolition of the Tier 1 Post-Study Work Visa, which had allowed student visa holders to stay on for two years of work after graduation. This was replaced by Tier 2 visas which required employer sponsorship, at a salary out of reach of most new graduates, and a scheme allowing doctoral graduates to stay for twelve months (HEC 2018: 19–20). Between 2012 and 2016, the number of graduates who stayed on to work in the UK plummeted from 38,605 to 6,037 (HEC 2018: 52). This new barrier to graduate work experience contrasted with the liberalization of post-study work rights in competitor countries Australia and Canada. Jo Attwooll of Universities UK told the HEC Inquiry:

> The number of new students recruited from India to Australian universities had a major boost following 2012 and enhancements to the Australian Post Study Work offer whereas Indian student numbers in the UK have gone in the opposite direction – this suggests that Australia's growth strategy has successfully recruited Indian students who might otherwise have gone to the UK. (HEC 2018: 40)

In May 2019, the OECD published the first edition of *OECD Indicators of Talent Attractiveness*, which measured the relative attractiveness of countries to international students, Masters/PhD graduates and foreign entrepreneurs, in terms of factors such as opportunities, future prospects, levels of pay and inclusiveness. The OECD noted that in OECD countries overall, dependence of economies on foreign talent was increasing. Between 2000–01 and 2015–16 the share of migrants in the tertiary-educated portion of working-age populations had increased from 11 to 16 per cent. It found that the most attractive countries for international students were Switzerland, Norway, Germany, Finland and the United States, with the UK bottom of the English-speaking countries in eleventh place. The most attractive countries for highly qualified workers were Australia, Sweden, Switzerland, New Zealand and Canada. When policies and regulations governing admission were taken into account the UK fell from tenth to sixteenth place (OECD 2019).

Conclusions

In 2015, the UK government fixed an export earnings target of £30 billion a year by 2020 (HEC 2018: 20). In 2019, it set a target for international enrolments of 600,000 a year by 2030 (British Council 2019: 13) but continued to restrict post-study work visas. Under the present settings it is hard to see either target being achieved. International education is still pulled between contrary forces. On one side are those in government, especially the Department of Education, and in higher education and elsewhere, who want the export industry to return to growth, and/or see international graduates as a source of skills. On the other side are those in government who want to retard the flow of students and send nearly all graduates home regardless of their economic potential.

From a bird's eye view it is a classic case of global flows pushing against the limits of a nationally framed world. Closer to the ground it looks more like a country shooting itself in the foot because of an inchoate fear of migrants and because leading politicians have chosen to work with that fear rather than working to overcome it. Instead of the national interest being pursued through adaptation to the global setting, it seems that the UK's national interest lie in a blind resistance to mobility in which UK international education has become collateral damage. It is an absurd situation. International students are scarcely the front line of tensions over migration and bearing down on these students and on global talent flows has made no economic or educational sense.

Nevertheless, the fact that talking tough about blameless cross-border students is seen by many UK politicians as electorally potent shows how migration anxiety is readily colonized by nativist politics and neo-imperial dreaming. Anxiety and nativism have become coupled in a self-reproducing system in which each feeds the other. This in turn points to the instability and potency of the underlying global/national tensions. Such tensions are inevitable. Good policy lies in managing them to minimize disruption and damage. Yet good policy does not always coincide with political advantage. For some politicians, temptations to exploit the global/national fault line are ever present.

In higher education it is widely expected there will be a swing back to openness, with the international education sector returning to growth amid a more supportive policy. Nevertheless, there is no cosmopolitan natural equilibrium; and even if growth returns the policy setting will not revert to the halcyon days of the 1999 Prime Minister's Initiative when higher education institutions were loosely global, national and local without a second thought. In future many higher education institutions will work harder on bringing their global mission into effective synergy with their service to local communities.

References

Barnet, G., Lee, M., Jiang, K. and Park, H. (2016), 'The Flow of International Students from a Macro Perspective: A Network Analysis', *Compare*, 46 (4): 533–59.

British Council (2019), *The Shape of Global Higher Education: International Comparisons with Europe*. https://www.britishcouncil.org/education/ihe/knowledge-centre/global-landscape/shape-global-higher-education-vol-4

Cunliffe, B. (2015), *By Steppe, Desert, and Ocean: The Birth of Eurasia*, Oxford: Oxford University Press.

Higher Education Commission (HEC), (2018), *Staying Ahead: Are International Students Going Down Under*, London: Policy Connect.

Higher Education Statistics Agency (HESA) (2019), *Data and Analysis*. https://www.hesa.ac.uk

Kharas, H. and Hamel, K. (2018), *A Global Tipping Point: Half the World Is Now Middle Class or Wealthier*, Brookings. https://www.brookings.edu/blog/future-development/2018/09/27/a-global-tipping-point-half-the-world-is-now-middle-class-or-wealthier/

Marginson, S. (2012), 'Including the Other: Regulation of the Human Rights of Mobile Students in a Nation-bound World', *Higher Education*, 63 (4): 497–512.

Marginson, S. (2014), 'Student Self-formation in International Education', *Journal of Studies in International Education*, 18 (1): 6–22.

Marginson, S., Nyland, C., Sawir, E. and Forbes-Mewett, H. (2010), *International Student Security*, Cambridge: Cambridge University Press.

Montgomery, C. (2010), *Understanding the International Student Experience*, Houndmills: Palgrave.

Organisation for Economic Cooperation and Development, OECD (2018), *Education at a Glance, 2018*, Paris: OECD.

Organisation for Economic Cooperation and Development, OECD (2019), 'How Do OECD Countries Compare in Their Attractiveness for Talented Migrants?', *Migration Policy Debates*, 19 May, Paris: OECD.

QS (2019), *World University Rankings*. https://www.qs.com/rankings/

Sassen, S. (2001), *The Global City: New York, London, Tokyo*, Princeton: Princeton University Press.

Times Higher Education (2019), *World University Rankings*. https://www.timeshighereducation.com/world-university-rankings

United Nations Educational, Social and Cultural Organization (UNESCO) (2019), *UNESCO Institute for Statistics Data on Education*. http://data.uis.unesco.org/

Universities UK (UUK) (2017), *The Economic Impact of International Students*. https://www.universitiesuk.ac.uk/policy-and-analysis/reports/Pages/briefing-economic-impact-of-international-students.aspx

Universities UK (UUK) (2019), *International Facts and Figures 2019*. https://www.universitiesuk.ac.uk/policy-and-analysis/reports/Pages/Intl-facts-figs-19.aspx

Universities UK (UUK), University Alliance, UKCISA, Russell Group, Million Plus and Guild HE (2019), *The Student Visa System: Principles to Reform*. https://www.universitiesuk.ac.uk/policy-and-analysis/reports/Pages/the-student-visa-system-principles.aspx

5

Feeling the Brexit Shock

European Connectedness and the Existential Crisis in UK Higher Education

Simon Marginson, Vassiliki Papatsiba and Xin Xu

Introduction

In June 2016, the UK electorate voted by 52 per cent to leave the European Union, though only 26 per cent of those holding university degrees agreed (Swales 2016: 8). Across the North, the Midlands and in Wales, Remain-voting university communities were isolated amid surrounding Leave-voting populations. Everything began to change, in British politics and in higher education. The EU referendum triggered a protracted negotiation over the terms of withdrawal. There was an increasingly bitter national debate, in which the political centre fell away and the contrary demands for a 'No Deal' Brexit, and a second referendum to overturn the first, both gained ground. Three years after the referendum the implications for higher education were still unclear.

What was clear was uncertainty about the future, and the fact the sector was newly vulnerable. Universities found themselves counting the costs of severing ties in Europe without knowing whether there would be a withdrawal agreement, what would be severed, how much change would occur, which mitigating strategies might be needed, whether there were new global opportunities outside Europe or things would shrink inwards and what it meant for the financial bottom line (UUK 2019).

Over the four decades since the UK voted to join the European Economic Community in 1975 the EU trajectory of 'ever closer union' was resisted in much of the country (Gifford 2014; Vasilopoulou 2016). Some in higher education were also resistant, albeit to a lesser extent, mainly because of the administrative burden of EU programmes and concerns about quality/prestige in parts of the EU. However, progressively, UK higher education has moved 'ever closer' to European universities, research networks and people. The extent of engagement has varied by region, university and discipline but includes almost all higher education institutions in the four nations. Higher education's engagement with European colleagues and students has often been sufficiently deep to change the lifestyle, values and identities of higher education people born in the UK. Of course, as will be discussed, with free cross-border labour mobility in the EU, in some universities one in four academics are citizens of non-UK Europe. European doctoral students are often vital to research.

Following the 2016 referendum the Economic and Social Research Council (ESRC) commissioned a set of research projects designed to investigate the consequences of Brexit and post-Brexit developments in different parts of UK polity and economy. These projects were grounded in the ESRC's UK in a Changing Europe programme. The Centre for Global Higher Education (CGHE) was awarded a grant for work on Brexit in higher education in the four UK nations,[1] with emphasis on migration-related aspects, resources for responding to Brexit-induced changes and financial sustainability. Between October 2017 and July 2018 the Centre's researchers conducted 127 semi-structured interviews on the effects of Brexit in 12 contrasting UK higher education institutions. The researchers (Simon Marginson, William Locke, Vassiliki Papatsiba and Ludovic Highman) also collected system-wide data on UK institutions engagement with Europe.

This chapter summarizes the UK universities' engagement with Europe and presents early findings from the Brexit-related research. These findings concern the emotions expressed by interviewees. The researchers did not set out to find how people felt about Brexit. Uncalled for, interviewees displayed a range of strong and mostly negative emotional responses, including pain, anguish, confusion and a sense of loss.

UK Universities and Europe

European Research Programmes

UK universities' work in European Framework research programmes is often described in financial terms. It is true that European funding has become essential to much research in UK but to focus only on the financial equation is to underestimate the transformative effects of long-term integration into Europe. UK research engagement in Europe is also logistical, cultural, demographic and, most importantly, intellectual.

Data for 2019 show the UK had the highest success rate in European Research Council grants, hosted 22.3 per cent of ERC funded researchers, attracted 20.5 per cent of talented researchers via the Marie-Sklodowska-Curie scheme, and coordinated almost one in five Horizon 2020 projects (European Commission 2019). Research works on the basis of collaborative networks, and the interim evaluation of Horizon 2020 showed the UK to be the most connected Horizon 2020 participant (European Commission 2017: 69), positioning UK universities favourably in the world's largest single pool of ideas and people, and drawing an immense flow of talent into the UK.

In the European Research Area's Seventh Framework Programme (FP7) cycle the UK contributed €5.4 billion to the €50 billion EU research and development budget. UK universities and other research organizations secured €8.8 billion in FP7 grants, a net gain of €3.4 billion. In Horizon 2020 the UK has so far spent about €3 billion and gained €6 billion. However, it has slipped to second place in Horizon 2020 funding after Germany, having lost first place in the aftermath of the Brexit Referendum.

In addition, UK research and innovation has been resourced by European structural funds, in two ways: European Regional Development Fund (ERDF) grants, which in 2007–13 provided €1.9 billion to UK research organizations compared to €7.0 billion provided by Framework Programme grants, and loans for research activities from the European Investment Bank (EIB). Whereas Framework Programme grants tend to favour the leading research universities, Structural Funds have been especially linked to poorer regions, notably Wales. 'All regions are benefitting from substantial flows of research income from EU government bodies' (Technopolis 2017: 1, 4, 10).

In total 12 per cent of the research income of UK higher education institutions was from EU sources in 2014–15, but this proportion varied by discipline. Research in the UK social sciences and humanities has especially benefitted from European resources as these disciplines are better funded in Europe than in the UK. While UK-based clinical medicine took in £119.9 million in European research funding in 2014–15, the largest amount to any discipline, this was only 7 per cent of UK research income in that discipline. Yet as Table 5.1 shows in archaeology the level of dependence was 38 per cent, in classics 33 per cent and in computing-related research 30 per cent (Technopolis 2017: 15–16, 18).

Table 5.1 UK Discipline-Based HESA Cost Centres Most Dependent on EU Funding: 2014–15

HESA Cost Centre	EU Share of Funding (%)
Archaeology	38
Classics	33
IT, Systems, Software Engineering	30
Media Studies	27
Law	26
Philosophy	25
Modern Languages	24
Anthropology, Development Studies	23
Business and Management	23
Chemistry	23
Area Studies	23
Politics & International Studies	21
Architecture, Building, Planning	21
Art & Design	21
Sociology	20

HESA = Higher Education Statistical Agency.

Source: Technopolis 2017: 16.

European research funding has also played a disproportionately large role in a group of middle-tier UK universities that are less UK STEM heavy than the peak of the Russell Group and less strong in domestic competition (Technopolis 2017: 3, 20).

Research Collaboration

In total, UK researchers collaborate more in Europe than in the English-speaking world. For example, Table 5.2, drawing on data sourced originally in Scopus, shows that in 2016 the number of papers co-authored with researchers from Germany, France and the Netherlands together equalled those with researchers from the United States and Canada.

Table 5.2 also demonstrates the propensity to collaborate – the rate at which UK researchers collaborate with other countries, relative to the overall patterns of the two countries. 1.00 indicates collaboration at the expected level, 0.50 a low propensity to collaborate and 1.50 a high propensity. With almost every country in Europe, UK researchers exhibit a higher than expected propensity to collaborate. This is not the case in North America, or in East Asian Southeast Asia or South Asia.

Table 5.2 Research Papers Co-authored by UK Researchers in Europe, the English-Speaking World, and Propensity to Collaborate with Each Country in the Pair Relative to the Overall Co-authorship Patterns of Both Countries (1.00 = expected rate of collaboration): 2016

Partner Country	Propensity to Collaborate	Co-authored Papers
Europe		
Ireland	2.16	2,621
Greece	1.74	2,531
Netherlands	1.50	8,039
Denmark	1.43	3,658
Hungary	1.43	1,274
Norway	1.40	2,720
Finland	1.28	2,317
Italy	1.27	10,023
Sweden	1.27	4,967
Belgium	1.26	4,174
Switzerland	1.21	5,720
Portugal	1.19	2,309
Spain	1.16	7,789
Poland	1.12	2,523
Germany	1.07	14,200
Austria	1.03	2,514
France	1.01	10,079
Czech Republic	0.96	1,535
Russia	0.77	2,335
Anglosphere		
New Zealand	1.35	1,640
South Africa	1.33	2,170
Australia	1.19	8,838
Canada	0.84	6,685
United States	0.77	25,858
East Asia		
Singapore	0.77	1,541
Japan	0.65	3,659
China	0.62	10,472
Taiwan	0.57	981
South Korea	0.45	1,589
South and Southeast Asia		
Thailand	0.94	862
Malaysia	0.84	1,428
Pakistan	0.76	847
India	0.67	2,494

Source: Authors, drawing on NSB 2018: Tables A5.43 and A5.44. The total number of co-authored papers with all countries in 2016 was 87,577.

Research Partnerships with Industry in Europe

Collaboration between UK universities and industry in continental Europe has become more important over time. Tijssen, van de Klippe and Yegros (2019) examine the 2008–17 research papers of forty-eight UK universities with high output, to discern co-publication between researchers in those universities and researchers in industry. While 14.7 per cent of the partner firms were within 100 kilometres of the university's headquarters and 21.3 per cent elsewhere in the UK or Ireland, 28.9 per cent were in continental Europe and 33.8 per cent elsewhere in the world. Over the ten-year period the most rapid increase in research cooperation, with average annual growth of 12 per cent, was with firms in Europe.

Many such collaborations were in public–private consortia which also involved multiple European university partners. Collaborations with firms located within 50 kilometres grew by a much lower 3 per cent per annum, and those elsewhere in the world by 11 per cent. Commenting on the possible implications of Brexit for UK higher education, Tijssen (2019) finds that 'UK universities have become increasingly embedded in the industry-relevant segment of the European Research Area and are therefore vulnerable'.

European Doctoral Students in UK

Like all national research systems, the UK research system relies on a continuing flow of postgraduate researchers. PhD students generate a high proportion of all research activity and also teach and co-publish with academic staff. Many later become academic staff. With British universities open to talent from all over the world, in 2017–18, 13.1 per cent of all research students (nearly all at doctoral level) were non-UK EU citizens and 28.5 per cent were other international students. Dependence on non-UK EU citizens was high in STEM disciplines, including mathematics, physical science, computer science and engineering (HESA 2019). Table 5.3 has details for the preceding year, 2016–17. Many of the EU research students worked in European research funded projects.

The role of EU postgraduate researchers peaks in the most research-intensive UK universities. In 2017–18, non-UK EU students constituted 40.1 per cent of all postgraduate researchers at each of Cambridge and Imperial, where there were very large concentrations of STEM researchers, and at least one-quarter of all postgraduate researchers at eleven of the twelve research universities in Table 5.4 (HESA 2019).

Table 5.3 Non-UK EU Citizens in UK Postgraduate Research Programmes, 2016–17

	Non-UK EU Research Students	Total Research Students	Non-UK EU Students as Proportion (%)
Science Fields			
Mathematics	645	2915	22.1
Physical Sciences	2205	12,750	17.3
Computer science	775	4870	15.9
Engineering and Technology	2210	14,150	15.6
Veterinary sciences	45	305	14.4
Biological sciences	1965	15,230	12.9
Architecture, Building, Planning	225	1950	11.5
Medicine allied subjects	935	8380	11.2
Medicine and Dentistry	910	8495	10.7
Agricultural sciences	95	885	10.7
TOTAL for all science fields	10,015	69,925	14.3
Non-Science Fields			
Social studies	1365	9055	15.1
Law	310	2245	13.8
Languages	775	5710	13.6
History and Philosophy	830	7435	11.2
Creative Arts and Design	455	4090	11.1
Business studies and related fields	725	6670	10.9
Mass communications	120	1205	10.0
Education	390	6180	6.3
Combined studies	0	15	0.0
TOTAL for all non-science fields	4970	42,595	11.7
Combined Total			
All fields	14,985	112,520	13.3

Source: Author, drawing on HESA 2019.

European Staff

The role of European citizens in UK university staffing is similar to that in postgraduate research, in that it peaks at the top of the Russell Group and in STEM. In 2017–18, there were 37,255 academic staff and 14,515 non-academic professional staff from EU countries other than UK. This represented 17.5 per cent of academic staff and 6.7 per cent of non-academic professional staff. The EU proportions had risen markedly from four years before in 2013–14 when they were 15.0 per cent and 5.2 per cent. In 2016–17, more than one-third of academic staff in economics and modern languages and more than one-quarter from mathematics, physics and chemical engineering were non-UK EU citizens (HESA 2019). The European share of recent appointments was much higher.

Table 5.4 Non-UK EU Citizens in UK Postgraduate Research Programmes, Twelve Largest Populations in Individual UK Universities, 2017–18

Institution	Non-UK EU Research Students	All Research Students	Non-UK EU Proportion (%)
University of Cambridge	1130	2820	40.1
University of Oxford	910	2495	36.5
Imperial College London	845	2105	40.1
University College London	845	2240	37.7
University of Edinburgh	745	1850	40.2
University of Manchester	470	1880	25.0
Kings College London	385	940	41.0
University of Nottingham	380	1295	29.3
University of Glasgow	335	1000	33.5
University of Birmingham	320	1110	28.8
University of Southampton	300	980	30.6
University of Sheffield	300	1295	23.2

Source: Author, drawing on HESA 2019.

As with postgraduate research, European research funding won by leading UK research universities has brought many European staff to UK. In 2016–17, 32.0 per cent of academic staff from Imperial (1,385 persons), 27.2 per cent from UCL (2,020), 26.1 per cent from Cambridge (1,555) and 25.1 per cent from Oxford (1,700) were from EU countries aside from UK. Dependence was greater in proportional terms at LSE (39.0 per cent), and Ulster (35.3 per cent) which recruited across the soft Irish border (HESA 2019).

European Students

In all in 2017–18 there were 139,150 non-UK EU students enrolled in British higher education institutions at all levels of study, 5.9 per cent of the total. These European students had larger weight in postgraduate research (13.1 per cent) than in taught postgraduate (6.7 per cent) and all undergraduate education (5.3 per cent) (HESA 2019). First degree students in England paid home country fees and accessed tuition loans. On 27 May 2019, the higher education minister Chris Skidmore announced that this arrangement would persist until at least the 2020–1 academic year.

In some institutions European students have had a larger presence, especially in Russell Group universities, in London, in Scotland where they pay no fees, and in some universities that have attracted EU students in order to boost their income (are thereby especially vulnerable to Brexit). There were 4,930 non-UK EU nationals at UCL in 2017–18, 4,080 at Kings, 3725 at

Edinburgh, 3,245 at Coventry, 3,175 Glasgow. The University of the Arts in London enrolled 2,460; LSE had 2,060. The highest proportional enrolments were at Aberdeen (19.9 per cent) where the 2,865 Europeans were one student in five, and LSE (17.7 per cent). Europeans played a much larger role at LSE at Masters level (HESA 2019). In addition to those enrolled full-time, there are the many temporary students who enter the UK via Erasmus and Erasmus Plus. The future of those programmes in UK will be determined by the character of the UK's exit from EU.

Financial Implications

Brexit has profound net financial implications for UK higher education institutions. Engagement with Europe creates a larger than otherwise portfolio of activity, with financing to match in the form of research programme funds, structural funds for research and European student fees. But disengagement means scaling back finance more than activity. First, as noted, the UK makes a large net financial gain from European research programmes. Second, when European student numbers drop in low-demand institutions where they cannot be readily replaced there are likely to be diseconomies of scale – similar fixed costs and facilities, less student income. Third, European structural funds have been a vital source of not only research funding but also infrastructure funding.

From 2007 to 2016, UK universities received €2,625 million in EIB loans. For example, in 2011, the University of Strathclyde received €100.9 million for restructuring its two main sites. In 2014, Ulster's relocation to Belfast City Centre received €182.6 million. Kent borrowed €94.3 million for teaching and research facilities. Imperial received €178.5 million in 2014; Oxford €278.8 million in 2015; UCL €365.7 million in 2015 and 2016; Edinburgh €257.0 million in 2016 (Technopolis 2017: Appendix D). This kind of funding is unlikely to be replicated by the UK government.

The Research: Emotions Associated with Brexit in UK Higher Education

The chapter now moves to the first findings from the Centre's Brexit project research. As noted, these findings concern the emotions expressed in the 127 interviews.

The Research on Brexit and UK Higher Education

The case studies were conducted in UCL, SOAS, Manchester, Sheffield Hallam, Durham, Keele, Exeter and Coventry in England; St Andrews and Aberdeen in Scotland; South Wales in Wales; and Ulster in Northern Ireland, over a period of time 16–25 months after the referendum decision. Four of the universities were from the Russell Group; five were from other pre-1992 universities, which accordingly were over-represented; and three from the post-1992 universities, which were under-represented.

Among the 127 interviewees, 44 were senior executives, 28 were academic leaders, 23 were senior administrators, 14 were other academics, 10 were from institutional governing bodies and 8 were students. There were 38 (29.9 per cent) women and 89 men. In the case of the 86 persons who were academics, academic leaders and senior executives, disciplines were identified: 42 were from the social sciences (including a small number of people from the humanities), 26 were from the sciences and 18 were from the health sciences.

The Importance of Emotions

Spontaneously shared emotions link the micro and macro levels of social practice (Boccagni and Baldassar 2015: 74; Zembylas 2012: 167). Though emotions are part of everyday life they are often heightened at moments of transformation and displacement, for example migration (Boccagni and Baldassar 2015) and unexpected loss. In the research on Brexit in UK higher education the drier financial or administrative concerns become mixed with more potent tropes like belonging and identity. During a shift of this magnitude people experience emotions on a shared as well as individual basis, and the forums of institutions have an amplification effect.

Emotions are often overlooked in social research. But actions are not always based on rational calculation. Identity, values and organic ties to communities understood as a sense of belonging, all shape regret or resistance in the face of changes seen as negative, like Brexit in UK higher education. Uncertainty is one of the emotions typical of moments of sharp change and transformation, as Ho notes in relation to migration (Ho 2014: 2214).

Balance of Emotions

As indicated, the power of emotion in relation to Brexit is shown by the fact that in the research, a barrage of emotional expression pushed through the framing of what was a fact-seeking investigation. Interviewees were asked about the likely effects of Brexit at institutional level, or in their part of the operation, and on the responses and strategies of the institution/unit in the face of the coming change. When the 127 interviews were coded using NVivo, clear emotions were listed as arising in all of them. In all, 1,784 instances of emotional expression were coded. Of these 1,418 (79 per cent) were categorized as negative, 284 (16 per cent) as positive and 82 (5 per cent) as neutral.

Remarkably, every interviewee expressed negative emotions at least once, 73 per cent expressed positive emotions and 42 per cent expressed neutral emotions. On average 11 negative emotions were expressed per interview, three positive emotions and two neutral emotions. Some interviewees expressed more than one kind of emotion in the same sentence. As Figure 5.1 and Table 5.5 show, neutral emotions included stoicism and resilience. Among those expressing such neutral emotions were some people who regarded Brexit as less of a problem than

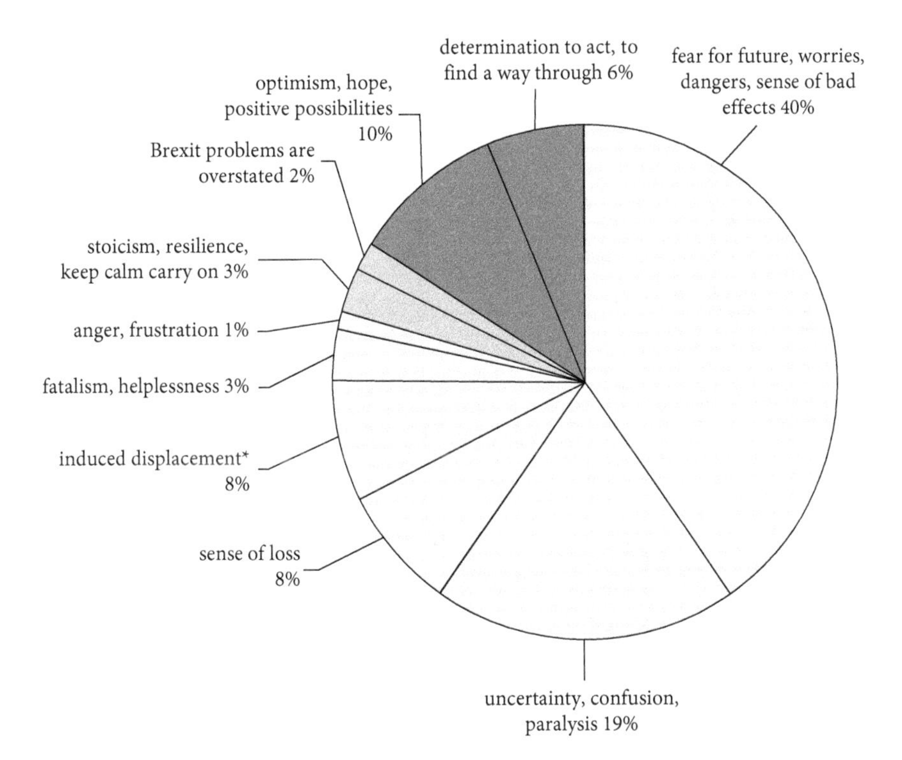

Figure 5.1 Coded emotions arising from CGHE interviews in 12 UK universities in 2017–18, concerning Brexit and higher education (n=1784).

*Includes loss, regret, sadness, distrust, disappointment, disillusionment, ironic detachment or unpleasant shock.

Source: Authors.

Table 5.5 Summary of Emotions Expressed in Brexit Project Interviews in 2017–18

Emotions	Number of Interviewees (n=127)	Proportion Interviewees (%)	Times Occurred (n=1784)	Proportion All Coded Emotions (%)	Average Times per Interview
Negative (79% of all coded emotions)					
Fears, worries, dangers, bad effects	122	96	720	40	5.90
Uncertainty, confusion, paralysis	106	83	347	19	3.27
Loss	71	56	138	8	1.94
Feeling of induced displacement*	59	46	136	8	2.31
Fatalism, helplessness	36	28	57	3	1.58
Anger, frustration	12	9	29	1	1.67
Neutral (5% of all coded emotions)					
Stoicism, resilience/keep calm carry on	33	26	50	3	1.52
Brexit problems overstated/not there	14	11	32	2	2.29
Positive (16% of all coded emotions)					
Positive possibilities, optimism, hope	76	60	173	10	2.28
Determination to act/find way through	59	46	111	6	1.88

While the coding was checked and rechecked, the assignment of expressed words to categories of emotion is fraught. Sound recording allows tone to be considered. Nevertheless, sorting imposes an undue 'flatness' on what is a complex of feelings in different contexts. Some expressed emotions are more strongly expressed, or clearer as to type, than are others.

* Includes loss, regret, sadness, distrust, disappointment, disillusionment, ironic detachment or unpleasant shock.

Source: Authors, with primary assignment of textual material to categories by Xin Xu.

most of the other interviewees considered it to be. Positive emotions included optimism, belief in unspecified post-Brexit opportunities, determination and a sense of personal or institutional agency.

Though there was some criticism of 'Remainers' and of negative talk of the effects of Brexit, there was no expression of unambiguous support for Brexit in the 127 interviews.

On average male interviewees expressed more emotions of each type than did females. Participants from the two Scottish universities tended to express more emotions in all categories; Northern Ireland interviewees the least. Participants from the post-1992 universities (Coventry, Sheffield Hallam, South Wales) expressed more emotions, and were more likely than others to be positive; while on average the participants from the five non–Russell Group pre-1992 universities (Aberdeen, Keele, SOAS, St Andrews, Ulster) expressed more negative and neutral emotions than did other interviewees.

Academic leaders and academics were more likely than were other interviewees to express emotions, and express negative and neutral emotions. Governing body members were the most likely to be positive. Students were less emotional than others. Among those interviewees who were ordered by discipline, the differences were small but the health sciences group was the least often negative and the most often positive.

Negative Emotions

As Table 5.5 suggests, while positive emotions often related to coping in the present, the negative emotions expressed by interviewees were mostly about looking back at the time of the referendum or looking forward to problems in the future. The word 'cloud' in Figure 5.2, which is dominated by the negative emotions, emphasizes the effects of Brexit for 'students', 'research' and 'people' and focuses strongly on 'European', 'collaborate' and 'funds'. Terms like 'concern', 'worry', 'losing' and 'problems' also stand out.

The largest single category, 40 per cent of all expressed emotions, was comprised by fears and worries about the anticipated consequences of Brexit. Almost all of the 127 interviewees (96 per cent) expressed such feelings at some point. Interviewees were anxious about

- people mobility problems;
- the attractiveness and reputation of UK higher education and research;
- the possibility that UK higher education would become less diverse, more 'insular' and 'isolated' and less collaborative than before;

- the outcomes of not being in the European research area;
- the potential for the UK to become distanced from European historical connections, culture, civilization and intellectual heritage.

Another 22 per cent of all responses, expressed by more than four interviewees in every five, embodied loss of personal agency after the referendum. These expressed feelings included uncertainty, confusion, paralysis, helplessness and fatalism. Participants associated uncertainty with the lack of reliable information, the lack of clear direction and the lack of trust in university leadership or the government. A further 16 per cent of emotions referred to displacement: a sense of loss, regret, sadness, distrust, disappointment, disillusionment, ironic detachment or unpleasant shock. Feelings of displacement or disconnection might also be read as diminished agency, as the wording of many of the quotes – and tones of voice in the associated voice recordings – suggest. The sense of what was being lost included collaboration opportunities, funding opportunities,

Figure 5.2 The word 'cloud' based on expressed emotions (n=1784).
Source: Authors.

collegial networks, friendships, mobility, freedom and agency, diversity and high academic capacity. Sense of loss was commonly associated with a sense of belonging in Europe, and with fear about the future. Such feelings were much more prevalent than anger or frustration, which were expressed by just 9 per cent of interviewees and comprised only 1 per cent of the expressed emotions.

Neutral Emotions

The main form of expressed neutral emotion was stoicism: we can get through this, keep calm and carry on. These feelings of resilience were associated with both a sense of helplessness and with mild optimism. However, while resilience was expressed by more than a quarter of all interviewees at some point, it constituted only 3 per cent of all expressed emotions. The theme of a further 2 per cent of responses, expressed by 11 per cent of interviewees, was the downplaying or denial of Brexit-related problems. Some of these interviewees said that they were 'relaxed' about issues that worried others.

Positive Emotions

Participants sometimes reported mixed feelings. Some were hopeful (the future will be great, we can find a way through), while acknowledging the challenges. Some were pessimistic (worried and wanting to find a way through) but tempered this with hope.

A total of 10 per cent of all the emotions, expressed by 60 per cent of interviewees, were optimistic in tone. Optimism was often linked to faith in collegial culture and belief that universities would continue to collaborate with other universities, confidence in the quality and resilience of British higher education, and potential opportunities to expand from a European-oriented vision to a larger international scope. Those emotions were linked to willingness to prepare for the outcome of Brexit, and to strategize in response to potentially undesirable impacts, although few senior executives or professors provided information about specific institutional or disciplinary strategies for the post-Brexit environment. (It is likely that some were reluctant to share plans before they could be announced.)

While 22 per cent of all expressed emotions were directly about loss of personal agency, and in another 16 per cent agency appeared to be diminished, 9 per cent asserted personal agency, as resilience (neutral) or determination (positive).

Conclusion

Emotions in social relational contexts are more than interesting. They matter in a practical sense. Discussing cross-border mobility, Zembylas (2012: 16) makes the argument that 'emotions work to align the subject and the nation-state in specific ways'. For example, emotional responses to Brexit in higher education have and will affect the resources and strategies of universities, including the extent to which they sustain or reforge links with universities, academics and students in Europe after Brexit takes place. Widely shared emotions, in government or in universities, help to set boundaries of the possible.

The strong and largely negative emotions expressed by interviewees during the Brexit project research are the flip side of UK higher education's thoroughgoing engagement in Europe. National exceptionalism runs deep in the UK. In this research few of the UK-born personally called themselves European. 'If you ask anybody … it's always been it starts at Calais,' as one interviewee put it. Yet some interviewees talked of an individual journey towards personal European identity, and many described the UK higher education sector, or their own institution, as 'European' or 'part of Europe'. In that respect higher education is different to most of the UK. Or it was until June 2016.

In higher education Brexit takes the form of a forced divorce. The couple, UK and EU higher education, are being pulled apart against their will. The absence of the machinery of European ties and the high-volume flows of people will leave a hole, and it is unclear how it will be filled. Most worrying is that Brexit, an agenda welcomed by few in higher education and with nothing positive to offer, appears to have robbed people of energy and agency. It will not stay like this. All things must pass and higher education in UK is always changing, as it is everywhere. University folk are inventive. Much of the alignment with Europe will be remade, partly by replacing institutionalized ties with customized ones. Eventually the hole will be filled locally and internationally. In the interim there will be the lost years – a hiatus with a sense of something diminished, withered or broken.

Note

1 ESRC Award number ES/R000166/1 – Brexit, trade, migration and higher education

References

Boccagni, P. and Baldassar, L. (2015), 'Emotions on the Move: Mapping the Emergent Field of Emotion and Migration', *Emotion, Space and Society*, 16: 73–80.

European Commission (2019), 'United Kingdom Horizon 2020 Country Profile'. https://webgate.ec.europa.eu/dashboard/extensions/CountryProfile/CountryProfile.html?Country=United%20Kingdom

European Commission, Directorate-General for Research and Innovation (2017), 'Interim Evaluation of Horizon 2020'. https://publications.europa.eu/en/publication-detail/-/publication/33dc9472-d8c9-11e8-afb3-01aa75ed71a1/language-en/format-PDF

Gifford, C. (2014), *The Making of Eurosceptic Britain*, Burlington: Ashgate.

Higher Education Statistics Agency (HESA) (2019), *Data and Analysis*. https://www.hesa.ac.uk

Ho, E. (2014), 'The Emotional Economy of Migration Driving Mainland Chinese Transnational Sojourning Across Migration Regimes', *Environment and Planning A*, 46: 2212–27.

National Science Board, NSB (2018), *Science and Engineering Indicators 2018*. https://www.nsf.gov/statistics/2018/nsb20181/assets/nsb20181.pdf

Swales, K. (2016). *Understanding the Leave Vote*. London: NatCen and The UK in a Changing Europe. http://natcen.ac.uk/our-reseach/research/understanding-the-leave-vote/

Technopolis Group (2017), *The Role of EU Funding in UK Research and Innovation*. https://royalsociety.org/~/media/policy/Publications/2017/2017-05-technopolis-role-of-EU-funding-report.PDF

Tijssen, R. (2019), 'Why Distance Matters for Collaboration with Industry', University World News, 25 May.

Tijssen, R., van de Klippe, W. and Yegros, A. (2019), 'Globalisation, Localisation and Glolocalisation of University-Business Research Cooperation: General Patterns and Trends in the UK University System', CGHE Working Paper 50. https://www.researchcghe.org/publications/working-paper/globalisation-localisation-and-glocalisation-of-university-business-research-cooperation-general-patterns-and-trends-in-the-uk-university-system/

Universities UK (UUK) (2019), 'Brexit and UK Universities'. https://www.universitiesuk.ac.uk/policy-and-analysis/brexit/Pages/brexit-and-universities.aspx

Vasilopoulou, S. (2016), 'UK Euroscepticism and the Brexit Referendum', *The Political Quarterly*, 87 (2): 219–27.

Zembylas, M. (2012), 'Transnationalism, Migration and Emotions: Implications for Education', *Globalisation, Societies and Education*, 10 (2): 163–79.

Part III

Financing and Widening Participation

6

Global Higher Education Financing

The Income-Contingent Loans Revolution

Bruce Chapman, Lorraine Dearden and Dung Doan

Introduction[1]

When the first official university in Europe was established in the late eleventh century in Bologna, loans were provided to some students. The first student loan system was formalized in 1240, by the Bishop of Lincoln at the University of Oxford. Many other universities followed suit, but it took until 1951 for the Colombian government to initiate the world's first national student loan scheme which is still in (faltering) operation.

Student loans can take two very different forms depending on how borrowers are obliged to repay their debts. First, and most common, loan repayments are determined with respect to time (a certain amount of money is repaid over a set number of years). This is known as a 'time-based repayment loan' (TBRL). Second, loans can be repaid when and only if a debtor's income exceeds a certain amount per period, and this is known as an 'income-contingent loan' (ICL).

Since 1989, when Australia first adopted ICLs nationally, the use of ICLs in other countries has been remarkable, including universal coverage of all domestic students in New Zealand (1992), England (1998) and Hungary (2001), and partial coverage in the United States (1994), Thailand (2006), South Korea (2011), Brazil (2015) and Japan (2017). Currently there are legislative reforms underway for introducing ICLs in Colombia, Thailand, Brazil, Japan and Malaysia.

To appreciate why these changes have happened, this chapter

- examines key conceptual student loan issues, concluding that the essential economics of student loans suggests major advantages of ICLs over TBRLs for borrowers, lenders and government;

- explains some important recent empirical methodological work originating from the Centre of Global Higher Education which has provided many governments with the evidential ballast and persuasion to move away from TBRLs and towards ICLs; and
- highlights a critical feature of ICL design, namely that when adopting ICLs, governments have substantial flexibility with respect to parameter choices to ensure that an ICL can be shaped efficaciously to suit the idiosyncratic characteristics of their country's unique context.

The Economics of Higher Education Financing

This section focuses on fundamental issues related to the role of government in subsidizing and providing higher education. We consider the equity of imposing a charge on students; the effects of charging on public-sector decisions concerning the provision of higher education places; the necessity of student loans; and the relative effects of different approaches to the collection of student debts.

Tuition and Equity

Should students contribute towards the costs of public higher education, or, should governments cover all the costs? While most governments charge tuition fees for public university services many in Europe do not, including Germany, Sweden and Denmark. These countries do not offer 'free higher education', since there is no such thing as 'free'. Universities are free to the students because there are no tuition fees but instead all the costs are borne by taxpayers.

Recent political experience illustrates this as a potent issue. For example, it is plausible that promises of university tuition fee abolition by both the UK and New Zealand Labour oppositions in recent (2017 and 2018) general election campaigns were important to their relative success. Furthermore, the state of New York has removed college tuition for the majority of students, and a recent US Democrat presidential candidate, Bernie Sanders, proposed this for public colleges.

What does economics have to say about so-called 'free' higher education? For economists, this is a clear equity issue. Not charging tuition fees for public higher education is regressive, because the majority of taxpayers financing it, non-graduates, are financially disadvantaged over their lifetimes compared to graduates. This observation pervades contemporary economics literature (e.g. Barr 1989) but was also made nearly 150 years ago by Karl Marx (1875).[2]

Unsurprisingly, many on the left of politics argue for tuition-free higher education, because of concerns that tuition fees limit the participation of the poor. But we believe that this concern can be overcome so long as there are no tuition fees *at the point of university enrolment*, and that after graduation loan repayments are only required when debtors' incomes are sufficient to facilitate payment. Thus there can be a resolution between the heart of the left and the distributional logic of economics, which is to require loan repayments if, and only when, graduates receive relatively high incomes; this is what an ICL achieves.

Charging Tuition and the Provision of Public University Places

The introduction of, or an increase in, tuition fees might encourage governments to provide the finances to sustain and expand the number of public university places. From an economics perspective, tuition fees mean the financing of higher education costs the government less per place, implying that *ceteris paribus* tuition fees result in better funded universities.

Some English empirical evidence supports this. Murphy, Scott-Clayton and Wyness (2019) show that the increases in both enrolments and per capita student funding, after tuition fees were first reintroduced in 1998, and when fees were increased to £3,000 in 2006 and £9,000 in 2012, were supported by ICLs. Murphy et al. (2019) argue that, despite these tuition increases, there was no diminution in access to higher education for those from disadvantaged backgrounds. This implies that an ICL system mitigates concerns about participation that might otherwise have existed from debt aversion associated with a TBRL.

Figure 6.1 reproduces Murphy et al.'s (2019) indicative evidence. It shows the spurt in enrolments, particularly for the youngest university entrants, following the 2006 and 2012 tuition fee increases. In a cost-sharing world, since the government finances only a proportion of each additional place, any given expansion requires lower government outlays than it would in a 'free'-higher education world. This explains the association between fee hikes and expansion in England.

Consistent with the English experience, the key motivation for the reintroduction of tuition charges in Australia in 1989 (previously abolished in 1974) was to finance a major expansion of university places (Chapman and Hicks 2018). As a result of tuition revenues, paid through an ICL, enrolments between 1989 and 2015 expanded by a factor of 2.5. However, more international evidence on such ICLs effects is needed to establish the policy validity of the presumed association, including examination of university expenditures in countries without tuition fees such as Norway, Denmark, Sweden and Germany.

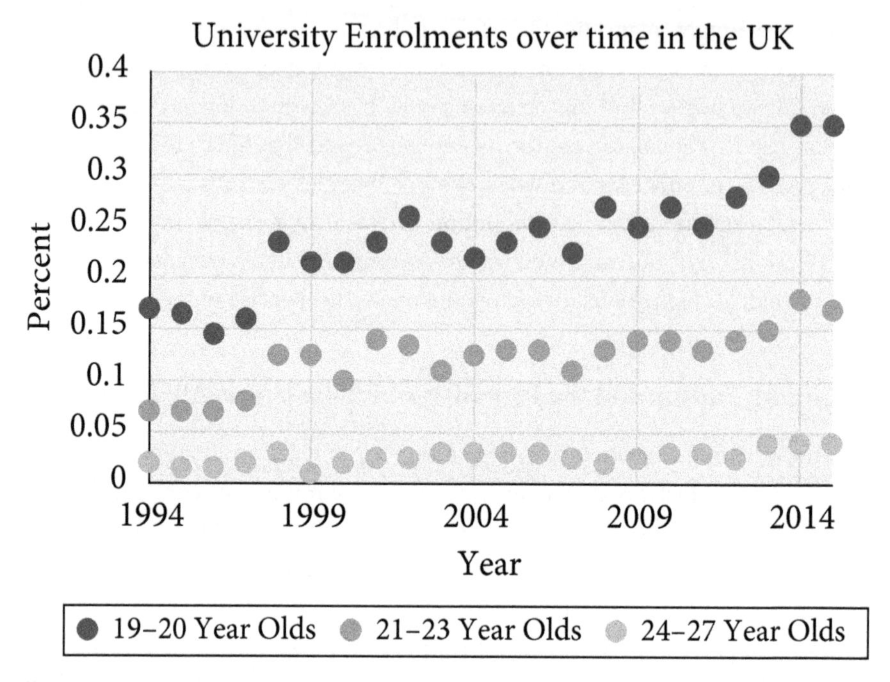

Figure 6.1 Domestic University Enrolment rates by age in the UK.
Source: Murphy, Scott-Clayton and Wyness (2019).

The Necessity for Government-Provided Student Loans

What would happen if countries with tuition fees had no government-provided loan scheme? There are two issues: the first relates to uncertainty and the second to the basic market failure inherent in university funding. With respect to the first Barr (1989), Palacios (2004) and Chapman (2014) highlight that

- enrolling students do not know fully their capacities for higher education – they cannot be sure of graduating;[3]
- students cannot be certain of future success in their area of study; and
- many prospective students, particularly those from low-education backgrounds, will not have much information about graduate earnings, partly because of limited contact with graduates.

Thus, there are important risks for both borrowers and lenders in financing tuition fees via loans. In addition, and critical for prospective lenders, student loans are different to mortgages because of the absence of collateral. If the borrower experiences difficulty with loan repayments or defaults, the lender cannot sell part of the investment to refinance a different educational path.

As a result the market, left to itself, will not deliver propitious outcomes for higher education financing. Credit constrained prospective students will be unable to access commercial loans. Consequently, without government intervention there cannot be equality of educational opportunity (Friedman 1955). Therefore, governments in almost all countries intervene in the financing of higher education through the provision and subsidization of student loans.

Comparing the Effects of Different Forms of Student Loans

What are the essential differences between a TBRL and an ICL, and do they matter? TBRL repayments are set at a constant amount per period for a fixed duration, but ICL repayments depend on an individual debtor's per period capacity to pay as reflected in their income.

With an ICL, no loan repayments are required if a debtor experiences low personal income, resulting from, for example, being unemployed, having a poorly paid job or caring full-time for an infant or aged parent. There is no prospect of loan default or financial hardship as a result of a debtor being unable to keep up repayments in hard times. This security cannot be achieved with a TBRL.

This distinction between the two types of loan is directly supported from a theoretical perspective by Ngo (2019), who, using a model of incomplete credit markets, concludes that an ICL is preferable to a TBRL since the former delivers greater consumption smoothing. Quiggin (2014) comes to the same conclusion with a somewhat different theoretical model.

Furthermore, ICLs have important advantages for government. These include the avoidance of administration and court costs in the event of borrower bankruptcy or default; the fact that more loan outlays can be recovered by not writing off the debts of borrowers who temporarily have low incomes (which can recover later); and the receipt of rapid loan repayments from debtors with high initial incomes. In Australia, for example, the median male graduate repays his debt in about ten years after graduating (Norton 2015).

In addition, so long as ICL debts are collected through employer-withholding (like income tax), the administration of ICLs is extremely simple. In Australia, England and New Zealand, the estimated costs of debt collection are less than 2 per cent of the annual revenue collected (Chapman 2014).[4] These costs are far lower than the public-sector administrative costs of TBRL systems, involving hundreds of officials mostly chasing delinquent borrowers, such as in Colombia, Thailand, Malaysia and the United States.

Student Loan Effects: Measurement

Empirical analyses of student loan-related issues have grown considerably over recent years, with positive implications for country-specific debates about student loan reform. This section examines two important aspects of these developments in concept and practice: the projection of graduates' lifetime incomes and the measurement of loan repayment burdens.

The Critical Importance of Predictions of Graduate Lifetime Incomes

A critical element of student loan analysis concerns graduate debtors' income, which determines whether and how much they can repay debts and how much the government needs to subsidize. Graduates at the bottom of the income distributions are more likely to face difficulty in repaying their debts. And since income varies over a debtor's life course, their risk of default or experiencing consumption hardship due to excessive repayment obligations is not constant over their lifetime. Therefore, reliable projections of graduates' lifetime incomes are essential for analysing student loan systems and the effects of loans on debtors' well-being.

There has been much recent methodological debate and progress within this area. Following Chapman and Lounkaew (2015), many analyses adopted a rather restrictive approach that employs the unconditional quantile regression method to project graduate lifetime incomes (Chapman and Sinning 2014; Chapman and Liu 2013; Chapman and Suryadarma 2013). However, Dearden (2019) explains that restrictions inherent in this approach can result in misleading inferences, and promotes instead the use of simple smoothing of raw income quantiles over a flexible polynomial function of age.

Furthermore, Dearden (2019) stresses that it is vital to account for the dynamics of income across the life course and to show the extent of changes in an individual's income over time which are critical to understanding loan effects. Studies often use cross-sectional (i.e. static) data to calculate lifetime incomes and therefore implicitly assume that debtors' incomes by sex and age remain unchanged over their lifetime, which cannot be accurate. An obvious way to address this is to use longitudinal data, but such data are unavailable in many countries.

When longitudinal data are available, several different approaches are possible (Chowdry et al. 2012; Crawford, Crawford and Jin 2014; Belfield et al. 2017; Britton, van der Erve and Higgin 2019). More recently Dearden (2019) explains a methodological approach which enables approximation of lifetime incomes even when there are just two observations for an individual.

A technical and detailed discussion of these methods is beyond the scope of this chapter. However, it is important to document these advances in the derivation of lifetime incomes and their significant policy implications. Specifically, they help both to demonstrate the adverse consequences of TBRLs and to explain the recent interest shown by several governments in the insurance benefits of ICLs.

Measuring Repayment Burdens in Concept

Accurate projections of graduate lifetime incomes methodologies are significant for calculations of loan repayment burdens, too. The 'repayment burden' (RB) is the most used empirical concept with respect to TBRLs which allows measurement of debtors' difficulties. It is conventionally measured as

$$\frac{L_{it}}{Y_{it}}$$

where L_{it} is the repayment amount of the loan in period t for debtor i and Y_{it} is debtor i's own income in period t. The ratio thus represents the financial consequences for individuals as a result of repaying the debt, and it has been an empirical norm in understanding the potential impact of TBRLs on debtors' financial well-being.

However, the ratio has important limitations in reflecting an individual's financial loan stress. Doan's work (in preparation, 2019) points out that by measuring RB as a proportion of debtor's own income, the repayment-to-income ratio relies on three critical assumptions that are quite restrictive and unlikely to hold in practice. They are: the borrower's own income is the only resource available to repay their debt and the role of intra-household allocation of resources is ignored; loan stress depends only on the size of income relative to the debt and does not depend on the absolute level of income; and, the possibility of a debtor being responsible for repaying both their own student loan and a family member's loan.[5]

In addition to the need for more accurate measurements and interpretations of RBs, there remain unexplored conceptual and behavioural issues behind RBs. For instance, the potential impacts of TBRL collection rules on various decisions made by young graduates, such as occupational choice, leaving their parental homes, getting married and having children. These aspects of how TBRLs affect debtors' welfare are clear candidates for future research, and matter for economic research and policy assessments of student loans (See Callender et al. in this volume for a discussion of the consequences of student loan debt on graduates' lives).

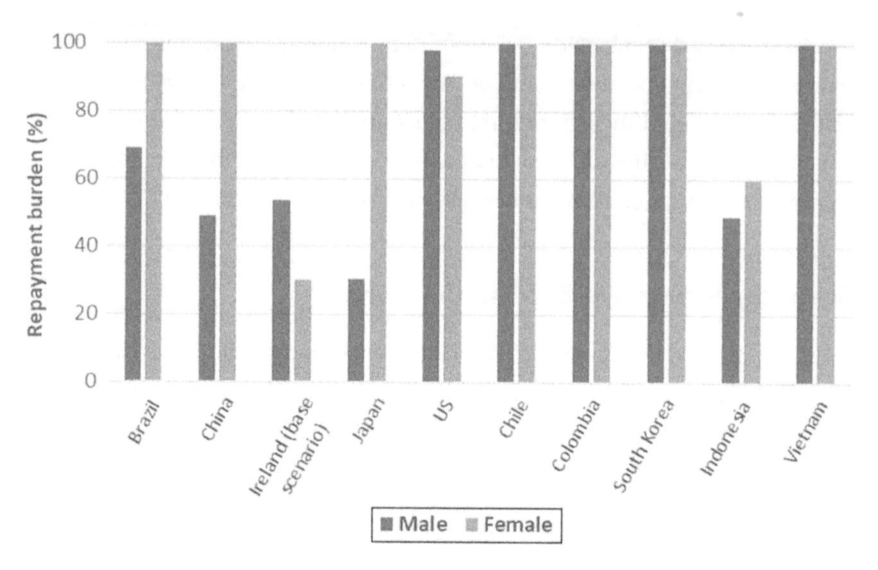

Figure 6.2 Estimated maximum TBRL RBs for the bottom 20 per cent of graduates aged twenty-three to thirty-one.

Source: Reproduced from Chapman and Doan (2019).

Measuring Repayment Burdens in Practice

Despite TBRLs differing widely between countries in terms of loan size and interest rates, research consistently illustrates that RBs can be excessively high for graduates at the bottom of the earnings distribution across quite different national environments. This is illustrated in Figure 6.2, which shows the results of RB calculations from ten countries, with the columns showing the maximum annual RBs for the poorest 20 per cent of young graduates aged twenty-three to thirty-one.[6]

Figure 6.2 shows two things: how very high RBs can be, and the potential for marked differences in RB calculations depending on the design characteristics of TBRLs. As examples, the maximum RBs for male graduates range from 30 per cent in Japan to 98 per cent in the United States; and for females they range from 30 per cent in Ireland to above 100 per cent in Brazil, China and Japan. Although not shown, in all cases bar one, RBs are highest in the first year after graduation, when graduate earnings are at the lowest, except for Japanese females.

In addition to the level of maximum RBs, several papers demonstrate the extent to which graduates might face 'unmanageable' debt, which is defined in some literature as having RBs in excess of 18 per cent of their income (Salmi 2003). Using this benchmark, an estimated 42 per cent of male and 75 per cent of female graduates in Japan will experience excessive RBs for at least one year over the term of their loans (Armstrong et al. 2019), with the corresponding figures in Brazil being 67 per cent for males and 86 per cent for females (Dearden and Nascimento 2019). Similarly, about 70 per cent of male and 67 per cent of female graduates in Ireland would face such excessive RBs in the first year of repayments (Chapman and Doris 2019). While there are limitations to using the repayment-to-income as a measure of RBs, these results indicate serious adverse effects of TBRLs on debtors' economic well-being.

All these findings suggest that under TBRLs, low-earning graduates are likely to face significant difficulties in repaying their debts, financial difficulties and higher risks of loan default. In case of default, the consequence for borrowers is a loss of credit reputation and access to future commercial loans. These findings have constituted key data for ongoing policy debates in Ireland (Chapman and Doris 2019), the United States (Barr et al. 2019), Malaysia (Hock-Eam, Ismail and Ibrahim 2014), Brazil (Dearden and Nascimento 2019), Japan (Armstrong et al. 2019) and Colombia (Penrose 2017). In contrast, all ICL schemes, by design, cap RBs at low levels (no more than 8 and 9 per cent in Australia and England, for instance), thus insuring debtors against default and the financial stress arising from adverse employment outcomes.

Undoubtedly, experiences of default have been an important motivation for the emerging interest in student loan reform in many countries with TBRLs. The policy issues for governments are that default significantly damages debtors' lives, and is extremely expensive for the public purse because once a borrower defaults they are unlikely to make future loan repayments.

It is no coincidence that the countries moving towards universal ICLs have experienced high levels of default with their poorly functioning TBRLs. As evidence shows, defaults as measured by the proportion of borrowers unlikely to repay their TBRLs are as follows: 25 to 30 per cent for the United States (Best and Best 2014), 60 to 70 per cent for Thailand (Lounkaew 2014), 35 to 50 per cent for Malaysia,[7] 50 to 60 per cent for Colombia (Penrose 2017) and 30 to 50 per cent for Brazil (Dearden and Nascimento 2019).

ICL: Subsidies and Design

ICL and Interest Rate Subsidies

International student loan policy reform involving moves to replace TBRLs with ICLs, requires analysis of the interest rate subsidies associated with particular design features of ICLs. This is critical because protecting borrowers against loan repayment hardship needs to be traded off against the costs of taxpayer subsidies.

Government subsidies arise when debtors do not repay their debt in full and/or when the amount they are obliged to repay is less than the true value of loan outlays. That is, when the present value of all their repayments is less than the present value of the government's loan outlays.[8]

Britton et al. (2019) calculate the ICL subsidy in an international comparative context which takes into account income dynamics by using simulations based on British panel data. Their results from the creative technique of imposing the collection parameters of different countries – England, Australia and New Zealand – to the British graduate income structures allow an isolation of the empirical characteristics of the graduate labour market from country-specific ICL parameters.

Britton et al. (2019) find that the extent of subsidies provided by governments and the distribution of such subsidies among debtors are the result of several factors: the level of debt relative to graduate earnings (influenced by the level of tuition fees); the variance of graduate earnings; and interest rates on ICLs relative to the government's cost of borrowing (particularly an issue in New Zealand where real interest rates on ICLs are negative). These findings are also supported by the results for the United States (Barr et al. 2019).

Designing Country-Specific ICLs

Many design parameters need to be considered when implementing ICLs including the level of tuition fees, the rate of interest, the level of loan surcharge and the first annual income level for the collection of the repayment (Barr et al. 2019). Consequently, governments can make fairly precise choices when balancing the generosity of the system for borrowers with taxpayer subsidies.

Importantly, propitious ICL design has critical country-specific dimensions, which is largely associated with the idiosyncratic characteristics of countries' graduate labour markets, budget constraints and public administration. A powerful example is the unique character of the Japanese female-graduate labour market (Armstrong et al. 2019). Because of the extraordinarily low incomes of married Japanese women, using the parameters of the English ICL system, for instance, would result in major shortfalls in the collection of ICL revenue in Japan. Armstrong et al. (2019) illustrate that for an ICL to be viable in terms of minimal subsidies, the first annual income threshold of debt repayment needs to be relatively low to maximize the prospect of Japanese female graduates repaying much of their debt before marriage.

A final important point for policy consideration concerning loan parameters is that countries with long-standing ICL systems (Australia, New Zealand and England) have made considerable changes to their ICL features since their ICLs were originally introduced. The following are noteworthy:

Australia: The first income threshold of repayment was initially set at $A21,000 per annum, but in real terms this was decreased by around 30 per cent in 1997, increased from the 1997 level by around 20 per cent in 2012 and decreased again in 2018 by around 15 per cent. The first rate of repayment was 1 per cent of annual income, which changed to 2, 4 and back to 1 in 1990, 2009 and 2018 respectively.

New Zealand: The annual rate of interest on ICL debt began at price inflation plus 3 per cent in 1992, changed to a lower and hybrid rate depending on income in 2000, and was set equal to zero in nominal terms in 2007.

England: Tuition fees were £1,000 for every full-time student year for a subset of undergraduate students in 1998, but this charge was increased to £3,000 in 2006 for all full-time undergraduates, to £9,000 in 2012, and is currently £9,250.

There are three broad conclusions concerning ICL parameter design. First, between countries there can be a divergence in myriad arrangements with respect to desirable combinations. Second, the variation in parameter values highlights an important policy issue in ICL student loan reform, which is that there is no single generic best scheme; instead, for propitious ICL reforms, design parameters need to be customized to optimize country-specific objectives and institutional characteristics, and ICL reform allows for this. Third, even within a particular country there have been major changes over time in ICL design settings, reinforcing that political and policy circumstances and dynamics often make any suggestion of a specific all-purpose ICL uninteresting.

Conclusion

There has been a quiet international transformation in approaches to student loan policy. This chapter has sought to explain, from a conceptual basis, why governments are moving away from TBRLs and towards ICLs. As well, we have examined recent innovations in empirical methodologies which facilitate an understanding of the consequences of different approaches to higher education financing.

If designed and collected properly, ICLs have major advantages over TBRLs because the former provide insurance for borrowers against repayment hardship and default. A clear benefit to governments interested in introducing ICLs is that they can be designed to suit the country's idiosyncratic characteristics; this then facilitates the opportunity for governments to find the right design mix with respect to the trade-off between equity and taxpayer subsidies. The international higher education financing reforms towards ICLs over the last thirty years should be considered to be unsurprising.

Notes

1 To some extent this chapter draws on previous work by the authors, including Barr, Chapman, Dearden and Dynarski (2019), Chapman (2014), Chapman and Doan (2019), Chapman and Dearden (2018), Dearden (2019), Doan (2017) and Doan (in preparation, 2019). The authors wish to thank the Centre for Global Higher Education, University College London and the College of Business and Economics (Australian National University) for financial support. All opinions are those of the authors.

2 Marx (1875) wrote: 'If in some states … higher education institutions are also "free", that only means in fact defraying the cost of education of the upper classes from the general tax receipts' (Ch. (iv)).

3 In Australia, for example, around 20–25 per cent of students end up without a qualification.

4 The importance of the point is given theoretical substance in Stiglitz (2014).

5 Doan (in preparation, 2019) proposes new measures of RBs to address these limitations.

6 These studies all report the estimations of RBs for existing TBRLs in the countries, except for the cases of Ireland, Indonesia and Vietnam, in which a hypothetical TBRL system was designed on the basis of typical features of such arrangements.

7 Malaysian government loan (PTPTN) documents, 2019.

8 See Chapman and Doan (2019) for the formula for the present value of repayments of an ICL.

References

Armstrong, S., Dearden, L., Kobayashi, M. and Nagase, N. (2019), 'Student Loans in Japan: Current Problems and Possible Solutions', *Economics of Education Review*, 71: 120–34.

Barr, N. (1989), 'Alternative Proposal for Student Loans in the United Kingdom', in M. Woodhall (ed.), *Financial Support for Students: Grants, Loans or Graduate Tax?*, 110–21, London: Kogan Page.

Barr, N, Chapman, B., Dearden, L. and Dynarski, S. (2019), 'The US College Loans System: Lessons from Australia and England', *Economics of Education Review*, 71: 32–48.

Belfield, C., Britton, J., Dearden, L. and van der Erve, L. (2017), 'Higher Education Funding in England: Past, Present and Options for the Future'. IFS Briefing Note BN211. Institute for Fiscal Studies, London.

Best, E. and Best, J. (2014), *The Student Loan Mess*. San Francisco: University of California Press.

Britton, J., van der Erve, L. and Higgin, T. (2019), 'Income Contingent Student Loan Design: Lessons from Around the World', *Economics of Education Review*, 71: 65–82.

Chapman, B. (2014), 'Income Contingent Loans: Background', in B. Chapman, T. Higgins and J. Stiglitz (eds), *Income-Contingent Loans: Theory, Policy and Prospects*, 12–29, New York: Palgrave McMillan.

Chapman, B. and Dearden, L. (2018), 'The International Transformation in Student Loan Systems', University World News, 11 April 2018, https://www.universityworldnews.com/post.php?story=20180411082843685.

Chapman, B. and Doan, D. (2019), 'Introduction to the Special Issue 'Higher Education Financing: Student Loans''', *Economics of Education Review*, 71: 1–6.

Chapman, B. and Doris, A. (2019), 'Modelling Higher Education Financing Reform for Ireland', *Economics of Education Review*, 71: 109–19.

Chapman, B. and Hicks, T. (2018), 'The Political Economy of the Higher Education Contribution Scheme', in B. Cantwell, H. Coates and R. King (eds), *Handbook of the Politics of Higher Education*, 248–64. Cheltenham: Edward Elgar Publishing Limited.

Chapman, B. and Liu A. (2013), 'Repayment Burdens of Student Loans for Vietnamese Higher Education', *Economics of Education Review* (Special Issue on Education Policy), 37: 298–308.

Chapman, B. and Lounkaew, K. (2015), 'An Analysis of Stafford Loan Repayment Burdens', *Economics of Education Review*, 45: 89–102.

Chapman, B. and Sinning, M. (2014), 'Student Loan Reforms for German Higher Education: Financing Tuition Fees', *Education Economics*, 22 (6): 569–88.

Chapman, B. and Suryadarma, D. (2013), 'Financing Higher Education: The Viability of Commercial Student Loan Scheme in Indonesia', in D. Suryadarma and G. W. Jones (eds), *Education in Indonesia*, 203–15, Singapore: Institute of Southeast Asian Studies.

Chowdry, H., Dearden, L., Goodman, A. and Jin, W. (2012), 'The Distributional Impact of the 2012–13 Higher Education Funding Reforms in England', *Fiscal Studies*, 33 (2), 211–35. doi: 10.1111/j.1475-5890.2012.00159.x

Crawford, C., Crawford, R. and Jin, W. (2014), 'Estimating the Public Cost of Student Loans', IFS Report R94, London: Institute for Fiscal Studies. doi: 10.1920/re.ifs.2014.0094.

Dearden, L. (2019), 'Evaluating and Designing Student Loan Systems: An Overview of Empirical Approaches', *Economics of Education Review*, 71: 49–64.

Dearden, L. and Nascimento, P. (2019), 'Modelling Alternative Student Loan Schemes for Brazil', *Economics of Education Review*, 71: 83–94.

Doan, D. (2017), 'Rethinking Student Loan Repayment Burdens: Evidence from Korea'. Presentation at ACDE Trade & Development Seminars, Australian National University, Canberra, 1 May 2017.

Doan, D. (in preparation, 2019), 'Rethinking Student Loan Repayment Burden', Research School of Economics, Australian National University.

Friedman, M. (1955), 'The Role of Government in Education', in R. A. Solo (ed.), *Economics and the Public Interest*, 123–44, New Brunswick, NJ: Rutgers University Press.

Hock-Eam, L., Ismail. R. and Ibrahim, Y. (2014), 'The Implication of Graduate Labour Market Performance in Designing a Loan Scheme for Malaysia', in B. Chapman, T. Higgins and J. E. Stiglitz (eds), *Income Contingent Loans*, 83–97, New York: Palgrave Macmillan.

Lounkaew, K. (2014), 'Modelling Aggregate Loans Recovery of the Student Loans Fund in Thailand', in B. Chapman, T. Higgins and J. E. Stiglitz (eds), *Income Contingent Loans*, 98–108, New York: Palgrave Macmillan.

Marx, K. (1875), 'Critique of the Gotha Program', *Die* Neue Zeit, 1 (18): 1890–91. Reprinted in Marx/Engels Selected Works, vol. 3, pp. 13–30. Moscow: Progress Publishers, 1970.

Murphy, R., Wyness, G. and Scott-Clayton, J. (2019), 'The End of Free College in England: Implications for Quality, Enrolments, and Equity', *Economics of Education Review*, 71: 7–22.

Ngo, L. (2019), 'Financing Higher Education in an Imperfect World', *Economics of Education Review*, 71: 23–31.

Norton, A. (2015), 'Years to Repay Student Debt as a Way of Setting Student Contribution'. https://andrewnorton.net.au/2015/04/08/years-to-repay-student-debt-as-a-way-of-setting-student-contributions/ (accessed 6 May 2019).

Palacios, M. (2004), *Investing in Human Capital: A Capital Market Approach to Student Funding*, Cambridge: Cambridge University Press.

Penrose, G. (2017), 'Colombia Higher Education Financing: An Analysis of Repayment Burdens'. Honours thesis, Research School of Economics, Australian National University.

Quiggin, J. (2014), 'Income Contingent Loans as a Risk Management Device', in B. Chapman, T. Higgins and J. Stiglitz (eds), *Income-Contingent Loans: Theory, Policy and Prospects*, 39–48, New York: Palgrave Macmillan.

Salmi, J. (2003), *Student Loans in an International Perspective: The World Bank Experience*. LCSHD Paper Series No. 44. Washington, DC: World Bank.

Stiglitz, J. (2014), 'Remarks on Income Contingent Loans: How Effective Can They Be at Mitigating Risk?', in B. Chapman, T. Higgins and J. Stiglitz (eds), *Income-Contingent Loans: Theory, Policy and Prospects*, 31–38, New York: Palgrave Macmillan.

7

Student Loan Debt

Longer-Term Implications for Graduates in the United States and England

Claire Callender, KC Deane, Ariane de Gayardon
and Stephen L. DesJardins

Introduction

The introduction of cost-sharing policies, especially tuition fees and student loans, has helped fuel the global expansion of access to higher education. One of the consequences is rising student loan debt. In this chapter we explore research on the effect of student loan debt on life after the first degree, including graduate education, career choices, homeownership, family formation, health and financial well-being. Most studies are from the United States (US), supplemented with United Kingdom (UK) data where available.[1]

We focus solely on student loan debt incurred during undergraduate studies, not graduate programmes (e.g. law school or medical school in the United States). 'Postsecondary education' refers to all students in baccalaureate degrees in the United States or first/Bachelor's degrees in the UK. 'Student loans' refers exclusively to publicly funded loans, administered and distributed by the federal government in the United States and the government-owned Student Loans Company in England. (In England, unlike in the United States, there is a negligible private market.)

Rising Student Loan Debt

The English Context

Higher education policy in the UK is devolved and differs between the four nations. The tuition fees and loans discussed here relate to full-time English domiciled undergraduate students at public UK universities which house most higher education students. All these students are eligible for government-backed loans covering all tuition fees, and maintenance loans towards their costs of living. (Part-time undergraduates, largely outside the discussion here, became eligible for tuition loans in 2012/13 and maintenance loans in 2018/19.)

Loans are income contingent. Repayment begins when earnings reach a specified annual income threshold (currently £25,000). Borrowers pay 9 per cent of annual income above this threshold until the loan is repaid or they reach thirty years of repayment, at which point outstanding debt is forgiven. The interest paid on these loans, also income contingent, ranges from the inflation rate to inflation plus 3 per cent. Loan repayments are collected through pay packets, like income tax.

A growing number of English domiciled undergraduates take out both maintenance loans (Figure 7.1) and tuition loans (Figure 7.2) and are borrowing larger sums (Figure 7.3). As of 2016/17, 90 per cent of eligible students took out a maintenance loan while 95 per cent took out a tuition fee loan (Bolton 2019). The dramatic increase in student loan debt is associated with rising government capped tuition fees, from £3,000 in 2006 to £9,000 in 2012, and then £9,250 in 2017/18. In 2018/19 nearly all universities charged the maximum level for all undergraduate full-time courses.

Estimates for 2017 indicate that average debt upon graduation would exceed £50,000 per student. The amount differed by family income. Students from the poorest 40 per cent of families would graduate with an average debt of

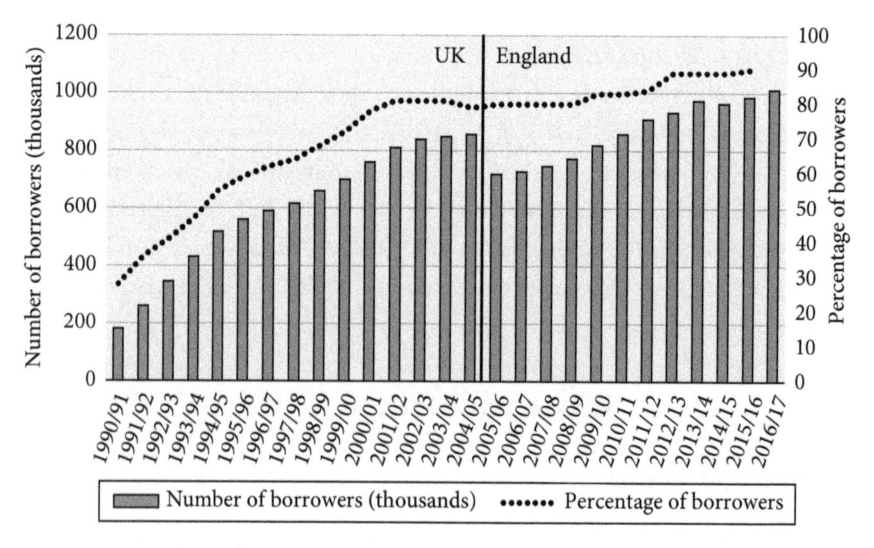

Figure 7.1 Undergraduates Maintenance Loan Take-up in the UK and England.
Source: Derived from Bolton 2018.

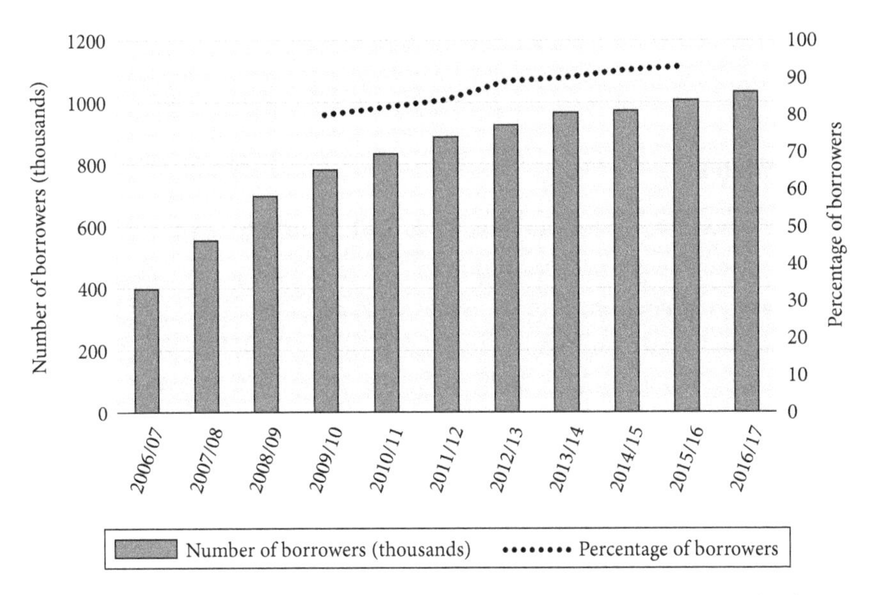

Figure 7.2 Undergraduate Borrowers Take-up of Tuition Fee Loans in England.
Source: Derived from Bolton, 2018.

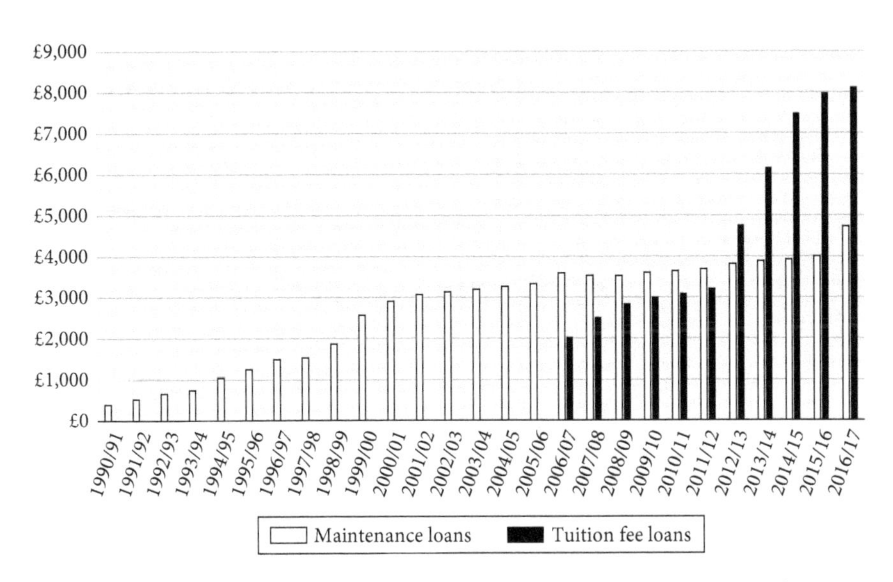

Figure 7.3 Average Value of Maintenance Loans and Tuition Fees Loans in the UK.
Source: Derived from Bolton 2018. In nominal GBP (£) values.

approximately £57,000, compared to £43,000 for students from the richest 30 per cent (Belfield, Britton, Dearden and van der Erve 2017: 17). An estimated 83 per cent of students would not repay their loans in full before the thirty-year mark when outstanding debt is forgiven, primarily because earnings would be too low to trigger full repayment (Belfield, Britton and van der Erve 2017). Student loan payments accompany the vast majority of graduates through most of working life.

United States

In the US students can borrow from both public and private sources with the majority of borrowing occurring through federal student loan programmes. The average graduate cumulatively borrowed approximately $15,000 in federal loans in 1996. In 2016, the figure was $22,000 (Figure 7.4). Because cumulative federal loan amounts exclude both private loans and federal loans borrowed by a student's parents, these amounts probably understate recent increases in cumulative borrowing at the undergraduate level. A separate analysis using income tax data found that from 2000 to 2014 the proportion of undergraduate borrowers with total federal and private student loan balances above $50,000 increased from 1.3 to 6.2 per cent (Looney and Yannelis 2015).

Both the proportion and the number of students borrowing rose between 1999 and 2015, the number swollen by enrolment growth of more than 4 million (Figure 7.5). The average amount borrowed per year was steady for much of the 1990s and early 2000s, then jumped substantially at the start of the 2008 recession (Figure 7.6). Borrowing behaviour differs across sectors in part because of the

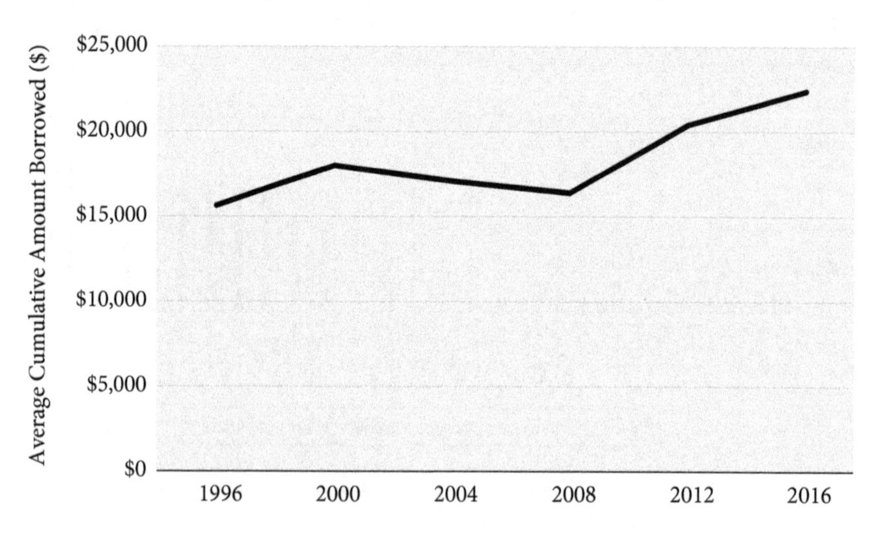

Figure 7.4 Cumulative Federal Loan Borrowing Among Graduates in the United States.

Source: Authors' calculations of NPSAS:96, NPSAS:00, NPSAS:04, NPSAS:08; NPSAS:12; NPSAS:16. (U.S. Department of Education National Center for Education Statistics 2018a)

In 2016 US dollars.

Note: Excludes private loans and Parent PLUS loans.

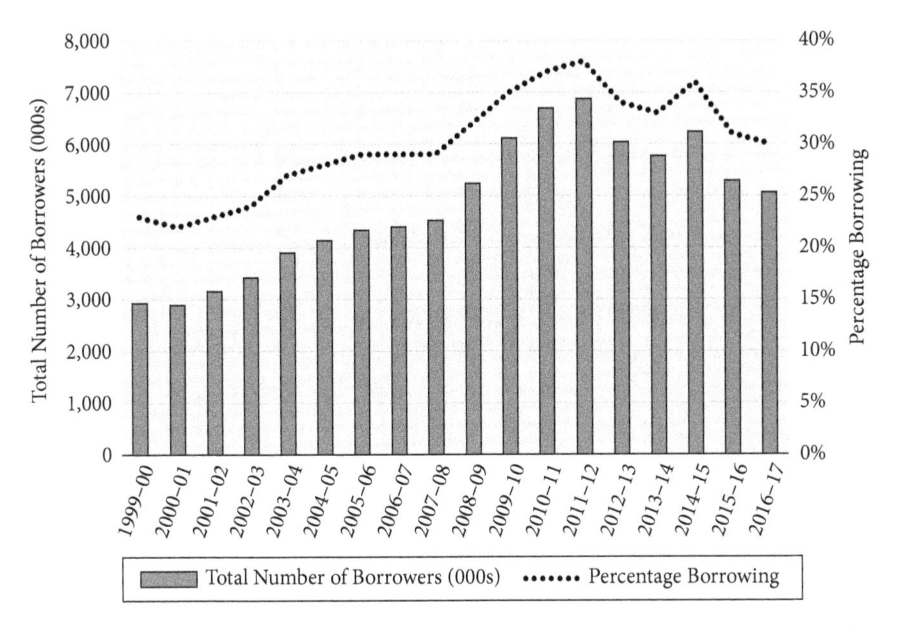

Figure 7.5 Change in the Number and Percentage of Undergraduates Borrowing in the United States.

Source: Baum et al 2017; U.S. Department of Education, National Center for Education Statistics 2018b.

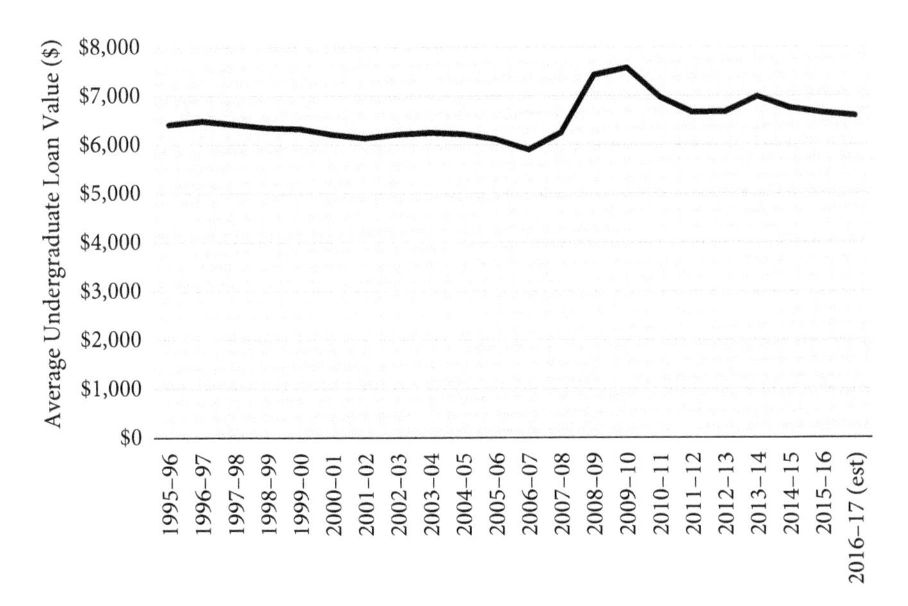

Figure 7.6 Change in Average Federal Loan Values per Undergraduate Borrower in the United States.

Source: Baum et al 2017.

In 2016 US dollars.

large variation in tuition fees. Among a recent cohort of graduates, nearly half of those who attended for-profit institutions had debt above $40,000, compared to 12 per cent from public institutions (Baum, Ma, Pender and Welch 2017).

Two surveys of graduate borrowers find that the average graduate expects to take nineteen years to pay off student loans (One Wisconsin Institute 2013). Over 60 per cent of borrowers aged thirty-five or younger expected their loans would be repaid after the age of forty (Citizens Bank 2016). However, repayment in the United States does not follow a single pattern. It differs across student characteristics, the amount borrowed and the repayment plan. Nearly 40 per cent of all black borrowers have defaulted on their student loans, compared to 12.4 per cent of their white peers (Scott-Clayton 2018). Among defaulters who entered repayment in 2010–11, 35 per cent owed less than $5,000 (Baum, Ma, Pender and Welch 2017).

Until recently, the overwhelming majority of borrowers repaid 'mortgage' style loans under a standard ten-year plan, on the basis of a fixed amount per month irrespective of income. Recently take-up of income-based repayment plans has increased. In 2016, about 5 million borrowers (one-fifth of all borrowers) were on income-based repayment plans compared to 700,000 in 2011 (U.S. Department of Education, Office of the Inspector General 2018). For low-income borrowers, income-contingent repayment plans could ease the monthly repayment burden. However, interest continues to accrue at a fixed rate. Monthly payments may not pay down the principal and the borrower might ultimately pay substantially more over the life of the loan than the amount originally borrowed. In addition, the US tax system treats forgiven loan balances as income, increasing taxation in the year of forgiveness. Moreover, the federal government loses money when a borrower repays student loans through an income-based plan. This cost rises as income-contingent loans spread (U.S. Department of Education, Office of the Inspector General 2018).[2]

Although this chapter is focused on undergraduates, postgraduate borrowing in the United States merits a brief mention. Of all borrowers with balances over $50,000 in 2014, 14 per cent had accumulated the full amount through postgraduate enrolment alone, and 47 per cent through undergraduate and postgraduate education combined (Looney and Yannelis 2015).

Effects: What the Evidence Suggests

Postgraduate Choices

Research findings on the effects of student loan debt on willingness to engage in postgraduate studies are mixed. Some studies find no relationship (Monks 2001;

Perna 2004; Rothstein and Rouse 2011), while others identify a negative relationship (Malcom and Dowd 2012; Zhang 2013). A small number of studies find a positive relationship but in relation to only some students (e.g. those with large debt, middle-income or male students: Azmat and Simion 2017; Kim and Eyermann 2006).

The proportion of survey respondents reporting that loan debt influenced their decision to attend graduate school ranges from 28 to 64 per cent in the United States (American Student Assistance 2015; Baum and O'Malley 2003; EdAssist 2016; Stone, Van Horn, and Zukin 2012) and 13–63 per cent in the UK (Purcell et al. 2012; Purcell and Elias 2010). In both countries the effects of debt on decisions about postgraduate study vary by student and institutional characteristics, including type of postgraduate degree (Perna 2004), undergraduate institution attended (Zhang 2013), debt already accumulated (Malcom and Dowd 2012; Monks 2001), student socio-economic status (Kim and Eyermann 2006) and ethnicity (Malcom and Dowd 2012; Purcell et al. 2012). The culture of loans – the availability and acceptability of taking loans for higher education in each student's social and economic context (Kim and Eyermann 2006) or social class (Malcom and Dowd 2012) – creates a unique set of factors affecting each decision that are hard to untangle.

Job Satisfaction and Career Choice

Worries about repayment of student loans may affect individuals' career decisions. UK studies indicate that student loan debt is correlated with graduates holding a job not of their first choice (Purcell et al. 2012; Purcell and Elias 2010). US research consistently finds a negative relationship between job satisfaction and student loan debt (Gervais and Ziebarth 2017), but indebted graduates are less likely to be unemployed or move jobs (Chapman 2016; Gervais and Ziebarth 2017). Graduates in the United States forego careers in education or sectors like entertainment (Chapman 2016). US studies on student loans and entrepreneurship agree that individuals with debt are more likely to avoid the financial risks of starting a business (Checovich and Allison 2016).

In research examining student loan debt in relation to earnings, there is no consensus on the direction of the relationship. Several US studies find that higher debt is related to lower earnings (Ji 2017; Price 2004). Others link higher debt to higher earnings (Chapman 2016; Rothstein and Rouse 2011). Many studies, including one from Canada and one from the UK, suggest no relationship (Gervais and Ziebarth 2017; Goodman, Isen, and Yannelis 2018; Purcell and Elias 2010; Zhang 2013).

A small number of studies find no relation between student loan debt and career choices, including non-graduate employment in the UK (Purcell et al. 2012), public-sector work in the UK (Zhang 2013), career-plan changing while enrolled (Monks 2001) and being on a temporary or permanent contract (Azmat and Simion 2017).

Homeownership

Most homes are purchased using mortgages. Individuals already holding and repaying debt may be less likely to access mortgages. Mortgage access in the UK requires a deposit and an income requirement. Student loan debt affects the affordability score though not the credit score. Research indicates that increased student loan debt does not change the age at which individuals reach the income requirements, but it delays accumulation of the required deposit by at least two years (Andrew 2010). In the United States, the borrower's debt-to-income ratio must fall below a specific threshold. In 2004, the average student loan debtor could not access typical home mortgages because of their debt-to-income ratio (Mishory and O'Sullivan 2012). It has been estimated that 11–35 per cent of the 8 per cent decline in homeownership between 2007 and 2015 can be explained by increased tuition fees and student loan debt (Bleemer et al. 2017).

There are negative relationships between student loan debt and owning a home (Elliott and Lewis 2015) and housing value and equity (Elliott and Lewis 2015; Hiltonsmith 2013; Zhan, Xiang and Elliott 2016). In US surveys, 38–71 per cent of respondents indicated that student loan debt delayed home purchase (Baum and O'Malley 2003; EdAssist 2016; Stone, Van Horn and Zukin 2012). There is some evidence debtors catch up with non-debtors by the age of thirty (Mezza, Sommer and Sherlund 2014). It is less clear whether the amount of debt is associated with less homeownership. Some US studies find a small negative relationship (Baum and O'Malley 2003; Bleemer et al. 2017; Mezza et al. 2015); others no relationship (Gervais and Ziebarth 2017; Gicheva and Thompson 2015; Marks 2009; Zhang 2013). A limitation is lack of data on variations by the geographic location of housing.

Some research indicates that lower home ownership among individuals with student loan debt is caused not by reduced eligibility for credit (Mezza et al. 2015), but student loan debtors self-selecting out of home purchase. Student loan debtors may have higher debt aversion and lower demand for other loans, including mortgages. This and the tightening of mortgage eligibility criteria may explain reductions in the supply of mortgages (Brown et al. 2014; Elliott and Lewis 2015).

Research in both the United States and United Kingdom suggests that student loan debt contributes to recent increases in students returning to the family home after graduation. In surveys, 13–43 per cent of respondents felt student loan debt prevented them from finding their own residence (Baum and O'Malley 2003; Purcell et al. 2012; Stone, Van Horn and Zukin 2012. See also Bleemer et al. 2014). However, Houle and Warner (2017) find no relationship between student loan debt and returning to live with family after graduation, and Marks (2009) finds a small negative relationship.

Family Formation

Research suggests that student loan debt can influence life choices like getting married and having children, with the latter affected by the concurrent costs of childcare and schooling.

The literature divides between studies finding a negative relationship between student loan debt and marriage (Gicheva 2016) and those finding no relationship (Gervais and Ziebarth 2017; Zhang 2013). In some US surveys, 14–21 per cent of respondents reported that student loan debt delayed marriage (EdAssist 2016; Stone, Van Horn and Zukin 2012). Studies suggest that debt influences marriage decisions differentially for men and women: the effect either only exists for women or is much stronger for women. Interestingly, a study examining student loan debt and marriage satisfaction found no relationship (Dew 2008).

Marks (2009) finds that student loan debt and the decision to have children are inversely related although Nau, Dwyer, and Hodson (2015) find this for women only. Recent US research highlights ethnic differences: a negative relation between student loan debt and first birth for Hispanic women, and marital first birth for white women; a positive relationship for black women (Min and Taylor 2018). Two studies fail to find a relationship between student loan debt and having children but these are limited: one examines self-reported expected lifetime fertility not the actual number of children (Yu, Kippen, and Chapman 2007); the other does not differentiate between various types of debt (Chiteji 2008).

Research studies have analysed marriage and fertility at specific points in time. Future research should analyse the temporal relationship between student loan debt and family formation to assess not only whether but also when people marry and have children.

Health

Debt is related to health issues, particularly mental health (Fitch, Hamilton, Basset and Davy 2011) including stress and associated depression and anxiety. In turn, mental health factors can directly and indirectly affect short-term and long-term physical health. Both United States and United Kingdom studies reveal that student loan debt is associated with poorer health among currently enrolled students (Morra, Regehr and Ginsburg 2008; Walsemann, Gee and Gentile 2015). However, literature on student loan debt and post-study health is scarce in the United States and non-existent in the United Kingdom. This important area is under-studied.

The US literature almost unanimously finds a negative relationship between student loan debt and health after leaving higher education. Student loan debt is related to healthcare hardship (Despard et al. 2016), lower psychological functioning (Walsemann, Gee and Gentile 2015), less mastery and self-esteem among older adults (Dwyer, McCloud, and Hodson 2011) and shorter sleep durations for black individuals (Walsemann, Ailshire and Gee 2016). These relationships could be moderated by factors like socio-economic background (Dwyer, McCloud and Hodson 2011; Walsemann, Gee and Gentile 2015), level of debt (Despard et al. 2016) and ethnicity (Walsemann, Ailshire and Gee 2016).

Lifetime Financial Well-Being

Whatever the student loan repayment scheme, debt-bearing individuals have less money for consumption, investment or savings, including savings for retirement.

Research in the United States and Canada finds an inverse relationship between student loan debt and wealth, with wealth mostly defined as net worth (Elliott and Nam 2013; Hiltonsmith 2013; Zhan, Xiang and Elliott 2016). Other research indicates a negative link between student loan debt and investments (Batkeyev, Krishnan, and Nandy 2016) and savings (Hiltonsmith 2013), though another study finds no link between overall debt and savings (Goodman, Isen and Yannelis 2018).

Studies also find student loan debt is positively associated with the incidence of financial distress, including financial struggle (Baum and O'Malley 2003), skipping or making late payments (Bricker and Thompson 2016; Despard et al. 2016; Gicheva and Thompson 2015), being denied credit (Bricker and Thompson 2016; Gicheva and Thompson 2015), and experiencing bank overdrafts, bankruptcy and food insecurity (Despard et al. 2016; Gicheva and Thompson 2015), with larger consequences for those not completing higher education.

US studies indicate an overwhelming inverse relationship between student loan debt and retirement preparedness. In surveys, 62–78 per cent of respondents felt student loan debt impaired their ability to save for retirement (EdAssist 2016). Student loan debt may lead to a society in which individuals are not only less financially prepared for retirement but delay it until an older age (Hiltonsmith 2013). Other findings include more retirees with outstanding debt (Jeszeck 2014), less retirement savings (Rutledge, Sanzenbacher, and Vitagliano 2016) and a higher proportion of individuals unable to maintain their lifestyle in retirement (Munnell, Hou and Webb 2016). However, there seems no relationship between student loan debt and participation in a retirement scheme (Rutledge, Sanzenbacher and Vitagliano 2016).

Conclusions

Calculations of the average pecuniary benefits of higher education rarely account for all costs including opportunity costs, tuition fees and the long-term servicing of student loan debt which eats into the graduate lifetime earnings premium – which itself varies by labour market conditions on graduation, institution attended, discipline and graduate background.

Student loan debt that affects many facets of individual lives also affects the future of society. Yet little is known about the incidence and magnitude of the relations between student loans and important life choices and events. Research so far reveals inconsistent findings concerning decisions to enrol in postsecondary education, choice of career, housing investment and family formation. Signs point to an almost universal negative relationship between student loan debt and physical and mental health, and preparedness for retirement. However, there are limitations in research designs that do not account for diverse backgrounds and personal circumstances. More longitudinal studies should be developed, to track the changing effects of loan debt over the life course. More qualitative studies could provide new insights into the pecuniary and non-pecuniary consequences of student loan debt.

Existing knowledge is overly reliant on US data which limits generalisability. For example, the differences between student loans in the United States and England have implications for behaviour. With income-contingent loans in England, the government, not students, bears financial penalties associated with low graduate earnings and non-repayment. On the other hand, graduates in England take far longer to pay off their loans than most in the United States. There is overreliance on descriptive surveys and secondary data analysis, especially in the United States where researchers cannot access the national data system with federal student loan information, or the private loan data covering a substantial part of the student loan market.[3]

There is also a dearth of studies that move beyond studying relationships between loan debt and important education and life-course outcomes, to making causal statements about these connections. Although researchers have made great strides in recent years in understanding the multifaceted ways in which student loans influence individuals' education and lifelong decisions and behaviours, there is much to learn.

Notes

1 For additional information about differences in English and United States' loan policies, as well as contextual and descriptive data about the life-course outcomes discussed in this chapter, see 'Graduate Indebtedness: Its Perceived Effects on Behaviour and Life Choices – a Literature Review' at: http://www.researchcghe.org/publications/key-findings-graduate-indebtedness-its-perceived-effects-on-behaviour-and-life-choices-a-literature-review/.

2 Currently the US Department of Education estimates that the present value of cash inflows is estimated to exceed the present value of cash outflows for the IBR plan.

3 Known as the National Student Loan Data System (NSLDS), which is housed within the U.S. Department of Education's Federal Student Aid office. Due to legal constraints, this database has been off limits for use by researchers.

References

American Student Assistance (2015), *Life Delayed: The Impact of Student Debt on the Daily Lives of Young Americans*, Boston: Author.

Andrew, M. (2010), 'The Changing Route to Owner Occupation: The Impact of Student Debt', *Housing Studies*, 25 (1): 39–62. https://doi.org/10.1080/02673030903361656

Azmat, G. and Simion, S. (2017), *Higher Education Funding Reforms: A Comprehensive Analysis of Educational and Labor Market Outcomes in England*. Discussion Paper Series No. 11083, Bonn: IZA Institute of Labor Economics.

Batkeyev, B., Krishnan, K. and Nandy, D. K. (2016), *Student Debt and Personal Portfolio Risk*, Northeastern U. D'Amore-McKim School of Business Research Paper No. 2777062, Boston: Northeastern University D'Amore-McKim School of Business. Available online: https://papers.ssrn.com/sol3/papers.cfm?abstract_id=2777062

Baum, S. and O'Malley, M. (2003), 'College on Credit: How Borrowers Perceive Their Education Debt', *Journal of Student Financial Aid*, 33 (3): 7–19.

Baum, S., Ma, J., Pender, M. and Welch, M. (2017), *Trends in Student Aid 2017*, Trends in Higher Education Series No. 00693–004, New York: The College Board.

Belfield, C., Britton, J. and van der Erve, L. (2017), *Higher Education Finance Reform: Raising the Repayment Threshold to £25,000 and Freezing the Fee Cap at £9,250*. IFS Briefing Note No. BN217, London: Institute for Fiscal Studies.

Belfield, C., Britton, J., Dearden, L. and van der Erve, L. (2017), *Higher Education Funding in England: Past, Present and Options for the Future*. IFS Briefing Note No. BN211, London: Institute for Fiscal Studies.

Bleemer, Z., Brown, M., Lee, D. and van der Klaauw, W. (2014), *Tuition, Jobs, or Housing: What's Keeping Millennials at Home?*. Staff Reports No. 700, New York: Federal Reserve Bank of New York.

Bleemer, Z., Brown, M., Lee, D., Strair, K. and van der Klaauw, W. (2017), *Echoes of Rising Tuition in Students' Borrowing, Educational Attainment, and Homeownership in Post-Recession America*. Staff Reports No. 820, New York: Federal Reserve Bank of New York.

Bolton, P. (2019), *Student Loan Statistics*. Briefing Paper No. 1079, London: House of Commons Library.

Bricker, J. and Thompson, J. (2016), 'Does Education Loan Debt Influence Household Financial Distress? An Assessment Using the 2007–2009 Survey of Consumer Finances Panel: Education Loans and Financial Distress', *Contemporary Economic Policy*, 34 (4): 660–77. https://doi.org/10.1111/coep.12164

Brown, M., Haughwout, A., Donghoon, L., Scally, J. and van der Klaauw, W. (2014), *Measuring Student Debt and Its Performance*. Staff Reports No. 668, New York: Federal Reserve Bank of New York.

Chapman, S. (2016), *Student Loans and the Labor Market: Evidence from Merit Aid Programs*. Working Papers No. 2016–04, Washington: The Washington Center for Equitable Growth. Available online: http://equitablegrowth.org/equitablog/student-loans-and-the-labor-market-evidence-from-merit-aid-programs/

Checovich, L. and Allison, T. (2016), *At the Extremes: Student Debt and Entrepreneurship*, Washington: Young Invincibles.

Chiteji, N. S. (2008), 'To Have and To Hold: An Analysis of Young Adult Debt', in S. Danziger and C. E. Rouse (eds), *The Price of Independence: The Economics of Early Adulthood*, 231–58, New York: Russel Sage Foundation. Available online: http://www.jstor.org/stable/pdf/10.7758/9781610441483.12.pdf

Citizens Bank (2016), *Millennial College Graduates with Student Loans Now Spending Nearly One-Fifth of Their Annual Salaries on Student Loan Repayments*, Press release. Available online: http://investor.citizensbank.com/about-us/newsroom/latest-news/2016/2016-04-07-140336028.aspx

Despard, M. R., Perantie, D., Taylor, S., Grinstein-Weiss, M., Friedline, T. and Raghavan, R. (2016), 'Student Debt and Hardship: Evidence from a Large Sample of Low- and Moderate-Income Households', *Children and Youth Services Review*, 70: 8–18. https://doi.org/10.1016/j.childyouth.2016.09.001

Dew, J. (2008), 'Debt Change and Marital Satisfaction Change in Recently Married Couples', *Family Relations*, *57*(1): 60–71.

Dwyer, R. E., McCloud, L. and Hodson, R. (2011), 'Youth Debt, Mastery, and Self-Esteem: Class-Stratified Effects of Indebtedness on Self-Concept', *Social Science Research*, 40 (3): 727–41. https://doi.org/10.1016/j.ssresearch.2011.02.001

EdAssist (2016), *Student Loan Debt: Who's Paying the Price*, Watertown, MA: Author.

Elliott, W. and Nam, I. (2013), 'Is Student Debt Jeopardizing the Short-Term Financial Health of US Households?', *Federal Reserve Bank of St. Louis Review*, 95 (September/October). Available online: https://www.researchgate.net/profile/William_Elliott5/publication/258126350_Is_Student_Debt_Jeopardizing_the_Short-Term_Financial_Health_of_U.S._Households/links/558aa0c208ae13db28c6cb49.pdf

Elliott, W. and Lewis, M. (2015), 'Student Debt Effects on Financial Well-Being: Research and Policy Implications', *Journal of Economic Surveys*, 29 (4): 614–36. https://doi.org/10.1111/joes.12124

Fitch, C., Hamilton, S., Bassett, P. and Davey, R. (2011), 'The Relationship Between Personal Debt and Mental Health: A Systematic Review', *Mental Health Review Journal*, 16 (4): 153–66. https://doi.org/10.1108/13619321111202313

Gervais, M. and Ziebarth, N. L. (2017), 'Life after Debt: Post-Graduation Consequences of Federal Student Loans', in *2017 Meeting Papers*, Edinburgh. Available online: https://www.biz.uiowa.edu/faculty/mgervais/workingpapers/student_loan.pdf

Gicheva, D. (2016), 'Student Loans or Marriage? A Look at the Highly Educated', *Economics of Education Review*, 53: 207–16. https://doi.org/10.1016/j.econedurev.2016.04.006

Gicheva, D. and Thompson, J. (2015), 'The Effects of Student Loans on Long-Term Household Financial Stability', in B. J. Hershbein and K. M. Hollenbeck (eds), *Student Loans and the Dynamics of Debt*, 287–316, Kalamazoo: W.E. Upjohn Institute for Employment Research.

Hiltonsmith, R. (2013), *How Student Debt Reduces Lifetime Wealth*, Debt-for-Diploma Series, New York: Démos.

Houle, J. N. and Warner, C. (2017), 'Into the Red and Back to the Nest? Student Debt, College Completion, and Returning to the Parental Home among Young Adults', *Sociology of Education*, 90 (1): 89–108. https://doi.org/10.1177/0038040716685873

Jeszeck, C. A. (2014), *Older Americans: Inability to Repay Student Loans May Affect Financial Security of a Small Percentage of Retirees*, No. GAO-14-866T, Washington: United States Government Accountability Office.

Ji, Y. (2017), 'Job Search under Debt: Aggregate Implications of Student Loans'. Available online: https://papers.ssrn.com/sol3/papers.cfm?abstract_id=2976040

Kim, D. and Eyermann, T. S. (2006), 'Undergraduate Borrowing and Its Effects on Plans to Attend Graduate School Prior to and after the 1992 Higher Education Act Amendments', *Journal of Student Financial Aid*, 36 (2): 5–21.

Looney, A. and Yannelis, C. (2015), 'A Crisis in Student Loans? How Changes in the Characteristics of Borrowers and in the Institutions They Attended Contributed to Rising Loan Defaults', *Brookings Paper on Economic Activity*, Washington: Brookings Institute.

Malcom, L. E. and Dowd, A. C. (2012), 'The Impact of Undergraduate Debt on the Graduate School Enrollment of STEM Baccalaureates', *The Review of Higher Education*, 35 (2): 265–305.

Marks, G. N. (2009), 'The Social Effects of the Australian Higher Education Contribution Scheme (HECS)', *Higher Education*, 57 (1): 71–84.

Mezza, A. A., Ringo, D. R. , Sherlund, S. M. and Sommer, K. (2015), *On The Effect of Student Loans on Access to Homeownership*, Finance and Economics Discussion Series No. 2016–10, 1–35, Washington: Board of Governors of the Federal Reserve System. Available online: http://www.federalreserve.gov/econresdata/feds/2016/files/2016010pap.pdf

Mezza, A. A., Sommer, K. and Sherlund, S. M. (2014, October 15), *Student Loans and Homeownership Trends*. Available online: https://www.federalreserve.gov/econresdata/notes/feds-notes/2014/student-loans-and-homeownership-trends-20141015.html

Min, S. and Taylor, M. G. (2018), 'Racial and Ethnic Variation in the Relationship Between Student Loan Debt and the Transition to First Birth', *Demography*, 55 (1): 165–88. https://doi.org/10.1007/s13524-017-0643-6

Mishory, J. and O'Sullivan, R. (2012), *Denied? The Impact of Student Debt on the Ability to Buy a House*, Washington: Young Invincibles. Available online: http://www.cgsnet.org/ckfinder/userfiles/files/Denied-The-Impact-of-Student-Debt-on-the-Ability-to-Buy-a-House-8_14_12.pdf

Monks, J. (2001), 'Loan Burdens and Educational Outcomes', *Economics of Education Review*, 20 (6): 545–50.

Morra, D. J., Regehr, G. and Ginsburg, S. (2008), 'Anticipated Debt and Financial Stress in Medical Students', *Medical Teacher*, 30 (3): 313–15. https://doi.org/10.1080/01421590801953000

Munnell, A. H., Hou, W. and Webb, A. (2016), *Will the Explosion of Student Debt Widen the Retirement Security Gap?*, Issue in Brief No. 16-2, Chestnut Hill: Center for Retirement Research at Boston College. Available online: http://research.prudential.com/documents/rp/IB_16-2_wm.pdf

Nau, M., Dwyer, R. E. and Hodson, R. (2015), 'Can't Afford a Baby? Debt and Young Americans', *Research in Social Stratification and Mobility*, 42: 114–22. https://doi.org/10.1016/j.rssm.2015.05.003

One Wisconsin Institute (2013), *Survey Results: Impact of Student Loan Debt on Homeownership Trends and Vehicle Purchasing*. Available online: https://drive.google.com/file/d/0B8LurBVUNQZfQVhYZWZvamlfd00/view

Perna, L. W. (2004), 'Understanding the Decision to Enroll in Graduate School: Sex and Racial/Ethnic Group Differences', *The Journal of Higher Education*, 75 (5): 487–527.

Price, D. V. (2004), 'Educational Debt Burden among Student Borrowers: An Analysis of the Baccalaureate and Beyond Panel, 1997 Follow-Up', *Research in Higher Education*, 45 (7): 701–37.

Purcell, K. and Elias, P. (2010), *The Impact of Paid and Unpaid Work and of Student Debt on Experience of Higher Education*, Higher Education Careers Services Unit. Available online: http://www.warwick.ac.uk/fac/soc/ier/futuretrack/findings/ft3.1_wp3_paid_work_and_debt.pdf

Purcell, K., Elias, P., Atfield, G. , Behle, H., Ellison, R., Luchinskaya, D. Snape, J. Conaghan, L., and Tzanakou, C. (2012), *Futuretrack Stage 4: Transitions into Employment, Further Study and Other Outcomes*, Higher Education Careers Services

Unit. Available online: http://www.hecsu.ac.uk/assets/assets/documents/Futuretrack_Stage_4_Final_report_6th_Nov_2012.pdf

Rothstein, J. and Rouse, C. E. (2011), 'Constrained after College: Student Loans and Early-Career Occupational Choices', *Journal of Public Economics*, 95: 149–163.

Rutledge, M. S., Sanzenbacher, G. and Vitagliano, F. M. (2016), 'How Does Student Debt Affect Early-Career Retirement Saving?'. Available online: https://papers.ssrn.com/sol3/papers.cfm?abstract_id=2839453

Scott-Clayton, J. (2018), *What Accounts for Gaps in Student Loan Default, and What Happens After*, Evidence Speaks, WA: Brookings Institute. Available online: https://www.brookings.edu/research/what-accounts-for-gaps-in-student-loan-default-and-what-happens-after/

Stone, C., Van Horn, C. and Zukin, C. (2012), *Chasing the American Dream: Recent College Graduates and the Great Recession*, Work Trends, John J. Heldrich Center for Workforce Development. Available online: https://eric.ed.gov/?id=ED535270

U.S. Department of Education, Office of the Inspector General (2018), *The Department's Communication Regarding the Costs of Income-Driven Repayment Plans and Loan Forgiveness Programs*, No. ED-OIG/A09Q0003, Washington: U.S. Department of Education.

U.S. Department of Education, National Center for Education Statistics. (2018a), *National Postsecondary Student Aid Survey: 1996, 2000, 2004, 2008, 2012, 2016.* Retrieved from https://nces.ed.gov/datalab/index.aspx

U.S. Department of Education, National Center for Education Statistics. (2018b), *Table 303.70: Total undergraduate fall enrollment in degree-granting postsecondary institutions, by attendance status, sex of student, and control and level of institution: Selected years, 1970 through 2027.* In Digest of Education Statistics (2017 ed.). Retrieved from https://nces.ed.gov/programs/digest/d17/tables/dt17_303.70.asp?current=yes

Walsemann, K. M., Gee, G. C. and Gentile, D. (2015), 'Sick of Our Loans: Student Borrowing and the Mental Health of Young Adults in the United States', *Social Science and Medicine*, 124: 85–93. https://doi.org/10.1016/j.socscimed.2014.11.027

Walsemann, K. M., Ailshire, J. A. and Gee, G. C. (2016), 'Student Loans and Racial Disparities in Self-Reported Sleep Duration: Evidence from a Nationally Representative Sample of US Young Adults', *Journal of Epidemiology and Community Health*, 70 (1): 42–8. https://doi.org/10.1136/jech-2015-205583

Yu, P., Kippen, R., and Chapman, B. (2007), 'Births, Debts and Mirages: The Impact of the Higher Education Contribution Scheme (HECS) and Other Factors on Australian Fertility Expectations', *Journal of Population Research*, 24 (1): 73–90.

Zhan, M., Xiang, X. and Elliott, W. (2016), 'Education Loans and Wealth Building Among Young Adults', *Children and Youth Services Review*, 66: 67–75. https://doi.org/10.1016/j.childyouth.2016.04.024

Zhang, L. (2013), 'Effects of College Educational Debt on Graduate School Attendance and Early Career and Lifestyle Choices', *Education Economics*, 21 (2): 154–75. https://doi.org/10.1080/09645292.2010.545204

8

Widening Participation in the UK

The Possibilities and the Limits

Vikki Boliver, Stephen Gorard and Nadia Siddiqui

Introduction

High rates of participation in higher education have become a hallmark feature of wealthy countries around the globe (Marginson 2016) and the United Kingdom (UK) is no exception. Currently, around half of all young people aged eighteen to age thirty participate in higher education in the UK (DfE 2017), up from just 5 per cent at the start of the 1960s and only 15 per cent by the late 1980s (Boliver 2011). As in many other countries, this expansion has been driven largely by the State and has been accompanied by a parallel drive to widen access to higher education and its benefits to all socio-economic groups. In the early 1960s, the UK government commissioned a committee on higher education to investigate the societal need for and economic viability of an expanded higher education system. Motivated by a concern to maintain the UK's competitive position within the international economy and a concern with matters of social justice, the Committee's report (better known as the 'Robbins Report') set out proposals for a substantial and rapid expansion of the UK higher education sector based on the 'guiding principle' that

> all young persons qualified by ability and attainment to pursue a full-time course in higher education should have the opportunity to do so. (Committee on Higher Education, 1965, p.49)

This sentiment has been echoed in virtually every UK government policy document relating to higher education in the intervening years, including the 1991 White Paper which set out plans for a second major wave of higher education expansion in the 1990s (DES, 1991), and the 2003 White Paper which proposed what was then an ambitious target for the higher education participation rate of 50 per cent (DfES 2003). The most recent higher education White Paper, published in 2016, went so far as to proclaim: 'We have gone from a higher education system that serves only a narrow band of people, to a broader, more diverse and more open system that is closer than ever before to fulfilling Lord Robbins' guiding principle that higher education 'should be available to all who are qualified by ability and attainment to pursue it'' (DBIS 2016: 7). However, the available evidence casts considerable doubt on this claim. This chapter considers why progress on widening participation has been so lamentable to date, and what scope there is for bringing about a step change in the future.

It must be said that decades of widening access policy have indeed succeeded in increasing the absolute rate at which those from socio-economically disadvantaged backgrounds participate in higher education. However, because participation rates have increased for all social groups to a similar degree, the socio-economic gap has reduced only slightly and in fact remains substantial. In 2014/15, the gap in the higher education participation rate was 10 percentage points smaller than it had been fifteen years previously, but the gap remains considerable at 33 percentage points for those whose parents held blue-collar jobs or were small-scale self-employed (NS-SEC categories 4–7) relative to those whose parents held white-collar jobs (NS-SEC categories 1–3). Similarly, the higher education participation rate for state-educated young people whose low family incomes qualified them to receive free school meals has improved in absolute and relative terms but remains 35 percentage points lower than that for other state-educated pupils (Harrison 2018).

Importantly, even this modest degree of progress on widening access to higher education in general has not been matched by equivalent improved access to the UK's most prestigious universities. Small increases in the absolute rates at which those from less advantaged backgrounds attend more prestigious universities have been matched by similar growth for more advantaged groups (Harrison 2018). Consequently, Russell Group universities – the self-proclaimed 'jewels of the crown' of the UK higher education system – saw that the proportions of their entrants who were from state-maintained schools, lower social class backgrounds or neighbourhoods with low overall rates of participation in higher education remained quite stable between 1997/8 and 2014/15 (Boliver 2015). At the hyper-prestigious universities of Oxford and Cambridge, one in three students still comes from fee-paying private schools, even though fewer than one in ten attend such schools nationally (Good University Guide 2019). The UK is not unique in this respect. Across the globe the most prestigious higher education institutions and programmes continue to be disproportionately accessed by students from the most advantaged socio-economic groups (Marginson 2016). Indeed, in the context of high rates of participation in higher education in general, the continued over-representation of socio-economic elites in forms of higher education that are perceived to be qualitatively 'better' is a key way in which inequality is 'effectively maintained' (Lucas 2001, Boliver 2016).

Widening access to higher education generally, and to more prestigious forms of higher education in particular, matters because of the potentially substantial returns to higher education credentials in the labour market. The average earnings of degree holders are more than 25 per cent higher than the earnings of non-graduates (Conlon and Patrignani 2011). Those holding degrees from Russell Group universities earn 10 per cent more than the average graduate after controlling statistically for a range of individual-level characteristics (Belfield et al. 2018). And although less than 1 per cent of the British public attended the universities of Oxford or Cambridge, Oxbridge graduates account for three-quarters of all senior members of the judiciary, and more than half of all government cabinet ministers and senior civil servants (Social Mobility Commission 2014). Unsurprisingly, therefore, widening participation in higher education is often regarded as a crucial means of increasing social mobility; that is, of ensuring that routes to positions of power and privilege are accessible to those from disadvantaged as well as advantaged backgrounds.

In this chapter we examine the obstacles to future progress on widening participation in the UK, focusing on the impact of socio-economic disadvantage on school attainment which renders many disadvantaged young people either ineligible for higher education or uncompetitive as university applicants. In light of this, we consider the possibilities for further and faster progress towards more equitable access to higher education via contextualized university admissions policies which involve substantial reductions in academic entry requirements for designated socio-economically disadvantaged applicants, and a commitment to nurturing the potential of disadvantaged students once at university where necessary. We also consider the limits of widening participation, highlighting first that even bold contextualized admissions policies will leave many disadvantaged people who lack post-sixteen qualifications outside the frame for university. We argue that widening participation policies should encompass this constituency of learner too by providing access to high-quality forms of second-chance education and to university courses with open admission policies. We conclude by discussing a further and more fundamental limitation of the dominant discourse on widening participation: the notion that a university degree is a prerequisite of access to a secure and well-paid job (Brown 2013). We push back on this assumption and ask why should it be so consequential for people's socio-economic prospects whether they went to university or not?

Obstacles to Widening Participation

By far the biggest barrier to widening participation in the UK is the persistent socio-economic gap in school attainment. For example, state-educated pupils whose low family income makes them eligible for free school meals perform significantly less well than their non-FSM peers in GCSE examinations taken at the age of sixteen, with an average 'Attainment 8' score of 35 out of 80 compared to 48 out of 80 (DfE 2018a). Unsurprisingly then, pupils eligible for free school meals are much less likely than non-FSM state school pupils to subsequently gain the level 3 (A-level and equivalent) qualifications often required for university admission by age nineteen, with rates of 36 per cent compared to 61 per cent. This disparity has remained constant for at least ten years (DfE 2018b). When those eligible for free school meals do obtain A-level or equivalent qualifications, they are less likely than their more advantaged peers to achieve the highest grades. The upshot is that the majority of socio-economically disadvantaged young people will not obtain the credentials required for admission to higher education, less still for admission to the most prestigious institutions. This is reflected in the findings of Chowdry et al (2008) whose analysis of linked administrative data showed that propensities to enrol in higher education can be explained entirely by pupils' academic attainment in various 'key stage' tests taken throughout their compulsory schooling careers.

There are a number of reasons for these differences in average attainment between socio-economic groups, some of which are beyond the scope of this chapter. But two things are clear. Disadvantaged students are more likely to face challenges that could hinder or disrupt their education, and they tend to have less support than they could, being more likely to be clustered in schools with others like them (Gorard 2018). Such social 'segregation' between schools in the UK is linked to reduced aspirations, and lower than expected participation in academic post-sixteen routes. Some aspects of policy, such as the Pupil Premium, are intended to help overcome the poverty gradient in school attainment. Others, such as the removal of the Education Maintenance Allowance in England, the promotion of selective grammar schools and the increasing differentiation of types of schools, may even work to exacerbate the situation.

Therefore, for the foreseeable future, applicants to higher education will continue to be stratified by socio-economic background and other characteristics linked to their prior attainment at school. If these qualifications are accepted as completely valid measures of ability and as entirely fair criteria on which to base admissions decisions, then the intakes to higher education will also be stratified by the same characteristics. However, if it is accepted, as it should be, that qualifications can be influenced by earlier and ongoing challenges in life, then these challenges must be taken into account as part of a fair university admissions system, perhaps going so far as to remove prior qualifications as an eligibility requirements altogether.

The Possibilities of Widening Participation

One promising means of partially redressing the impact of socio-economic circumstances on school achievement is the use of contextualized admissions policies involving significantly reduced academic entry requirements for clearly socio-economically disadvantaged learners. Contextualized admissions policies of this kind duly recognize that the prior school attainment of disadvantaged learners is unlikely to do full justice to their academic potential (Schwartz 2004; CoWA 2016), making it intrinsically unfair to measure the worth of all applicants against a single academic standard. The philosophical case for contextualized admissions rests on the philosopher John Rawls's distinction between 'formal equality of opportunity' and 'fair equality of opportunity' (Rawls 1971). The former equates fairness with equal treatment regardless of background or circumstances, also known as procedural justice. The latter, in contrast, equates fairness with differential treatment depending on background or circumstances, with that differential treatment explicitly intended to redress (at least partially) the lack of a 'level playing field' due to entrenched socio-economic inequality, hence its association with the term 'distributive justice'. In terms of its philosophical underpinnings, contextualized admissions has much in common with the affirmative action movement in the United States, albeit with a focus on socio-economic rather than race-based (and by implication socio-economic) inequality.

It is important to note that a contextualized approach to undergraduate admissions is made more practically possible than might otherwise be the case because academic entry requirements have been rising over the course of the past two decades, not out of pedagogical necessity, but because a buoyant 'market' in applicants has enabled universities to increase the 'price' of entry (CoWA 2016; Boliver, Gorard and Siddiqui 2017). As such, universities now routinely ask prospective students for more than is minimally necessary in order to successfully complete a degree programme. The upshot of this is that allowing socio-economically disadvantaged students to enter higher education programmes with somewhat lower qualifications than 'standard entry requirements' should not place such students at high risk of academic failure. Of course, it does not mean that such students can be expected to thrive at university as a matter of course. On the contrary, contextually admitted students from disadvantaged backgrounds may need additional support to fill in gaps in knowledge, to augment their academic study skills and to navigate the unfamiliar terrain of university teaching and assessment. Without these forms of support there may be a heightened risk of dropout (Van Stolk et al. 2007, Crosling, Thomas and Heagney 2008). As such, universities admitting contextually disadvantaged students will need to ensure that these forms of support are in place if such students are to realize their potential (Boliver, Powell and Moreira 2018). It is important to recognize, however, that while a number of costly initiatives have been implemented to address student retention (Morris Rutt and Yeshanew 2005, West et al. 2009), these initiatives have yet to be rigorously evaluated, and so we do not yet know with any certainty what constitute the most effective support mechanisms for socio-economically disadvantaged students.

What is clear, however, is that even moderately progressive contextual admissions policies could make a marked difference to student intakes, not least those of the most academically selective institutions. According to our calculations (Boliver et al. 2017a), a reduction of two A-level grades in entry requirements at the thirty most selective universities in the UK (e.g. from AAB to BBB at A-level) could increase the number of FSM-eligible students at these universities by 50 per cent (from around 1,500 to around 2,250 each year). A three grade reduction in entry requirements at Scotland's most selective institutions (e.g. from AAABB to BBBBB in Highers) would more than double the pool of eligible FSM-eligible learners (Boliver et al. 2017b).

Contextualized admissions has the clear potential to bring about a genuine step change in widening participation; but only if it is possible to distinguish between applicants who are genuinely contextually disadvantaged and those who are not. In Scotland, where universities have recently been mandated to take a contextualized approach to admissions (CoWA 2016), one of the most commonly used indicators of contextual disadvantage is whether an applicant lives in one of Scotland's 20 per cent or 40 per cent most deprived neighbourhoods as measured by the Scottish Index of Multiple Deprivation, referred to as SIMD20 and SIMD40 (Boliver et al. 2017b). Similarly, among the UK's thirty most academically selective universities, one of the most commonly used indicators is whether an applicant lives in an area with a young higher education participation rate which is among the lowest 20 per cent nationally, according to the POLAR measure (Boliver et al. 2017a). The widespread use of SIMD and POLAR is unsurprising considering that these are the indicators currently favoured by the Scottish and UK governments respectively (Scottish Government 2014; HESA 2018). However, the use of area-level proxies for socio-economic disadvantage, rather than individual-level measures, runs the risk of ecological fallacy; that is, of incorrectly assuming that the characteristics of individuals can be accurately inferred from the average characteristics of those who live in the same locale. There is abundant evidence to suggest that this risk is in fact very high: for example, the supporting documentation for SIMD states that only around one in three people living in a deprived area are income deprived, and that two out of three people who are income deprived do not live in deprived areas (Scottish Government 2016). Similar observations have been made in relation to the English IMD (DCLG 2015) and the UK-wide POLAR measure (McCaig and Harrison 2015). Consequently, contextual admissions policies which make use of area-level indicators may inadvertently benefit many who are not actually disadvantaged, while simultaneously offering no benefit to many genuinely disadvantaged individuals and potentially even making admissions chances worse for this group (Boliver, Gorard and Siddiqui 2017; Gorard et al. 2017). Similar problems arise where school attended is used as a basis for contextualized admissions. Our analyses show that the most valid indicators are those based on individual circumstances or characteristics, with this information being formally verified to ensure its reliability. Suitable indicators include whether a prospective student was eligible for free school meals or had spent time in local authority care. Both categories clearly capture socio-economic disadvantage, and are known to be the lowest attaining students at every stage in education (Gorard 2018). Although not all disadvantaged individuals will have been in receipt of free school meals (Hobbs and Vignoles 2009), ever having been in receipt of free school meals has been shown to be a strong predictor of GCSE attainment, very nearly as good as reliable survey-based measures of parental occupation and education (Ilie, Sutherland and Vignoles 2017). While free schools meal data is already available and highly trustworthy, parental occupation and education data is not already available and not easily verified.

The Limits of Widening Participation

One major limitation of the contexualized admissions approach, of course, is that it only concerns what Gorard et al. (2007) has called the 'usual suspects' – students who are very like those that already go to university. Even if academic entry requirements are reduced by three or four grades for socio-economically disadvantaged applicants, a large proportion of young people from these backgrounds will remain outside the frame for university, owing to a lack of post-sixteen qualifications, or indeed any qualifications at all in some cases. Contextualized admission, and indeed almost any current form of widening participation initiative, is irrelevant to them. This re-emphasizes the point that the contextualized admissions approach is only a partial and temporary solution, and must be conducted in parallel with greater efforts to provide a threshold entitlement to a minimum level of education for everyone, and to reducing the poverty attainment gap at school.

Widening participation policy should therefore also include accessible high-quality second-chance routes into higher education for those with limited post-sixteen qualifications. This could involve more universities which do not require their students to have any prior academic credentials (like the Open University), or more courses at traditional universities with open admission policies, or better 'second chance' access to existing courses at traditional universities. Perhaps, we will come to realize that prior qualifications are a poor way of selecting students for university which also lead to social inequalities at a wider level. They appear to be an odd proxy mixture of both talent (capability, motivation and determination) and socio-economic background and other characteristics (hence the level of stratification). It is not permitted, in the UK, to select students by age, sex or ethnicity, and it is not desirable practice to pick them in terms of prosperity either. Yet this is, partly, what is being done when selecting applicants using the proxy of qualifications (Walford 2004). This is the point recognized by the contextualized admissions approach – an attempted focus on the talent and untapped potential, not on the socio-economic background. But if qualifications are not to be trusted, then perhaps all courses should be open access as suggested by Gorard et al (2007) and repeated recently by Blackman in his development of the idea of the comprehensive university (2017).

A further major limitation of the widening participation discourse as currently constituted is that it can be seen as effectively a tool of legitimation for economic inequalities between 'winners' (graduates) and 'losers' (non-graduates). Going to university is a highly regarded endeavour, and it is represented as an essential prerequisite of a secure and well-paid job. The unspoken corollary is that it is acceptable that non-graduates are consigned to insecure and poorly paid jobs as long as the competition to avoid that fate has been deemed fair, and socio-economic origin does not determine socio-economic destination. But this kind of 'social mobility' approach (that never refers to the 'losers') cannot assume equal material conditions for all (Boliver and Byrne 2013). There is a wider social responsibility to reduce the socio-economic gap in school attainment highlighted earlier as the main barrier to WP, and to make it less consequential to have gone or not gone to university.

Conclusion

So, widening participation *to* higher education in the UK chiefly involves longer-term action to reduce the gap in early school attainment between social and economic groups. This is where the problem of access lies. In the shorter-term, it involves open access to high-quality opportunities for potential students beyond the traditional age. The selection *within* higher education is a bigger problem, and it is here that adjustments made at the admissions stage could be most effective. Contextualized admissions to highly selective universities would be easier to achieve in a context of an expansion of places at universities. Otherwise, there is a danger that one kind of unfairness is simply replaced with another (Cliffordson and Askling 2006). Either way, the indicators used for contextualized admission must be accurate and appropriate; they must relate to the individual student and not to their area or school. The Office for Students could play a valuable role here, by encouraging UK universities to take a more research informed approach to the design of their contextualized admissions policies, and to be bolder in adjustments they make to academic entry requirements for those from disadvantaged backgrounds. However, we also suggest a need for a national debate on precisely why higher education in the UK is, and remains, internally selective. It is unlikely that the current UK government and others similarly wedded to a highly marketized higher education system will be keen to start this kind of conversation.

Acknowledgement

This work was supported by the Scottish Funding Council (grant number 0/H15031) and the ESRC (grant numbers ES/N01166X/1 and ES/P002579/1).

References

Belfield, C., Britton, J., Buscha, F., Dearden, L., Dickson, M., van der Erve, L., Sibieta, L., Vignoles, A.,Walker, I. and Zhu, Yu (2018), *The Relative Labour Market Returns to Different Degrees*, London: Institute for Fiscal Studies.

Blackman, T. (2017), *The Comprehensive University: An Alternative to Social Stratification by Academic Selection*, London: Higher Education Policy Institute.

Boliver, V. (2011), 'Expansion, Differentiation, and the Persistence of Social Class Inequalities in British Higher Education', *Higher Education*, 61 (3): 229–42.

Boliver, V. (2015), 'Lies, Damned Lies, and Statistics on Widening Access to Russell Group Universities', *Radical Statistics*, 113: 29–38.

Boliver, V. (2016), 'Critically Evaluating the Effectively Maintained Inequality Hypothesis', *British Journal of Education, Society & Behavioural Science*, 15 (2): 1–9.

Boliver, V. and Byrne, D. (2013), 'Social Mobility: The Politics, the Reality, the Alternative', *Soundings: A Journal of Politics and Culture* (Winter 2013) (55): 50–9.

Boliver, V., Gorard, S. and Siddiqui, N. (2017), 'How Can We Widen Participation in Higher Education? The Promise of Contextualised Admissions', in R. Deem and H. Eggins (eds), *The University as a Critical Institution?*, 95–10, Rotterdam: Sense Publishers.

Boliver, V., Crawford, C., Powell, M. and Craige, W. (2017a), *Admissions in Context: The Use of Contextual Information by Leading Universities*, London: Sutton Trust.

Boliver, V., Gorard, S., Powell, M. and Moreira, T. (2017b), *Mapping and Evaluating the Use of Contextual Data in Undergraduate Admissions in Scotland*. Scottish Funding Council. Durham: Durham University.

Boliver, V., Powell, M. and Moreira, T. (2018), 'Organisational Identity as a Barrier to Widening Access in Scottish Universities', *Social Sciences*, 7 (9): 151.

Brown, P. (2013), 'Education, Opportunity and the Prospects for Social Mobility', *British Journal of Sociology of Education* 34 (5–6): 678–700.

Chowdry, H., Crawford, C., Dearden, L., Goodman, A. and Vignoles, A. (2008), *Widening Participation in Higher Education: Analysis Using Linked Administrative Data*, London: Institute for Fiscal Studies.

Cliffordson, C. and Askling, B. (2006), 'Different Grounds for Admission: Its Effects on Recruitment and Achievement in Medical Education', *Scandinavian Journal of Educational Research*, 50 (1): 45–62.

Committee on Higher Education (1965), *Report* (The 'Robbins Report'), London: HMSO.

Conlon, G. and Patrignani, P. (2011), *The Returns to Higher Education Qualifications*. London: Department for Business, Innovation and Skills.
CoWA (2016), *A Blueprint for Fairness. The Final Report of the Commission on Widening Access*. Edinburgh: Scottish Government.
Crosling, G., Thomas, L. and Heagney, M. (2008), *Improving Student Retention in Higher Education: The Role of Teaching and Learning*, London: Routledge.
DBIS (2016), *Higher Education: Success as a Knowledge Economy*, London: HMSO.
DCLG (2015), *The English Index and Multiple Deprivation (IMD) 2015 – Guidance*, Department for Communities and Local Government. London: Department for Communities and Local Government.
DES (1991), *Education and Training for the 21st Century*, London: HMSO.
DfE (2017), *Participation Rates in Higher Education: Academic Years 2006/2007 –2015/2016 (Provisional)*, London: Department for Education.
DfE (2018a), *Revised GCSE and Equivalent Results in England, 2016 to 2017*, London: Department for Education.
DfE (2018b), *Level 2 and 3 Attainment in England: Attainment by Age 19 in 2017*, London: Department for Education.
DfES (2003), *The Future of Higher Education*, London: HMSO.
Good University Guide (2018), *The Sunday Times: Good University Guide 2019*. Available at: https://www.thetimes.co.uk/article/good-university-guide-in-full-tp6dzs7wn
Gorard, S. (2018), *Education Policy: Evidence of Equity and Effectiveness*, Bristol: Policy Press.
Gorard, S., Boliver, V., Siddiqui, N. and Banerjee, P. (2017), 'Which Are the Most Suitable Contextual Indicators for Use in Widening Participation to HE?' *Research Papers in Education*, 34 (1): 1–31.
Gorard, S., with Adnett, N., May, H., Slack, K., Smith, E. and Thomas, L. (2007), *Overcoming Barriers to HE*, Stoke-on-Trent: Trentham Books.
Harrison, N. (2018), 'Patterns of Participation in a Period of Change. Social Trends in English Higher Education from 2000 to 2016', in R. Waller, N. Ingram, and M. R. M. Ward (eds), *Higher Education and Social Inequalities: University Admissions, Experiences, and Outcomes*, Abingdon: Routledge.
HESA (2018), *Widening Participation Summary: UK Performance Indicators 2016/17*, Cheltenham: Higher Education Statistics Agency.
Hobbs, G. and Vignoles, A. (2009), 'Is Children's Free School Meal "Eligibility" a Good Proxy for Family Income?', *British Educational Research Journal*, 36 (4): 1469–3518.
Ilie S, Sutherland A, Vignoles A (2017), 'Revisiting Free School Meal Eligibility as a Proxy for Pupil Socio-economic Deprivation', *British Educational Research Journal*, 43: 253–74.
Lucas, S. R. (2001), 'Effectively Maintained Inequality: Education Transitions, Track Mobility, and Social Background Effects', *American Journal of Sociology*, 106: 1642–90.

Marginson, S. (2016), 'High Participation Systems of Higher Education', *Journal of Higher Education*, 87 (2): 243–71.

McCaig, C. and Harrison, N. (2015), 'An Ecological Fallacy in Higher Education Policy: The Use, Overuse and Misuse of "Low Participation Neighbourhoods"', *Journal of Further and Higher Education*, 39 (6): 793–817.

Morris, M., Rutt, S. and Yeshanew, T. (2005), *Evaluation of Aimhigher: Excellence Challenge: Pupil Outcomes One Year On*. Available online at: http://webarchive.nationalarchives.gov.uk/20130323033617/https://www.education.gov.uk/publications/eOrderingDownload/RR649.pdf

Rawls, J. (1999 [1971]), *A Theory of Justice*, Oxford: Oxford University Press.

Schwartz, S. (2004), *Fair Admissions to Higher Education: Recommendations for Good Practice. The 'Schwartz Report'*. Report of the Admissions to Higher Education Steering Group, Nottingham: DfES.

Scottish Government (2014), *One Scotland: The Government's Programme for Scotland 2014–15*, Edinburgh: Scottish Government.

Scottish Government (2016), *Introducing the Scottish Government Index of Multiple Deprivation 2016*, Edinburgh: Scottish Government.

Social Mobility Commission (2014), *Elitist Britain*. London: Social Mobility Commission.

Van Stolk, C., Tiessen, J., Clift, J. and Levitt, R. (2007), *Student Retention in Higher Education Courses. International Comparison*. Available at https://www. nao. org. uk/wp-content/uploads/2007/07/0607616_international. pdf, accessed November, 27, 2017.

Walford, G. (2004), 'No Discrimination on the Basis of Irrelevant Qualifications', *Cambridge Journal of Education*, 34 (3): 353–61.

West, A., Emmerson, C., Frayne, C. and Hind, A. (2009), 'Examining the Impact of Opportunity Bursaries on the Financial Circumstances and Attitudes of Undergraduate Students in England', *Higher Education Quarterly*, 63 (2): 119–40.

Part IV

Teaching and Learning

9

Teaching Excellence

Principles for Developing Effective System-Wide Approaches

Paul Ashwin

Introduction

There is nothing new about teaching excellence in higher education (Skelton 2005). What is striking is the variety of international contexts in which teaching excellence is being explored and policies and practices are being established – in Europe, North and South America, Africa and Asia (e.g. see Courtney 2014; Land and Gordon 2015). The focus of attempts to develop teaching excellence has shifted over time. Initially the emphasis was on the development of excellent individual teachers, or 'teacher excellence' (Sherman et al. 1987; Kreber 2002; Gunn and Fisk 2013), and on promoting teaching excellence across departments and institutions (e.g. see Elton 1998; Frost & Teodorescu 2001). However, more recently attempts are being made to devise approaches to system-wide teaching excellence.

In this chapter, I explore system-wide attempts to promote and measure teaching excellence. First, I discuss the challenges of defining teaching excellence and then examine international approaches to promoting teaching excellence across systems of higher education. I identify and review two broad approaches to enhancing system-wide teaching excellence. Based on the limitations of these two approaches, I advance three principles that can inform the development of effective system-wide approaches to teaching excellence. I conclude the chapter by working through one example of what an approach that is aligned with these principles could look like. The intention is not to offer the definitive approach to teaching excellence but rather to demonstrate that it is possible to develop approaches that align with these principles. Taking these principles seriously is important if system-wide schemes of teaching excellence are to lead to the sustained enhancement of university teaching.

The Meaning of 'Teaching Excellence' in System-Wide Approaches to Promoting Teaching Excellence

While teaching excellence is always about 'exceptional performance' (Elton 1998; Little et al. 2007), the nature of this performance is contested. Skelton (2005) argues for four meta-understandings of teaching excellence: 'traditional', where excellence is focused on cultural reproduction and is located in the disciplinary knowledge of the teacher as subject expert; 'performative', where excellence is focused on system efficiency and located in rules and regulations that are enforced by the teacher; 'psychologized', where excellence is focused on effective learning and is located in the individual relations between students and teachers; and 'critical', where excellence is focused on emancipation and is located in the material conditions that are produced by participatory dialogue between an informed citizenry and critical intellectuals.

In thinking about system-wide schemes of teaching excellence, it is important to be clear that the meaning of 'teaching excellence' is relational. The meaning changes as we move from considering the teaching practices of an individual academic to thinking about the teaching practices across a department, to deliberating about teaching practices across an entire system of higher education. This is more than simply a reflection of the contested nature of the concept of teaching excellence. It is that the foregrounded features of teaching excellence change as we move between these scales. For example, when considering individual teaching excellence, it is possible to have a notion of teaching excellence that is focused on how an academic's teaching practices improve over time based on their reflections on their teaching practices (e.g. see Ashwin and Trigwell 2004). However, when reflecting on teaching excellence at the system level, three elements must be taken into account if the notion of teaching excellence is to be meaningful.

First, teaching excellence can only make sense at the system level if it is based on public accounts of teaching excellence. These public accounts of excellence require some definition or framework through which excellence can be understood. These public claims for excellence need to be supported by stronger evidence than is required at the individual level (Ashwin and Trigwell 2004). This makes questions about the evidence of teaching excellence much more prominent in system-wide approaches to teaching excellence.

Second, a key debate is whether exceptional performance is identified by distinguishing who is better than others (norm-referenced excellence), or by reference to particular intrinsic qualities that indicate excellence (criterion-referenced excellence) (Strike 1985; Greatbatch and Holland 2016). Within system-wide approaches to teaching excellence, there are difficulties with adopting either option. A purely norm-referenced approach, which is generally used when institutions are in competition with each other (Strike 1985), faces the danger of becoming meaningless because it is simply about being better than others rather than about the intrinsic quality of teaching (Strike 1985; Readings 1996). This has led some to reject the notion of excellence because what is wanted is an improvement in quality across the sector rather than a few examples of excellence (Evans 2000). The danger of a criterion-based only approach is that either the criteria of excellence are framed in a way that excludes some individuals or groups from ever being considered excellent, or they present the possibility that everyone can be considered excellent. Both options threaten the credibility of the claim to have identified teaching excellence. This suggests that within system-wide approaches, teaching excellence needs to be both norm and criterion-referenced.

Third, given the costs of generating this evidence across a system, there is no point in gathering evidence unless it leads to improvements in teaching practices. The desire to enhance teaching across the system also brings us back to the need to offer a definition of teaching excellence. If one is to have a coherent sense of what constitutes enhanced teaching practices then there is a need to be clear about what higher quality (or excellent) teaching looks like.

These elements of system-level teaching excellence mean that there are three key questions that need to be considered when examining such schemes. First, how is teaching excellence defined? Second, how is teaching excellence measured? Third, how does the teaching excellence scheme lead to the enhancement of teaching and learning?

Approaches to Promoting System-Wide Teaching Excellence

There are two broad approaches to promoting system-wide teaching excellence: The first, which I call 'exemplar approaches', focus on identifying particular cases of teaching excellence, whether at the level of the individual teacher, department or subject grouping, or institution. The second, which I refer to as 'mapping approaches', attempt to gauge the level of teaching excellence across the system of higher education.

Exemplar approaches focus on either individual teachers or centres of teaching excellence. There are many national schemes that identify excellent individual teachers (e.g. see Skelton 2004, 2005; Leibowitz, Famer and Franklin 2012; Behari-Leak and McKenna 2017; Efimenko et al. 2018). These schemes tend to be based on a nomination by students, colleagues or the institution and on the individual then producing a portfolio that makes a case for their teaching excellence. This is then assessed in comparison with other applicants, and excellent teachers identified and rewarded. There are also a number of national schemes that identify centres of teaching excellence, such as those in the UK (see Trowler, Ashwin and Saunders 2014), Finland (see Kauppila 2016) and Norway (see Andersen et al. 2019) and the 'Competition for Teaching Excellence' (*Wettbewerb Exzellente Lehre*) in Germany (Brockerhoff, Stensaker and Huisman 2014). The German scheme focuses on the institutional level while the others are more focused on particular subject groupings. However, they all have a common structure in which units compete to be awarded excellence status based on an assessment of their previous achievements and their plans for developing excellence further. They are similar to individually based schemes with the main difference being that they operate at a departmental or an institutional level.

Mapping approaches seek to assess teaching excellence across the whole system of higher education rather than identifying particular instances of teaching excellence. All teaching across the system is evaluated, which can be national or international in scope. The two main examples of this approach have assessed institutions on their success in supporting students to achieve certain defined outcomes. The OECD's unsuccessful piloting of the AHELO (Assessment of Higher Education Learning Outcomes) (see Ashwin 2015 for a discussion and critique) attempted to develop an international assessment of teaching excellence. The Teaching Excellence Framework (TEF) in England (see Ashwin 2017 for a full explanation) seeks to assess teaching excellence across a national system of higher education.

The following sections of this chapter assess existing exemplar and mapping approaches in relation to the three questions outlined earlier: How is teaching excellence defined? How is teaching excellence measured? How does the teaching excellence scheme lead to the enhancement of teaching and learning? This assessment is of system-wide approaches to teaching excellence that are currently adopted with the intention to formulate principles to help develop more effective approaches to system-wide teaching excellence in the future. In the final section of the chapter, I offer an approach to teaching excellence that meets these principles in order to show that they provide a practical way of developing system-wide approaches to teaching excellence.

How Is Teaching Excellence Defined?

Under exemplar approaches, teaching excellence tends to be defined by those who are applying to be awarded the status of 'excellence'. In some cases, applicants are asked to respond to particular dimensions related to excellence, or the applicant has to pass a threshold to be considered excellent. However, the nature of the applicants' excellence is something that they develop in their case for excellence. The logic of such approaches is that applicants develop an account of the ways in which they are excellent and then support this with evidence. This allows the space for a variety of different definitions of teaching excellence to flourish.

In contrast, under current mapping approaches to teaching excellence, the approach has been to identify the expected outcomes of excellent teaching. If we take the TEF as an example, universities are assessed on a series of metrics. These have changed between different iterations of the TEF but generally include students' views of teaching, assessment and academic support as reported in the National Student Survey (NSS), student dropout rates and rates of employment and salary levels. In order to prevent student intake determining the outcomes on these measures, institutional performance has been benchmarked against the demographic characteristics of their students and based on this, their performance flagged when it was statistically significantly better or worse than the benchmark. Assessors initially assess institutions' performance based on the number of flags obtained, and then examine contextual information and the institution's narrative case for the excellence of their teaching. This institutional submission gives the space for institutions to develop a case for their particular version of excellence in a similar way to Centres of Excellence schemes, but performance on the common metrics is the most important contributor to institutions' overall performance. This means that while the TEF does not seek to define teaching excellence, the metrics that are used to measure teaching excellence do imply a particular view of the outcomes of high-quality teaching.

Therefore, we can see that in both exemplar and mapping approaches to teaching excellence, a definition of teaching excellence tends not to be developed. Rhetorically this can be explained in terms of not wanting to set limits on teaching excellence and allowing individuals or institutions to develop their own accounts of excellence. However, this points to a central contradiction in such approaches. How can system-wide schemes claim to have identified incidents of teaching excellence if they do not know what teaching excellence is? The answer is that they are based on implicit views of what constitutes teaching excellence, even if this is not made explicit from the outset. This lack of explicit criteria for excellence means that such schemes tend to be norm-referenced and thus face the danger of emptiness identified earlier.

Given the importance of defining teaching excellence, on what basis can a definition be developed? While different schemes might define teaching excellence differently, what should be invariant is that any definition of teaching excellence is explicitly aligned with the educational purposes of higher education and show how it contributes to the successful education of students. This suggests that the first principle for system-wide teaching excellence schemes is:

Principle 1. Definition: System-wide schemes of teaching excellence need to offer a definition of teaching excellence that reflects the educational purposes of higher education.

How Is Teaching Excellence Measured?

As discussed earlier, under exemplar approaches to teaching excellence, applicants tend to develop their own accounts of teaching excellence. This shapes the measurement of teaching excellence with individuals or institutions providing their own evidence to support these accounts. There may be particular types of evidence that are requested or encouraged, such as the outcomes of student evaluations of teaching, but these tend to be tailored to the account of the applicant who selects which measures to focus on and explains the ways in which they are significant.

We have already seen in the previous section how mapping approaches to teaching excellence tend to focus on common measures of student outcomes, whether these are the ones selected in the TEF or students' performance in common tests such as in AHELO. Unsurprisingly, given their design, much of the discussion of mapping approaches focus on issues of measurement.

These discussions tend to be fuelled by two measurement myths: 'big data' and 'the silver bullet'. The myth of big data is the belief that measurement will be improved if we increase the points of measurement across students' experiences of higher education and combine them. Thus there are moves to combine measures of students' skills, competencies, content knowledge and personal development to gain a precise insight into the nature of teaching excellence. The problem with this way of thinking is that it misunderstands the kinds of measures that we have at our disposal. There are two aspects to this misunderstanding. First, it fails to take account of the process of 'commensuration' (Espeland & Stevens 1998; Espeland and Sauder 2007), through which qualities are transformed into metrics. This involves stripping out the context from the measures, and converting different qualities into numbers, which leads to the view that these measures can be combined and related in an unproblematic manner. This leads to the second aspect of this misunderstanding: it treats skills and competencies as if they are precise ways of measuring students' gains from education. In reality, they have the precision of a sledgehammer. For example, where do skills end and competencies begin? What is the difference between developing personally and gaining new knowledge? These measures overlap in a myriad of ways because they are different ways of describing the same educational processes, rather than separate aspects of an educational experience. The level of overlap means that they cannot be combined into a precise account of students' experiences and any attempt to do so is doomed to failure.

The myth of the silver bullet accepts that there is no meaningful way to combine different measures. Instead, it looks for one single measure that is often related to a high-quality outcome, though it does not capture everything about quality. The problem with this is that any silver bullet will ricochet against Goodhart's Law (for a discussion in relation to performance measures in higher education, see Elton 2004), that once a measure becomes a performance indicator it ceases to be a good measure. Though a factor may have co-varied with quality in the past, the moment it becomes a high-stakes performance measure, institutions will seek to address it, often at the expense of quality more generally. The most likely outcome is that the relationship between the factor and overall quality is lost as those assessed try to 'fix' their performance on the measures. As Elton (2004) argues, focusing on measures of processes as well as on outcomes helps to address the tendency of institutions to try to 'fix' outcome measures. This is because this creates a situation where the simplest way to 'fix' the system is to actually engage in processes that will enhance the quality of teaching and learning. This is not to argue that we should not include outcome measures but rather that these need to be underpinned by measures that provide evidence about how these outcomes have been achieved.

Dealing with the myths of big data and the silver bullet means that we need to have a range of separate measures of teaching excellence that focus on both the process and outcomes of high-quality teaching. Clearly any measures need to offer evidence about the extent to which the definition of teaching excellence discussed in the previous section has been achieved. Thus the second principle is:

Principle 2. Measurement: Measures of system-wide teaching excellence need to be aligned to the definition of teaching excellence and focus on educational processes as well as educational outcomes.

How Does Teaching Excellence Lead to Enhancement?

Exemplar and mapping approaches tend to be based on different views of how they lead to the enhancement of teaching. Exemplar approaches are based on a contagion model of change (Trowler, Ashwin and Saunders 2014). The underlying theory is that, if the best individual, department or institutions can be identified and rewarded, then they will share their excellent practices and help to encourage others to become excellent. Exemplar approaches tend to emphasize the importance of recognizing and rewarding excellence. While these schemes can play a role in signalling the importance of teaching, raising its profile and can provide significant benefits to individuals and departments, their long-term effects tend to be felt more by a small group of specialists who benefit from engaging with them rather than changing every day teaching and learning across the whole system (Trowler, Ashwin and Saunders 2014).

Current mapping approaches to teaching excellence are based on a competition model of change. Here the idea is that the best institutions will be rewarded and the others will improve their practices, lose students or cease to offer degree programmes (e.g. see DBIS, 2015). The problem with such an approach is that, for enhancement to occur, it relies on both the measures of teaching excellence being valid, precise and accurate and applicants using these measures to inform their choice of degree programme. Neither of these appears to be the case. We have seen the problem with measurements of teaching excellence in the previous section, and studies consistently show that students tend not to make their choices in this way and that choice processes are structured by applicants' social background (see Reay, David and Ball 2005; Haywood and Scullion in press).

This suggests that both exemplar and mapping approaches are based on flawed theories of change. An alternative approach can be developed based on our discussion of Goodhart's Law in the previous section. If we include in our measures of teaching excellence an indication of the extent to which institutions are engaged in practices that research has shown support high-quality teaching and learning then this is likely to lead to institutions improving their practices.

Based on this review of how system-wide teaching excellence can lead to enhancement, the third principle is developed:

Principle 3. Enhancement: Improving performance on measures of teaching excellence should only be possible due to improvements in teaching practices.

Towards the Development of a Principled Approach to System-Wide Teaching Excellence

The review of international approaches to system-level teaching excellence in this chapter has resulted in the elaboration of three principles that are intended to underpin their future development.

A difficulty with such principles is that they can be seen as an unachievable ideal rather than providing a practical way of informing the development of system-wide teaching excellence schemes. In order to address this difficulty, this final section of the chapter outlines an approach to system-wide teaching excellence that meets these principles. This is not an existing scheme but an example that is intended to show that it is possible to design a scheme that meets the following three principles:

Principle 1. Definition: System-wide schemes of teaching excellence need to offer a definition of teaching excellence that reflects the educational purposes of higher education.

If we seek a definition of teaching excellence that reflects the purposes of higher education, then one option is to focus on how students are transformed by their engagement with the knowledge they encounter in their degree courses. Knowledge is central to the transformational nature of undergraduate degrees, in which students change their sense of self through their engagement with disciplinary and professional knowledge. This involves students relating their identities to their disciplines and the world, and seeing themselves implicated in knowledge. It does not always happen. It requires students to be intellectually engaged with their courses and to see it as an educational experience and is dependent on both students and the quality of their educational experience (Ashwin, Abbas and McLean 2014, 2016, 2017; McLean, Abbas and Ashwin 2018). This supports a view of teaching excellence as the provision of educational experiences that successfully support students in this process of transformation.

Based on this, teaching excellence can be understood as designing ways in which particular students can develop an understanding of particular bodies of disciplinary and/or professional knowledge (Ashwin et al. 2015 based on Shulman 1986). Such an approach positions teaching excellence as a collective endeavour rather than as an individual endeavour. Teaching excellence is about how programme teams design their degree programmes in ways that explicitly take account of the previous knowledge and experiences of students who are studying the course. This involves being explicit about how and why the knowledge, which students are offered access to, is important and powerful and how it enables students to understand and change the world. Finally, it involves having a sense of who students will become through their engagement with this knowledge; how this will enable them to contribute to society including, but not limited to, their employment.

This offers a way of understanding of teaching excellence that is focused on higher education's role in producing and making accessible knowledge for society. Rather than being focused on excellent individuals, it is about how programme teams collectively produce degree programmes that can transform students (Ashwin et al 2015). This view of teaching excellence would support a system-wide mapping approach to teaching excellence that examines the extent to which degree programmes help students to develop these kinds of transformational relationships to knowledge.

Principle 2. Measurement: Measures of system-wide teaching excellence need to be aligned to the definition of teaching excellence and focus on educational processes as well as educational outcomes.

So how could teaching excellence as defined above be measured? One way would be to measure teaching excellence by examining the processes by which degree programmes are designed and developed over time. This would involve process measures that offer an insight into how programme teams use evidence about their programmes provided by metrics to evaluate the effectiveness of the design of their programmes. This would include an examination of how programmes are designed to take account of who the students are who are studying it, and how they are designed to help students develop transformative relationships to the disciplinary and/or professional knowledge that underpins the programme. It would also include outcome measures that examine the impact of this design on students' learning outcomes, as well as examining what graduates contribute to society after they complete the programme. Providing evidence of such complex processes and outcomes would require a mix of quantitative and qualitative measures, which could be both norm and criterion-referenced. This could draw on some metrics that are used across the higher education system but would also require that programme teams develop qualitative accounts of how the programme was designed in an evidence-informed manner.

Principle 3. Enhancement: Improving performance on measures of teaching excellence should only be possible due to improvements in teaching practices.

The approach outlined previously would align with Principle 3 because programme teams would be asked to develop accounts of how they have developed their programmes based on the available evidence. The advantage of an approach that measures how programme teams use evidence to design, and improve the quality of, their degree programmes is that it would directly lead to enhancements in that quality. In writing accounts of the design of their programmes, programme teams would collectively reflect on these processes, which is a key aspect of developing reflective approaches to teaching (Ashwin et al. 2015). The combination of process and outcome measures would ensure that the changes in the design of the programme were related to changes in student outcomes.

The brief discussion of ways of meeting the three principles gives an example, albeit limited given space constraints, of how a system-wide teaching excellence scheme could be developed that attempts to meaningfully capture teaching excellence while leading to the enhancement of the quality of teaching. It is important to be clear that developing any system-wide scheme of teaching excellence is difficult. All such schemes will have limitations and lead to unexpected responses that can result in perverse incentives and unintended consequences. However, a great strength of the approach outlined is that it foregrounds the difficulty of developing meaningful measures of educational processes and outcomes. It highlights how such measures can only be developed through collaborative conversations between academics, students and other contributors to the educational processes rather than suggesting that assessing and measuring teaching excellence is a transparent and straightforward enterprise.

References

Andersen Helseth, I., Alveberg, C., Ashwin, P., Bråten, H., Duffy, C., Marshall, S., Oftedal, T. and Reece, R. (2019), *Developing Educational Excellence in Higher Education*, Oslo: NOKUT. https://www.nokut.no/siteassets/sfu/developing-educational-excellence-in-higher-education_2019.pdf.

Ashwin, P. (2015), 'Missionary Zeal: Some Problems with the Rhetoric, Vision and Approach of the AHELO Project', *European Journal of Higher Education*, 5 (4): 437–44.

Ashwin, P. (2017), *Making Sense of the Teaching Excellence Framework Results: Centre for Global Higher Education Policy Briefing 1*, London: Centre for Global Higher Education. Reprinted on Times Higher Education, TEF results page: https://www.timeshighereducation.com/news/teaching-excellence-framework-tef-results-2017

Ashwin, P. and Trigwell, K. (2004), 'Investigating Educational Development', in P. Khan and D. Baume (eds), *Enhancing Staff and Educational Development*, 117–31, London: Kogan Page.

Ashwin, P., Abbas, A. and McLean, M. (2014), 'How Do Students' Accounts of Sociology Change over the Course of Their Undergraduate Degrees?' *Higher Education*, 67: 219–34.

Ashwin, P., Abbas, A. and McLean, M. (2016), 'Conceptualising Transformative Undergraduate Experiences: A Phenomenographic Exploration of Students' Personal Projects', *British Educational Research Journal*, 42 (6): 962–77.

Ashwin, P., Abbas, A. and McLean, M. (2017), 'How Does Completing a Dissertation Transform Undergraduate Students' Understandings of Disciplinary Knowledge?' *Assessment & Evaluation in Higher Education*, 42 (4): 517–30.

Ashwin, P., Boud, D., Coate, K., Hallett, F., Keane, E., Krause, K.-L., Leibowitz, B., MacLaren, I., McArthur, J, McCune, V. and Tooher, M. (2015), *Reflective Teaching in Higher Education*, London: Bloomsbury Academic.

Behari-Leak, K. and McKenna, S. (2017), 'Generic Gold Standard or Contextualised Public Good? Teaching Excellence Awards in Post-colonial South Africa', *Teaching in Higher Education*, 22 (4): 408–22.

Brockerhoff, L., Stensaker, B. and Huisman, J. (2014), 'Prescriptions and Perceptions of Teaching Excellence: A Study of the National "Wettbewerb Exzellente Lehre" Initiative in Germany', *Quality in Higher Education*, 20 (3): 235–54.

Courtney, S. (2014), *Global Approaches to Developing Teaching Excellence Frameworks: A Review of the Literature*, Manchester: Manchester University.

DBIS (Department for Business Innovation and Skills) (2015), *Fulfilling Our Potential: Teaching Excellence, Social Mobility and Student Choice*, London: Department for Business Innovation and Skills.

Efimenko, E., Roman, A., Pinto, M., Remião, F. and Teixeira, P. (2018), 'Enhancement and Recognition of Teaching and Learning in Higher Education', *Journal of the European Higher Education Area*, 2: 99–118.

Elton, L. (1998), 'Dimensions of Excellence in University Teaching', *International Journal for Academic Development*, 3: 3–11.

Elton, L. (2004), 'Goodhart's Law and Performance Indicators in Higher Education', *Evaluation & Research in Education*, 18 (1–2): 120–28.

Espeland, W. and Stevens, M. (1998), 'Commensuration as a Social Process', *Annual Review of Sociology*, 24 (1): 313–43.

Espeland, W. and Sauder, M. (2007), 'Rankings and Reactivity: How Public Measures Recreate Social Worlds', *American Journal of Sociology*, 113 (1): 1–40.

Evans, C. (2000), 'Against Excellence', *Educational Developments*, 1 (2): 7.

Frost, S. and Teodorescu, D. (2001), 'Teaching Excellence: How Faculty Guided Change at a Research University', *The Review of Higher Education*, 24 (4): 397–415.

Greatbatch, D. and Holland, J. (2016), *Teaching Quality in Higher Education: Literature Review and Qualitative Research*, Department for Business, Innovation and Skills.

Gunn, V. and Fisk, A. (2013), *Considering Teaching Excellence in Higher Education 2007–2013: A Literature Review Since the CHERI Report 2007*. York: Higher Education Academy.
Haywood, H. and Scullion, R. (in press), 'It's Quite Difficult Letting Them Go, Isn't It? "UK Parents" Experiences of Their Child's Higher Education Choice Process', *Studies in Higher Education*, 1–15.
Kauppila, O. (2016), 'Excellence in Teaching: Centres of Excellence in Finnish University Education 2010–2012', *The Online Journal of Quality in Higher Education*, 3 (1): 14.
Kreber, C. (2002), 'Teaching Excellence, Teaching Expertise, and the Scholarship of Teaching', *Innovative Higher Education*, 27 (1), 5–23.
Land, R. and Gordon, G. (2015), *Teaching Excellence Initiatives: Modalities and Operational Factors*, York: Higher Education Academy.
Leibowitz, B., Famer, J. and Franklin, M. (2012), *Teaching Excellence Awards in South Africa: A National Study*. http://www.che.ac.za/sites/default/files/publications/teaching_awards_in_south_africa_20121127.pdf
Little, B., Locke, W., Parker, J. and Richardson, J. (2007), *Excellence in Teaching and Learning: A Review of the Literature for the Higher Education Academy*, York: HEA.
McLean, M., Abbas, A. and Ashwin, P. (2018), *Quality in Undergraduate Education: How Powerful Knowledge Disrupts Inequality*, London: Bloomsbury.
Readings, B. (1996). *The University in Ruins*. Cambridge, MA: Harvard University Press.
Reay, D., David, M., and Ball, S. (2005), *Degrees of Choice: Class, Race, Gender and Higher Education*, Stoke-on-Trent: Trentham Books.
Sherman, T., Armistead, L., Fowler, F., Barksdale, M. and Reif, G. (1987), 'The Quest for Excellence in University Teaching', *The Journal of Higher Education*, 58 (1): 66–84.
Shulman. L. (1986), 'Those Who Understand: Knowledge Growth in Teachers', *Educational Researcher*, 15 (2): 4–14.
Skelton, A. (2004), 'Understanding "Teaching Excellence" in Higher Education: A Critical Evaluation of the National Teaching Fellowships Scheme', *Studies in Higher Education*, 29: 451–68.
Skelton, A. (2005), *Understanding Teaching Excellence in Higher Education: Towards a Critical Approach*, London: Routledge
Strike, K. (1985), 'Is There a Conflict Between Equity and Excellence?' *Educational Evaluation and Policy Analysis*, 7 (4): 409–16.
Trowler, P., Ashwin, P. and Saunders, M. (2014), *The Role of HEFCE in Teaching and Learning Enhancement: A Review of Evaluative Evidence*, York: Higher Education Academy.

10

Assessment for Social Justice

Achievement, Uncertainty and Recognition

Jan McArthur

Introduction

Assessment for social justice (McArthur 2016, 2018) argues for a philosophical reinterpretation of the role that assessment can play in furthering greater social justice within and through higher education. It thus extends the more well-known concept of assessment for learning and traditional associations of assessment with the concept of fairness. This is not to say that fairness is not important, but rather that the realm of social justice is wider and more complex than fairness alone.

Assessment for social justice takes seriously the implications of assessment for learning; that is, that assessment is a powerful force in shaping how and what students learn (Brown and Knight 1994; Boud and Falchikov 2007; Biggs and Tang 2011). Thus, if we are committed to greater social justice within and through higher education, it follows that we need to think carefully about the role of assessment. I do not envisage assessment for social justice as a policy to be adopted, top-down by those in power. Rather it reflects a disposition to find those fissures of resistance (McArthur, in press) through which radical social change can be enacted.

My understanding of social justice draws on the work of third-generation critical-theorist Axel Honneth (e.g. 1996, 2004, 2014) and the idea of justice as mutual recognition. Social justice encompasses the recognition of people in terms of their intrinsic worth *and* their place within society: it therefore relates dialectically to the individual and the social spheres. Honneth identifies three realms of recognition beginning with primary relationships (love recognition), legal rights (respect recognition) and then the traits and abilities through which one can make a positive contribution to the social sphere (esteem recognition). Taken together these three realms of recognition reflect the foundations upon which a person is able to act and be recognized as a valued member of society. Misrecognition, or the lack of any of these three aspects, is the source of injustice.

This chapter focuses particularly on the concept of esteem recognition and seeks to consider the different ways students might understand their own achievements from undertaking assessment tasks. Here, achievement is taken to be the attribution of value to a particular assessment task. Why is it worth doing? For esteem recognition to be nurtured through assessment requires students to have opportunities to develop the traits and abilities which position them to positively contribute to the broader social world, to be recognized for so doing, and to recognize this achievement in themselves. This idea rejects students understanding their academic achievement in terms of marks or grade point averages (Kohn 2011; Pippin 2014) and focuses instead on how assessment practices equip them to be productive and positive members of society. Clearly then this also goes beyond notions of employability and the like, for these concepts lack the critical notion of a social good beyond mere maintenance of the economic sphere: the economic realm is important to social justice, but not in isolation.

To demonstrate the ways in which assessment might contribute to the conditions of esteem recognition I draw on preliminary data from a project on Understanding Knowledge, Curriculum and Student Agency (UKSA). This project is a longitudinal study of chemistry and chemical engineering students, and it is also a comparative study of two institutions in each of three national contexts: the United Kingdom, South Africa and the United States. This project is still ongoing, so I will draw only on the first-year data from the two UK institutions; however, the issues that emerge in terms of assessment for social justice are global in nature.

In the first part of this chapter I expand on the concept of assessment for social justice, including its theoretical foundations. I then provide a brief overview of the UKSA project from which I draw data. That data then forms the basis of the latter part of the chapter in which I propose a spectrum of different ways in which students might accord value, or a sense of achievement, to their assessment practices. I consider each of these in terms of the possibilities for esteem recognition. In addition, I give two small case studies, drawn from the UKSA project, which demonstrate the possibilities for designing assessments congruent with the notion of esteem recognition.

Assessment for Social Justice

Assessment for social justice argues for a cultural change in the values that underlie assessment and which then shape assessment practices, and a radicalized sense of the purposes of assessment. There are two theoretical foundations for assessment for social justice. The first, as already outlined, is Honneth's conceptualization of social justice in terms of mutual recognition, and the three realms of recognition – love, respect and esteem. Recognition is mutual – it is about giving and receiving. And it involves an interplay between the individual and the social realm. Thus Honneth states:

> What is just, is that which allows the individual member of our society to realize his or her own life objectives in cooperation with others, and with the greatest possible autonomy. (Honneth 2010: 13)

The second foundation is drawn from social practice theorist Theodor Schatzki (e.g. 1996, 2002, 2013) and particularly his notion of 'general understandings' as *senses of worth* which shape a practice; for example, the perceived beauty of a well-crafted item that informs the way artisan craftspeople go about their work, or a commitment to courtesy that shapes the way someone does their weekly shop in a busy supermarket. In Schatzki's terms, therefore, I suggest five general understandings – senses of worth – which should help shape assessment practices, if we are committed to greater social justice: trust, honesty, responsibility, forgiveness and responsiveness (for a full analysis see McArthur 2018). In this chapter I focus particularly on the idea of responsiveness, which refers to both the ways in which students engage with knowledge and the ways in which assessment practices are interrelated with the social world in which they are situated. I focus on responsiveness because of its strong connection to esteem recognition. This term is used to convey a sense of the dialectical connection between students and the social world in which they live. Assessments should be responsive both to what students bring to the assessment practice (rather than it simply being 'done' to them) and to the broader social realm in which they are located. Thus, it focuses on the extent to which the students gain recognition for engagement with socially useful knowledge, and see themselves as having developed the skills and attributes associated with that knowledge. In Honneth's terms, there is a sense of solidarity: of contribution to a common social good.

Understanding Knowledge and Student Agency Project

In this chapter I draw upon the first-year student data from the UK side of the UKSA project. The two UK universities were chosen to reflect different institutional types. University 1 is a research-intensive, selective university which ranks highly in all the main league tables and was awarded Gold (the highest level) in the Teaching Excellence Framework (TEF). University 2 is a teaching-oriented university which also received Gold in the TEF; however, it ranks less highly in major league tables (although it does rank highly in terms of work placements in industry).

A total of sixty-six students were interviewed in their first year, with roughly equal numbers across the two institutions and two disciplines. Forty-two of these students will become our case study students to follow through future years of study. Quotes used throughout this text identify student participants in terms of their university, then discipline and then participant number; for example, U1-C-12 would signify University 1, Chemistry and participant number 12.

A defining feature of the experiences of students in both disciplines and both institutions is the way in which assessment is integrated into the curriculum with numerous, regular assessment points, using a variety of assessment activities, including lab reports, tests, presentations, multiple choice questions, essays and final exams. Students were asked to talk about different assessment experiences, share an actual piece of assessed work and consider the overall purposes of assessment.

Chemistry and chemical engineering were chosen because, in Biglan's (1973) terms, they are both hard and non-life disciplines, and there has been a relative lack of research into teaching and learning aspects of such disciplines. However, academics we have spoken with in the course of this project have rejected the classification of their disciplines as 'non-life' because they regard their work as having human interest at its heart. This point raises a broader one about the relationship between such disciplines and social justice.

There is some evidence that STEM (science, technology, engineering and maths) students in general have, upon commencement of their degrees, less of an orientation towards social justice issues than non-STEM students (Garibay 2018; Nicolls et al. 2007) and less of a sense of social agency, that is of being able to effect positive social change, upon completion of their degrees (Garibay 2015, 2018). This suggests that we might have to think in particular ways about how these chemistry and chemical engineering students are given opportunities for genuine esteem recognition. I suggest that all STEM subjects, including chemistry and chemical engineering, have a powerful role to play in the movement towards greater social justice. And as we will explore in the next section, data from this project suggests real possibilities for realizing esteem recognition in these disciplines, despite their 'non-life' categorization.

There is also much to learn from the first-year experience. First-year knowledge is often foundational and preliminary, especially in STEM subjects, and thus the opportunities for esteem recognition arguably only grow as students progress through their degrees, with more opportunities to develop socially useful traits and abilities the closer one gets to graduation. But the demand for greater social justice should be true for all students, whatever their level or discipline. My aim, therefore, in this chapter is to discuss the nascent sense of esteem recognition evident in the perceptions and experiences of some of these first-year chemistry and chemical engineering students.

Towards Esteem Recognition: Achievement across a Spectrum

In this section I propose a typology, generated from the UKSA data, of ways in which students associate assessment with achievement. This spectrum of categories involves differing possibilities for the assessment tasks to engender genuine esteem recognition – that is, to develop knowledge and skills through which they can make a positive contribution to the social whole, to be recognized for doing so and to recognize this achievement in themselves. The aim of this typology is to highlight the ways in which students might move from an inward-looking approach to assessment to a more outward, responsive conceptualization, and how this in turn nurtures the conditions of esteem recognition.

Achievement Represented by Grades Obtained

For some students, assessment achievement is seen largely in terms of grades obtained; however, Kohn (2011) argues that grades diminish students' interest in learning, make students risk averse and reduce the quality of work. Clearly, then, a focus on grades alone is likely to impair the possibilities for esteem recognition. In fact, we found very few students among our sixty-six respondents who associated achievement solely in terms of the grade received. However, there is no doubt that all cohorts of students were very focused on their grades and regularly liked to check progress towards their desired degree outcome. One student described the transition from school, where he was very grade-focused, to university where other forms of achievement came into play:

> For an assessment, for example, when I was in high school, I used to think the purpose of an assessment was just to show the teachers that you can do it. Look I'll get this mark. Since I've come to university, I've seen that it's about making the knowledge stronger in your head. (U2-E-22)

Achievement Represented by Knowledge Learnt

The previous quote nicely introduces this idea of achievement in terms of the knowledge actually learnt. This form of achievement holds more promise in terms of genuine esteem recognition. It suggests a tangible value in understanding disciplinary knowledge. What is less clear, and more varied between participants, is the extent to which this knowledge engagement is then linked to traits and abilities which have a social value.

Of our sixty-six first-year students, fifty-seven describe some relationship between assessment and learning. This ranged from a fairly general level associated with monitoring or checking on learning to a more active sense of assessment enhancing learning, and finally to making a connection between assessment now and learning in terms of future engagement with knowledge and/or professional practice.

Students criticized assessment methods that placed technique or memorization above actual learning – focusing in particular on traditional, unseen and time-limited exams as an assessment method. For example,

> I think the problem with exams is you learn to pass an exam, you don't learn the subject matter whereas I've learnt more in physical chemistry from doing the coursework. I've learnt so much more than I have probably revising for any test I've ever done. (U2-C-27)

The actual learning of disciplinary knowledge is clearly valued by this student. He added that the value of coursework lies in: 'it's challenging your understanding rather than your ability to memorise a few equations' (U2-C-27).

Students who referred to this form of achievement displayed pride in genuine understanding, but the usefulness of this is implicit rather than explicit. Personal improvement could be linked with increased learning through assessment practices, but again the link to any external dimension is implicit only:

> For me, it will be a way of enhancing yourself, an assessment puts you in a position where you can feel 'Okay, fine am I doing okay or do I need to read more books or do I need to do?'... So I do love assessment to be honest. ... It does help me a lot to improve myself. (U2-C-30)

Achievement Represented by Practical Application of Knowledge

The practical application of their disciplinary knowledge opens up another form of potential esteem recognition for these students. Here they are clearly able to *do something* with the knowledge they have learnt, but the broader social relevance of this application is again much more implicit than explicit.

In particular, labs were generally regarded as a positive form of assessment and learning, with students valuing highly the practical application of knowledge they had learnt:

> They [assessments] really help us improve what we are capable of, what we learn, actually apply the concepts. (U1-E-27)

There is a strong sense that in the practical application of knowledge students must demonstrate actual understanding, again in contrast to mere memorization. For example,

> I quite like working in a lab, and I enjoy working accurately and making sure everything happens that is meant to happen. … I also like doing the lab reports because I like to see how things that I've learnt in the lectures actually work, physically. I can actually see it happening. (U1-C-29)

What is implicit, given the strong connections between these two disciplines and the professional realm, is the wider relevance of this application. But for students in this category, this is implicit, and certainly not linked to any stated social justice aims.

Achievement Represented by Future Application of Knowledge in Social Sphere

In this category we see students move closer still to what is meant by esteem recognition, as they begin to categorize the application of their disciplinary knowledge in terms of the actual social sphere. In the previous section, assessment was valued when it involved the application of knowledge; in this section there is that added dimension of foreseeing this application in real contexts. Again, these students are not necessarily talking about socially just applications, and indeed their responses have a fairly strong utilitarian quality. These responses therefore not only take us closer to realizing esteem recognition through assessment practices but also highlight where more work is required to make links to broader social contribution rather than simply technical competence. For example, this student sees assessment as helping learn the rules of the game, as they will apply in industry:

> It's to, kind of, help us all learn certain rules that we can apply to industry. In industry, you wouldn't be putting four significant figures on a reading you're giving to your manager. You need to be concise and quite accurate. (U2-E-6)

We can infer social usefulness from this comment, such as the contribution engineers make due to their commitment to accuracy, but it is not explicit in any way. Another student talked about his experience with celluloid:

> Celluloid, in itself, isn't actually that good to use in industry, but you can make something called celluloid fibres, which are quite useful. (U1-E-23)

So we have an explicit sense of assessment involving doing something useful, but as yet still no link to broader society, except as implied by the notion of usefulness. What is most strong here is a responsiveness not to the social sphere as such but to the disciplinary community. But this is interesting because according to Garibay (2018) those STEM students who do see themselves as having a role in terms of social betterment, do so through the practices of disciplinary research, rather than social or political activism.

Achievement Represented by Future Application of Knowledge in Social Sphere for the Social Good

The final category takes us closest to esteem recognition. Indeed, this is exactly what the notion of a responsive assessment is all about and the links to the social good become clear and explicit. Perhaps unsurprisingly, this was not a form of achievement which featured in our students' responses. One might infer social good by comments such as one about a particular assignment (the transport project discussed in the following paragraphs) focusing on reducing pollution, but this student did not make the explicit link themselves. Where there is scope for further development lies with the sense of broader social usefulness and explicitly working towards greater social justice. However, I believe these nascent signs of esteem recognition, indicated by the spectrum of forms of achievement, demonstrate the potential for realizing the aims of assessment for social justice in these, and other, disciplines. They demonstrate the ways students might think about assessment and how these can be channelled towards explicit consideration of the social good, which is essential for esteem recognition and essential for furthering social justice.

Two Examples of Assessment That Can Nurture Esteem Recognition

To reinforce the point made previously, I now turn to two illustrative examples of responsive assessment tasks that, I believe, have potential in terms of assessment for social justice. The first comes from chemical engineering at University 1, where students are asked to solve a real-world problem. The second example from chemistry at University 2 introduces students to the practices of being part of a research community.

The Transport Project – Solving Real Problems

At University 1 the chemical engineering students undertook an assignment based on alternative forms of transport between the city centre and the university campus:

> We had to think up a transport system for getting students from the city to the campus without using buses. We had to go through all the costing, all of the specific Engineering principles of it, so how big the motor needed to be, how much energy it required, and all of that kind of thing. That was quite interesting. (U1-E-22)

This is a very good example of a form of assessment that is responsive to the social world in which it is situated, and which offers students the chance to develop genuine esteem recognition. Because this is a local problem, relating to their own university and campus, it affords opportunities for solidarity – in working towards a common social goal. Engaging in this type of real-world problem is also regarded by some students as a form of scaffolding for engagement with increasingly complex disciplinary knowledge.

Because students had to pick one option from the three on offer there is a sense of helpful uncertainty here: in other words they are having to make judgements between alternatives, not simply work out some of the more technical details. They must make an informed judgement. This is an essential part of a responsive form of assessment and one that can engender genuine recognition. It reflects the difference between what Hardarson (2017) refers to as open or closed aims in assessment. A closed aim is self-contained, an end in itself and fits well with memorization or learning technique in isolation. An open aim requires judgement and a more active relationship with knowledge. But there are also fewer certainties; there is no 'right' answer. To develop genuine esteem recognition students need these opportunities to engage with less certain, open aims, even in the first-year context.

The Graphene Project – Being Part of a Research Community

Chemistry students at University 2 undertook a lab-based project over several weeks in which they had to grow the material graphene and then perform certain tests upon it. In addition, their work had to be written up in the style of the Royal Society of Chemistry and they had to engage with several papers from the academic literature. The whole project was inspired by a recent piece of research published by academics at Warwick University, examining new ways of producing graphene. So a defining feature of this project is that students are engaging with contemporary research from their discipline. Here is one student's explanation of the project:

> We did four weeks in the lab growing graphene and testing that. You had to make your own labs, what concentrations to use, what volumes of gas and pressure and then you went through the CVD machine, you grew your own graphene on some copper or nickel. … Then you dissolve that in your own concentration of ammonium sulphate which you had to make up from your own calculations then tested it yourself on the infrared and UV-vis see what you made. Then you write your own four page report with detail from other research and other theories. (U2-C-5)

Note the way the student repeatedly takes responsibility for decisions in this lab, asserting himself into the role of chemist, making decisions about each stage of the work, and positioning his work in the broader research field. Looking at examples of some students' graphene projects it is striking the level of professionalism, competence and confidence achieved in first year. It is clear that some students thrived in the more uncertain atmosphere of an unscripted experiment.

Like the transport project, this assessment offered students the opportunity to make decisions for themselves. And it is through this form of independence and responsibility that students can achieve esteem recognition:

> Really enjoyed it … . We got to choose whatever molarity we wanted, I thought that was brilliant freedom. And then also the next the lab we could adjust that, so then in the report we got to write about how we improved it ourselves. (U2-C-19)

A particular strength of the graphene project, and its link to esteem recognition, lies in the way it uses contemporary research literature. It challenges the common assumption that first-year students need to be protected from the complexity of disciplinary knowledge. As one student observed about the lecturer's advice on reading a journal article,

> He just said, 'Read it, if you don't understand all of the words just make a sheet, write down any words you don't understand and find the meaning.' It

> got everyone to read through an actual paper because when you first come to university, you're not going to have read a full research paper or any sort of journal or anything. … I think I read through it like seven times. I knew exactly what was going on and then when I've read other papers to apply to other lab reports I've done, I've known some of the words from that. I'm building up my knowledge from the littlest of things. (U2-C-4)

We should not, however, underestimate the challenges involved in an assessment such as this. Without a set lab script to follow the outcomes are uncertain and one student at least found this unsettling and felt it was inappropriate in the first year, as she also argued that it was unreasonable to expect them to find journal literature. This raises an important social justice issue in terms of whether we protect students from uncertain knowledge and filter the undergraduate curriculum in order to ensure certainty and stability. But to do this would irreparably degrade the quality of disciplinary knowledge with which they get to engage. The answer to this student's concerns is not to make all assessment safe and risk-free but to normalize the ways in which disciplinary knowledge is dynamic, contested and difficult to know (McArthur 2013).

Conclusion

Enabling students to connect their work to the wider social world is an essential feature of esteem recognition, and thus greater social justice. Not only for the students themselves – that is, recognition of their achievement – but for the wider society as students come to associate what they do with contributions to that society. This necessarily encourages students to become critical users of this disciplinary knowledge, moving beyond implicit assumptions that they are doing something positive through its application, to actually questioning the role that the professions, and the associated disciplinary knowledge, have in contributing to the social good.

I am not suggesting that every assessment must always meet the criteria of enabling students to associate their achievements directly with the social good. Some assessments, particularly in disciplines such as these, will be about partial knowledge and building blocks towards more complex applications. As Hardarson (2017) argues, higher education will involve a mixture of closed and open aims. However, what this project suggests is that there is considerable scope for students to engage with open aims, complex and uncertain knowledge, even at the first-year level. There must be some opportunity in some way for this in order to fulfil the demands of assessment for social justice. To be clear, this is therefore about both what is just for the individual student and what contributes to greater social well-being and justice.

Certainly these students demonstrate that in disciplines such as chemistry and chemical engineering there can be a strong desire to connect disciplinary knowledge with actual usefulness and to far transcend the association of assessment achievement purely with grades awarded, despite other research suggesting students are very grades-oriented. What remains is to both make more explicit the nature of social usefulness and in so doing problematize it. A commitment to greater social justice cannot be passed on intact as some form of directive. It must be developed iteratively, through that responsiveness to both knowledge and the social world in which we apply that knowledge. If higher education is going to contribute to greater social justice then we cannot ignore the central role that assessment plays in shaping students' engagement with knowledge, and their associated perceptions of achievement and their place and contributions within society.

Acknowledgement

The Understanding Knowledge, Curriculum and Student Agency project team is Paul Ashwin (project leader), Alaa Abdalla, Ashish Agrawal, Margaret Blackie, Jenni Case, Benjamin Goldschneider, Janja Komlijenovic, Jan McArthur, Nicole Pitterson, Kayleigh Rosewell and Renee Smit.

References

Biggs, J. and Catherine T. (2011), *Teaching for Quality Learning at University*, Maidenhead: Open University Press.

Biglan, A. (1973), 'The Characteristics of Subject Matter in Different Academic Areas', *Journal of Applied Psychology*, 57 (3): 195–203.

Boud, D. and Nancy, F. (2007), 'Introduction: Assessment for the Longer Term', in D. Boud and N. Falchikov (eds), *Rethinking Assessment in Higher Education*, Abingdon: Routledge.

Brown, S. and Knight, P. (1994), *Assessing Learners in Higher Education*, London: Kogan Page.

Garibay, J. C. (2015), 'STEM Students' Social Agency and Views on Working for Social Change: Are STEM Disciplines Developing Socially and Civically Responsible Students?' *Journal of Research in Science Teaching*, 52 (5): 610–32

Garibay, J. C. (2018), 'Beyond Traditional Measures of STEM Success: Long-Term Predictors of Social Agency and Conducting Research for Social Change', *Research in Higher Education*, 59: 349–81.

Hardarson, A. (2017), 'Aims of Education: How to Resist the Temptation of Technocratic Models', *Journal of Philosophy of Education*, 51 (1): 59–72.

Honneth, A. (1996), *Struggle for Recognition*, Cambridge: Polity Press.

Honneth, A. (2004), 'Recognition and Justice: Outline of a Plural Theory of Justice', *Acta Sociologica*, 47 (4): 351–64.

Honneth, A. (2010), 'The Political Identity of the Green Movement in Germandy: Social-Philosophical Reflections', *Critical Horizons*, 11 (1): 5–18.

Honneth, A. (2014), *The I in We: Studies in the Theory of Recognition*, Cambridge: Polity Press.

Kohn, A. (2011), 'The Case Against Grades', *Educational Leadership*, 69 (3): 28–33.

McArthur, J. (2013), *Rethinking Knowledge in Higher Education: Adorno and Social Justice*, London: Bloomsbury.

McArthur, J. (2016), 'Assessment for Social Justice: The Role of Assessment in Achieving Social Justice', *Assessment and Evaluation in Higher Education*, 41 (7): 967–81.

McArthur, J. (2018), *Assessment for Social Justice*, London: Bloomsbury.

McArthur, J. (in press). 'Theodor Adorno: Restless, Fractured and Uncomfortable Thoughts', in A. Fulford and R. Barnett (eds), *Philosophers of the University*, London: Springer.

Nicholls, G. M., Wolfe, H., Besterfield-Sacre, M., Shuman, L. J. and Larpkiattaworn, S. (2007), 'A Method for Identifying Variables for Predicting STEM Enrollment', *Journal of Engineering Education*, 96 (1): 33–44.

Pippin, T. (2014), 'Roundtable on Pedagogy: Response: Renounce Grading?' *Journal of the American Academy of Religion*, 82 (2): 348–55.

Schatzki, T. R. (1996), *Social Practices: A Wittgensteinian Approach to Human Activity and the Social*, Cambridge: Cambridge University Press.

Schatzki, T. R. (2002), *The Site of the Social: A Philosophical Account of the Constitution of Social Life and Change*, University Park: Pennsylvania State University Press.

Schatzki, T. R. (2013), 'A Primer on Practices', in J. Higgs, R. Barnett, S. Billett, M. Hutchings and F. Trede (eds), *Practice-Based Education: Perspectives and Strategies*, 13–26, Rotterdam: Sense Publishers.

11

MOOCs and Professional Development

The Global Potential of Online Collaboration

Diana Laurillard and Eileen Kennedy

Introduction

This chapter focuses on the way digital interventions are opening up new roles for universities. In particular we report on the potential of massive open online courses (MOOCs) as a powerful form of digital intervention transforming the University's relationship to professional development and knowledge exchange, and helping to deliver on the UN's (United Nations 2015) Sustainable Development Goals (SDGs).

The chapter begins with a discussion of the potential and limitations of MOOCs as a model for online education. We assess the extent to which MOOCs can be effective for undergraduates and professionals, and argue that while MOOCs may not currently be viable for teaching the former en masse, they could be developed as an effective mechanism for creating collaborative online professional development. We present a series of case studies of teacher professional development (TPD) MOOCs to illustrate this potential, particularly for addressing the global crisis in TPD (Moon and Villet 2017). We draw on a second set of case studies of MOOCs for healthcare professionals to explore the extent to which MOOCs can bring researchers and end users into a closer, more participative research model. We show how these digital interventions enable universities to go beyond the unidirectional forms of dissemination, towards dialogic engagement with current research processes on the large scale.

Meeting the Global Challenge for the Digital University

Digital technology has the greatest impact when it contributes to addressing our greatest challenges in global inequality. The UN's Agenda 2030 sets out for the first time an explicit role for higher education within Sustainable Development Goal 4 (SDG4), that is to provide 69 million teachers to enable every child access to primary and secondary education (UNESCO 2016). Higher education can also meet other SDGs through training professionals in fields such as healthcare, education and engineering. To do this, however, higher education needs to scale in a way that is inconceivable without digital technology (Laurillard et al. 2018).

This chapter explores some of the ways digital technology could potentially enable higher education to deliver on the SDGs. Digital methods have completely transformed university research in all disciplines over the last few decades, but they have not yet transformed the way researchers interact with research users. We therefore examine how MOOCs might provide new forms of genuine knowledge *exchange* (rather than one-way dissemination) between higher education and professionals on a massive, global scale. We argue that this could be a future model for a way in which higher education could act as a global common good (UNESCO 2015), because it emphasizes the participation of both academics and professionals in the construction of shared knowledge products through engagement in an online space.

To begin this process, we explore the limitations of MOOCs as an equivalent to traditional university education and show the extent to which they might meet the aims of a new approach to public engagement. We examine a series of case studies from a range of MOOCs. We use multiple methods which include cycles of design-based research (Anderson and Shattuck 2012) that involve embedding pedagogical theory and findings from previous studies into the design of MOOCs, and evaluating the success of the learning design through the analysis of quantitative data from the platform and qualitative data from participant contributions during the course and interviews with selected participants. In this chapter we present evidence from MOOCs we have designed and evaluated ourselves as well as from MOOCs designed by others. The next section reviews findings from existing research to argue for a move away from conceiving of MOOCs as having potential for scaling up undergraduate campus-based higher education to considering their merits for delivering a new kind of collaborative online knowledge exchange with professionals.

MOOCs as a Method for Online Education

The development of platforms for MOOCs in 2012 brought the potential of large-scale online education to the attention of university leaders and education policy-makers for the first time. The distance learning Open University in the UK[1] has been the most successful higher education contribution to adult education in the world, raising the education ambitions and achievements of over 2 million learners. Yet, distance learning was never seen as a key strategic issue for higher education. When a few top universities began to experiment with MOOCs, all top universities took an interest in what this meant for them (Hollands and Tirthali 2014). This new type of course offered high-quality teaching from respected academics, and because they were free, open to all and online, the numbers of learners were indeed massive, sometimes over 100,000. For the universities that entered the market the primary value was marketing, although the costs were not obviously commensurate with the return in terms of profit from additional student recruitment. This was an opportunity for innovation, however, and led many academics, oblivious to the negative bottom line, to experiment with online learning, and thereby discover methods that could be of value to their campus learners as well (Macleod et al. 2015).

The great expectations of MOOCs, that they could solve the problem of widening participation in higher education, were quickly thwarted. The data on MOOC demographics showed that MOOC participants were not typical undergraduates: the great majority (80 per cent) were graduate or postgraduate professionals (Hollands and Tirthali 2014).

Moreover, the pattern of participation in MOOCs was very different from typical university courses, whether face to face or online, showing high levels of attrition with participation steadily falling as the course progressed (Clow 2013). Further analysis indicated, however, that patterns of engagement in MOOCs were related to participants' motivations which were not the same as undergraduates' (Kizilcec and Piech 2013). Comparisons with persistence in other course contexts, therefore, are untenable since they make the assumption that motivations are driven by pay-offs, such as qualifications, that do not hold for MOOCs (Kizilcec and Schneider 2015). In addition, enrolment requires neither cost nor commitment, as degree courses do. It is closer to the 'enquiry' stage of degree enrolment. Lack of time is the principal reason given for dropout (Kizilcec and Halawa 2015) and over half of participants do not enrol with the intention of gaining a certificate (Kizilcec and Schneider 2015). For time-poor professionals, the goal may simply be to engage as much as is feasible and justified alongside their other commitments.

As a method for online education, MOOCs are a less viable proposition for undergraduates. Being massive and open, MOOCs are not able to support all of the conditions for learning to take place as identified by Laurillard (2012), since individual feedback from the tutor is not available at scale and must be supplemented by peer learning and self-regulated learning. While self-regulated learning is a behaviour that needs to be carefully scaffolded in undergraduate education (e.g. through dialogic tutor feedback), in MOOCs it must already be highly developed for students to be successful (Kizilcec, Pérez-Sanagustín and Maldonado 2016; Littlejohn et al. 2016). This means that MOOCs can only provide an effective learning environment for the small elite of persistent and high achieving current undergraduates who exhibit most self-regulation (Nicol and Macfarlane-Dick 2006).

However, professionals are more likely to be self-regulated learners, and MOOCs can provide a high-quality version of the typical course for professional development, that is the latest ideas and techniques on video, access to digital resources, and the engagement with other professionals, that is so important for them together. The real potential of MOOCs is not, therefore, in the direct provision of higher education to all learners, but in scaling up support to a much wider range of professionals.

In this the next section we explore the feasibility of two ways of using MOOCs for collaborative professional development. The first relates to TPD. We examine case study data from four current TPD MOOCs that we designed and evaluated. Teachers, through their engagement with MOOCs, can then provide local access to high-quality education for a wider range of learners, showing how MOOCs can contribute to meeting SDG4. The second is an exploration of the way MOOCs can be used as a form of large-scale public engagement in professional development in the health sector, focusing on MOOCs delivered by UCL and the London School of Hygiene and Tropical Medicine (LSHTM), thus contributing, potentially, to SDG3 on promoting health and well-being.

Teacher Professional Development on the Large Scale

Introduction

The UN's SDG4 sets the goal for universal basic education, one that fits with the mission and value statements of most universities in relation to their role in the world. Universities are responsible for educating the professionals who will provide the UN's specified nine years of basic education. The expansion of basic education over the last half-century has been unprecedented, to the extent that most children now have access to basic education (World Bank 2018). Even so, global higher education is very far from meeting the extension to nine years for the new goal. UNESCO reports the need for sixty-nine million more teachers by 2030 to meet the scale of the educational challenges across the world, and states that 'for education to be transformative in support of the new sustainable development agenda, "education as usual" will not suffice' (UNESCO 2016: 160). We can only tackle this issue at present by considering an alternative to the current models for supporting the professional development of teachers.

In this section we explore the potential of MOOCs for supporting teachers in all sectors to collaborate on innovative digital methods that are designed to improve learning outcomes. We have analysed data for four current MOOCs provided by universities, all of which aimed to support teachers to use blended learning. These are the following:

- ICTPEd: ICT in Primary Education, on Coursera, for primary school teachers and policy-makers.
- PTET: Progressing Technology Enhanced Teaching, on EU Schoolnet Academy, for school teachers.
- BLE: Blended Learning Essentials, on FutureLearn, for the vocational education sector.
- PBL: Blended Learning for Project-Based Learning, on Learning Cell (at Beijing Normal University), for school teachers.

These analyses explore the extent to which a teacher community collaborates through learning from each other in discussion, and through reviewing each other's practice.

Engaging Professionals in Learning from Each Other

MOOCs always offer a discussion environment, but their success appears to be dependent on the pedagogic design. If there is a specific topic for focused peer discussion, and not just an option to comment, then teachers are more likely to engage in that step. While early MOOCs generated only 2–3 per cent participation in forums, the ICTPEd teacher professional development MOOC used focused peer discussions and achieved significantly higher participation at 39 per cent (Laurillard 2016), and an 81 per cent rating of 'usefulness' (Laurillard 2014). The course had around 600 active participants from the DfID 'low-income countries' (Laurillard 2015).

Similarly, the PTET MOOC for EU teachers had high participation. The post-course survey showed 90 per cent 'agree/strongly agree' that 'the forum discussions were useful for my learning'. In the PBL course 44 per cent of participants completed all the steps, which includes participating in discussions, and evaluated the discussion forums at 4 out of 5 on a 1–5 scale. In the BLE MOOC, 21 per cent of participants in the final week generated nearly 2,000 comments in the discussions focused on specific topics in the video case studies and shared contributions. The post-course survey item 'Focused discussion questions' had an 83 per cent rating of liked/strongly liked. In interviews with participants after the course, participants explained that the discussions made them feel like they had company, creating a common space where 'people didn't seem to be worried about putting up their comments' (Participant 16).

The only negative comment related to the large numbers contributing to discussions.

Even in the best cases cited, less than half the active participants contribute to discussions. However, in all cases forum ratings are high in the post-course survey, suggesting that teachers do derive high value from both the actual and vicarious experience of the debates among their peers. Further research is needed to ascertain the extent to which the teachers are learning from each other in these discussions. At this stage, we can show that the design of these courses is at least able to foster the valued peer discussion needed for collaborative knowledge-building.

Peer Reviewing of Practice

Forum discussion is not sufficient for building knowledge from practice, however. It may succeed in 'creating joint reference … as a platform for further exploration' (Crook 1996: 225), but developing community knowledge requires a tougher process of peer review of each other's practice. We analysed the data from the TPD courses to explore the feasibility of this.

Platform data shows that teachers are willing to prepare and submit short pieces of work that typically require at least an hour of effort, and to collaborate in the review process, and discussion comments often show a clear intention to make use of the resources. The process elicits sufficient contributions, such as learning designs, for it to help with knowledge-building, for example 1,300 for ICTPEd, more than 900 for BLE, 2,500 for PBL. However, the review process must be carefully designed to allow and elicit critique – advice on improvement is much more highly valued by recipients than scores alone.

Surveys and activity evaluations showed that participants in all four courses who performed reviews rated the process of doing a peer review higher than receiving one – more is learnt from reflecting on an alternative approach to the same task.

The idea of collaborating to build knowledge of effective teaching practices rests on the extent to which teachers value each other's ideas and feedback. We tested this in the PTET survey, where 72 per cent of respondents rated participants' submitted examples as useful/very useful, and 88 per cent rated the process overall as useful/very useful.

Both the large-scale quantitative data and the small-scale interview studies provide evidence of a teacher community able to discuss, review and learn from each other's practice, orchestrated by, but not wholly dependent on, the course team. These examples show that the format of a MOOC can be developed into a potentially powerful and valuable tool for a professional community to own and maintain its own process of community knowledge development. The next section will examine the possibility of extending this model to other disciplines by using MOOCs as a tool for public engagement.

Research Impact through Professional Development

Introduction

Studies of MOOCs drawn from the health sector illustrate their potential as tools for public engagement in research findings, which also create access for professionals working in the more challenging global contexts. In recent years, the rise of the research impact agenda in universities has attracted critical discussion (Gunn and Mintrom, 2016; McCowan 2018; Upton, Vallance and Goddard 2014). The challenges of measuring research impact, particularly that of research that falls outside of STEM subjects, and the fear that this may undermine some forms of academic inquiry, has led to calls for an emphasis on the *process* of knowledge exchange rather than its outcomes (Upton, Vallance and Goddard 2014). We argue that MOOCs designed to engage practitioners in the field with the results of university research projects have a distinctive contribution to make to this debate. MOOCs can achieve a depth and breadth of dialogic engagement, substantially shifting the 'linear relationship' of knowledge transfer to genuine knowledge exchange (McCowan 2018) and reflection-in-action (Schön 1987).

MOOCs as Professional Development

Ebola in Context

In November 2014, LSHTM[2] fast-tracked the creation of their *Ebola in Context: Understanding Transmission, Response and Control*[3] MOOC in response to the

2014–16 Ebola epidemic. The *Ebola in Context* MOOC was created in 7 weeks and hosted on the FutureLearn platform. The course offered health professionals in the field a rigorous, multidisciplinary perspective on the principles of infectious disease transmission, the social context of the Ebola epidemic, treatment and control measures, and the challenges of implementation and innovation in an emergency. In three runs, more than 12,000 participants were actively engaged. The top-ten countries of origin for the participants included five countries with cases of Ebola, including more than 300 from Sierra Leone, thus reaching many of the target audience.

The *Ebola in Context* participants were atypical for FutureLearn in that, 69 per cent were health professionals, contrasting with the 13 per cent average from that sector.[4]

The rate of conversion from 'Learners' (those who start the course) to 'Active Learners' (who complete at least one step), was 84 per cent, contrasting with the FutureLearn average of 66 per cent.

In response to the urgent global demand the LSHTM MOOC created highly successful public engagement with their research, and engaged committed professional learners who could put that knowledge into action from more than 180 low- and middle-income countries (LMICs).

Global Blindness

A longer-term approach to evaluation has been adopted by another LSHTM MOOC, *Global Blindness: Planning and Managing Eye Care Services* (Parsley et al. 2017) created to provide professional development to meet the global need for improved access to effective eye care.

The *Global Blindness* MOOC attracted far fewer initial learners than *Ebola in Context*,[5] but a post-course survey attracted 139 responses, 94 per cent of whom were healthcare professionals, with 82 per cent living in LMICs. The results showed that 85 per cent could apply their learning at work, and many had gained career advantage from the MOOC. Critically, 70 per cent had reused the course resources to guide proposal writing, and 65 per cent were guiding others about eye care, multiplying the impact of the MOOC.

Perioperative Medicine in Action

The UCL MOOC *Perioperative Medicine in Action* shows how the commitment of the participant and the value accorded to certification can combine to create a self-sustaining, university-practitioner knowledge exchange environment.

Perioperative medicine is an emerging, multidisciplinary approach, so the MOOC targets a range of health professionals, aiming to prevent deaths or prolonged complications following surgery. A distinguishing feature of the *Perioperative Medicine in Action* MOOC is its endorsement by the Royal College of Anaesthetists and the World Federation of Societies of Anaesthesiologists, which lend value to the Certificate of Achievement. 20 per cent of participants paid for the certificate, generating £94,000, compared to 7 per cent for *Global Blindness* participants, whose certificates have no such professional endorsement.

Perioperative Medicine in Action is therefore a financially sustainable MOOC as a vehicle for knowledge exchange. The income begins to cover both ongoing support and development costs.

Summary

The case studies from the health sector show that these forms of interactive and collaborative MOOCs are able to bring researchers and end users, including those from LMICs, into a close, participative research model. It is a means of using an online intervention to bring the global to the local, as a more participative form of professional development and knowledge exchange.

A New Model for Professional Development and Research

When the scale of a problem is massive, we must look to solutions that can work on a massive scale. The MOOC platforms do that, and our analysis shows that high-quality professional development courses are thus feasible on the large scale. They reach professional participants across the globe, including the Global South, as illustrated by all these courses, and in terms of effectiveness, both quantitative and qualitative data show that professionals recognize the value for their local beneficiaries.

Measuring the reach of MOOCs to participants' local groups is difficult. A single MOOC could achieve 10,000 active participants, given that in three runs of BLE there were over 35,000 active participants. Each participant could share their knowledge with their local group of, say, twenty-five learners. On these modest assumptions, therefore, the reach would extend to a quarter of a million beneficiaries, which is a substantial number. The arithmetic is simple; the practice happens, but its value is hard to verify. Consequently, research now focuses on the second-order effects of MOOC participation. Meanwhile, the projected estimate is sufficiently large, with respect to the very large-scale ambitions for professional development, to provide the motivation for this.

The MOOC provides an alternative to the 'cascade model' that has been the typical format for the rapid and affordable training of professionals on the large scale, especially in education. It is hierarchical and uses experts to train a selected national group of professionals, such as teachers, who then transmit their learning to other regional groups, who transmit to local groups, sometimes across several levels. It tends to fail because of the loss of value in the transmission: the initial group does not always understand the material (Ono and Ferreira 2010), the top-down structure is too inflexible to respond to needs at the grassroots level (Suzuki 2008), and the training does not always include the crucial participation, collaboration and ownership of the original form (Kennedy 2005), summarized neatly as 'if you are too far away from the source you can easily avoid getting soaked' (McDevitt 1998: 428).

Instead, we propose a 'local inclusion model' using MOOCs, because

- the initial group is all professionals who need training, a MOOC being open to all;
- there is no loss of value as there are no intervening levels;
- the course value is direct; and
- participants are explicitly invited to discuss solutions and collaborate on adapting them to local conditions.

Thus all participants experience the full value of direct access to the guidance, and the participation, collaboration and ownership of the outputs.

If this model is to be fully effective, two key conditions must be fulfilled: equity and affordability. Our recent report defines equity in education in terms of digital access, language and culture, gender, geographic location and the quality of the learning experience itself. There are actionable solutions for policy-makers, platform providers, universities, international agencies and national ministries who are willing to take on the challenge to make digital learning achieve equity in education on the large scale (Laurillard et al. 2018).

The report also argues that the model must be affordable for these stakeholders. One strand of this research has developed a new form of costing modeller for conventional, blended or online courses, including MOOCs (Kennedy et al. 2015). The approach enables providers to model teaching costs, learning benefits and fee income across multiple course iterations, and adjust costs and design elements to fit local conditions of affordability. If a sufficient percentage of participants in the Global North are motivated and able to pay for certificates (e.g. because they are endorsed to provide credit), it is conceivable that these participants could subsidize those less able to pay in the Global South. For the local inclusion model to be fully productive and affordable, policy-makers and providers would need to 'model and plan for income streams that will offset the true costs of online learning' (Laurillard et al. 2018: 23).

MOOCs have an interesting role in the context of universities providing a public good. Typically, they operate on an economies of scale model, where the development cost, of providing videos, reading materials, computer-assessed tests, peer discussion and peer review, is the same, no matter how many learners take part. In this case they are public goods (Marginson 2018) because, unlike normal university courses, they are non-excludable (not confined to single buyers, as is clean air regulation) and non-rivalrous (consumable by any number without being depleted, as is knowledge). While participants are required to make an account with a MOOC provider, this is free, and potential de facto exclusions based on language are rapidly disappearing as MOOCs become available in multiple languages. But insofar as they attempt to offer learner support, such as highly labour-intensive tutor-assessed assignments, or individuals commenting in discussions, they attract commensurate costs that would be unsustainable without charging, and for these elements, they become a private good.

MOOCs can offer an affordable public good by providing free or low-cost certified education to professionals on the large scale with personalized learning only in the form of peer collaboration. And as we have seen, the returns to the providers that are possible from the low-cost certificate suggest that financial sustainability could be feasible in some professional areas.

Conclusions

In this chapter we have set out the evidential basis for universities to plan a major role in transforming professional development. We have presented evidence of the willingness of teachers and health professionals to engage in this, to engage with and learn from each other, and to use and adapt what they learn within their own context. We have also shown evidence of knowledge exchange between researchers and their end users through engagement with their findings in MOOCs.

MOOCs being massive and open, present a new opportunity to universities to tackle the immensely large-scale problem of equity in education. The global potential of MOOCs is to widen access not to undergraduate education but to professional education. Using them to orchestrate knowledge exchange and professional community knowledge development would enable universities to contribute significantly to the global challenges facing education.

Notes

1. http://www.open.ac.uk/about/main/
2. London School of Hygiene and Tropical Medicine
3. https://open.lshtm.ac.uk/course/view.php?id=8
4. FutureLearn averages for participant demographics and activity across all their courses are provided in their restricted-access partner website.
5. https://iceh.lshtm.ac.uk/oer/

References

Anderson, T. and Shattuck, J. (2012), 'Design-Based Research: A Decade of Progress in Education Research?' *Educational Researcher*, 41 (1): 16–25. https://doi.org/10.3102/0013189X11428813

Clow, D. (2013), 'MOOCs and the Funnel of Participation', in *Proceedings of the Third International Conference on Learning Analytics and Knowledge - LAK '13*, 185, New York: ACM Press. https://doi.org/10.1145/2460296.2460332

Crook, C. (1996), *Computers and the Collaborative Experience of Learning: A Psychological Perspective*, London: Routledge.

Gunn, A. and Mintrom, M. (2016). 'Higher Education Policy Change in Europe: Academic Research Funding and the Impact Agenda', *European Education*, 48 (4), 241–57. https://doi.org/10.1080/10564934.2016.1237703

Hollands, F. and Tirthali, D. (2014), *MOOCs: Expectations and Reality*. Retrieved from Teachers College, Columbia University, New York: https://files.eric.ed.gov/fulltext/ED547237.pdf

Kennedy, A. (2005), 'Models of Continuing Professional Development: a Framework for Analysis', *Journal of In-service Education*, 31 (2): 235–50.

Kennedy, E., Laurillard, D., Horan, B. and Charlton, P. (2015), 'Making Meaningful Decisions About Time, Workload and Pedagogy in the Digital Age: The Course Resource Appraisal Model', *Distance Education*, 36 (2), 177–95.

Kizilcec, R. F. and Halawa, S. (2015), 'Attrition and Achievement Gaps in Online Learning', in *Proceedings of the Second (2015) ACM Conference on Learning @ Scale - L@S '15*, 57–66, New York, NY: ACM Press. https://doi.org/10.1145/2724660.2724680

Kizilcec, R. F., Pérez-Sanagustín, M. and Maldonado, J. J. (2016), 'Self-Regulated Learning Strategies Predict Learner Behavior and Goal Attainment in Massive Open Online Courses', *Computers & Education*, 104. https://doi.org/http://dx.doi.org/10.1016/j.compedu.2016.10.001

Kizilcec, R. F. and Piech, C. (2013), *Deconstructing Disengagement : Analyzing Learner Subpopulations in Massive Open Online Courses Categories and Subject Descriptors*, Stanford. Retrieved from http://lytics.stanford.edu/deconstructing-disengagement/

Kizilcec, R. F. and Schneider, E. (2015), 'Motivation as a Lens to Understand Online Learners', *ACM Transactions on Computer-Human Interaction*, 22 (2), 1–24. https://doi.org/10.1145/2699735

Laurillard, D. (2012). *Teaching as a Design Science: Building Pedagogical Patterns for Learning and Technology*, New York and London: Routledge. https://doi.org/10.4324/9780203125083.

Laurillard, D. (2014). *Anatomy of a MOOC for Teacher CPD*, London. Retrieved from UCL Institute of Education, London http://citeseerx.ist.psu.edu/viewdoc/download?doi=10.1.1.687.5940&rep=rep1&type=pdf

Laurillard, D. (2015), 'How Should Professors Adapt to the Changing Digital Education Environment?', in E. De Corte, L. Engwall and U. Teichler (eds.), *Emerging Models of Learning and Teaching in Higher Education: From Books to MOOCS?* Stockholm: Wenner-Gren.

Laurillard, D. (2016). 'The Educational Problem That MOOCs Could Solve: Professional Development for Teachers of Disadvantaged Students', *Research in Learning Technology*, 24 (1063519): 1–17. https://doi.org/10.3402/rlt.v24.29369.

Laurillard, D., Kennedy, E., Wang, T., Escorcia, G. and Hooker, M. (2018). *Learning at Scale for the Global South*, Quezon City, Philippines.

Littlejohn, A., Hood, N., Milligan, C. and Mustain, P. (2016). 'Learning in MOOCs: Motivations and Self-Regulated Learning in MOOCs', *Internet and Higher Education*, 29. https://doi.org/10.1016/j.iheduc.2015.12.003.

McCowan, T. (2018), 'Five Perils of the Impact Agenda in Higher Education', *London Review of Education*, 16 (2): 279–295. https://doi.org/10.18546/LRE.16.2.08.

Macleod, H., Haywood, J., Woodgate, A. and Alkhatnai, M. (2015). 'Emerging Patterns in MOOCs: Learners, Course Designs and Directions', *TechTrends*, 59 (1): 56–63. doi:https://doi.org/10.1007/s11528-014-0821-y.

Marginson, S. (2018). *Higher Education and the Common Good*, Melbourne: Melbourne University Press.

McDevitt, D. (1998), 'How Effective Is the Cascade as a Method for Disseminating Ideas? A Case Study in Botswana', *International Journal of Educational Development*, 18 (5): 425–8.

Moon, B. and Villet, C. (2017), 'Can New Modes of Digital Learning Help Resolve the Teacher Crises in Sub-Saharan Africa?' *Journal of Learning for Development*, 4 (1): 23–35.

Nicol, D. J. and Macfarlane-Dick, D. (2006), 'Formative Assessment and Self-Regulated Learning: A Model and Seven Principles of Good Feedback Practice', *Studies in Higher Education*, 31 (2): 199–218. https://doi.org/10.1080/03075070600572090.

Parsley, S., Patel, D., Stroud, J. and Lynch, S. (2017). 'Exploring the Use of Text Mining to Support Social Learning in an International, Open, Online Course', In *RIDE 2017 Learning and Teaching in a Digital Age: MOOCs, OERs and Innovation*, London: CDE.

Ono, Y. and Ferreira, J. (2010). 'A Case Study of Continuing Teacher Professional Development through Lesson Study in South Africa', *South African Journal of Education*, 30 (1): 59–74.

Schön, D. A. (1987), *Educating the Reflective Practitioner*, San Francisco: Jossey-Bass.

Suzuki, T. (2008), The Effectiveness of the Cascade Model for In-service Teacher Training in Nepal Paper presented at The 6th International Conference on Education and Information Systems, Technologies and Applications. http://www.iiis.org/cds2008/cd2008sci/EISTA2008/PapersPdf/E964RM.pdf

United Nations. (2015). 'Transforming Our World: The 2030 Agenda for Sustainable Development. https://doi.org/10.1007/s13398-014-0173-7.2F.

UNESCO. (2015), *Rethinking Education: Towards a global common good?* Paris.

UNESCO. (2016). Education for People and Planet: Creating Sustainable Futures for All. Retrieved from Paris, France: https://en.unesco.org/gem-report/report/2016/education-people-and-planet-creating-sustainable-futures-all/page#sthash.SDYhmB9I.dpbs.

Upton, S., Vallance, P. and Goddard, J. (2014), 'From Outcomes to Process: Evidence for a New Approach to Research Impact Assessment', *Research Evaluation*, 23 (4): 352–65. https://doi.org/10.1093/reseval/rvu021.

World_Bank. (2018), World Development Report *2018: Learning to Realize Education's Promise.* Retrieved from Washington, DC: http://www.worldbank.org/en/publication/wdr2018.

Part V

Graduates and Work

12

Graduate Employment and Underemployment

Trends and Prospects in High Participation Systems of Higher Education

Francis Green and Golo Henseke

Introduction

The modern-day graduate labour market is sometimes conceived as a straightforward race (Goldin and Katz 2008). It is an apt metaphor, in that virtually everywhere there has been a rising supply of graduates in the labour force following the massification of higher education, and at the same time a rising demand for college-educated workers. Moreover, competition is ingrained in both markets and races. Yet this market is not a typical micro-market, which would be expected to have an equilibrating price-mechanism ensuring that the race remains close. Any equilibrating forces for graduate labour act on a timescale of, not months but, decades; and price incentives are only one of the many factors affecting supplies and demands for graduates. It is, therefore, easy for the two sides of the market to drift apart. Given the vast resources involved in higher education, its 'public good' character, and its pivotal role in shaping students' lives, the potential for substantive, persistent mismatches between supplies and demands for graduates is a significant social and economic concern.

Our aim in this chapter is to build a comparable picture of recent graduate labour markets, examining in particular the disequilibrium trends. Underemployed graduates (those working in non-graduate jobs), while on average better paid than non-graduates, generally experience a wage penalty and report lower job satisfaction, compared with graduates doing graduate jobs. Relatively few can break out of underemployment within a reasonable time. We focus on countries in Europe where, despite efforts at cross-national convergence, there is a variety of higher education and further education systems, as well as economies with varying degrees of development. Covering the period from 2005 to 2015, our analyses draw on micro-data from the European Labour Force Survey (EU-LFS) and the OECD's Survey of Adult Skills (PIAAC).

There are three parts to the picture: growth of the graduate labour supply, trends in graduate jobs and growth of graduate underemployment. We pose the question: 'How do the growth rates of graduate supplies and of high-skilled jobs vary across these countries?' We then examine the prevalence of graduate underemployment, asking how that varies across countries and whether, as pessimists fear, it is increasing.

The Growth of the Graduate Labour Supply

In all but the poorest countries across the globe, mass participation in tertiary education participation has emerged in recent decades as a ubiquitous phenomenon. The gross tertiary enrolment ratio, the number of students in tertiary education as a percentage of the population in the five-year age band after the official secondary school graduation age, which was 32 per cent in 2012, has been growing by one percentage point a year, and appears to face no social, political or economic limits in the foreseeable future (Marginson 2016). Multiple socio-economic and political factors – some common to all countries, others with distinctive national specificites – lie behind the aspirational surge to acquire tertiary education. Nowhere is there any significant sign of an end to this trend, nor even of any convergence to a world-system logic of rising participation.

The long-term consequences for labour markets are assured: a rising supply of graduate labour. The pace of expansion, however, varies across countries. In order to begin to understand how graduate labour markets differ, it is useful first to picture the range of growth in supply. Where is the fastest growth to be found, and where the slowest? Which countries are likely to grow fastest in future? And, in the light of the Bologna process and other convergent regulatory pressures (Powell and Solga 2010), is there any convergence in the labour force, whereby the countries with the faster-growing supply of graduates are catching up with others who were ahead of the game, or is there some divergence, with countries pulling apart?

Taking all our twenty-six European countries together, the proportion of tertiary-educated workers in the labour force rose from 26 per cent in 2005 to 34 per cent in 2015. Figure 12.1 shows considerable variation in 2015 in the level of attainment of tertiary education among the labour force aged thirty to fifty-nine.

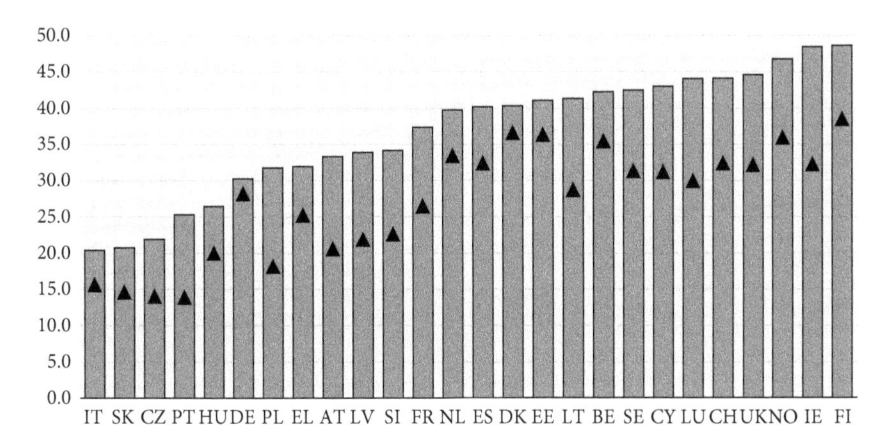

Figure 12.1 Supply of tertiary-educated labour in Europe (percentage of the labour force aged thirty to fifty-nine), 2005 and 2015.

Key: AT Austria, BE Belgium, CH Switzerland, CY Cyprus, CZ Czech Republic, DE Germany, DK Denmark, EE Estonia, EL Greece, ES Spain, FI Finland, FR France, HU Hungary, IE Ireland, IT Italy, LT Lithuania, LU Luxembourg, LV Latvia, NL Netherlands, NO Norway, PL Poland, PT Portugal, SE Sweden, SI Slovenia, SK Slovak Republic, UK United Kingdom.

Source: European Union Labour Force Survey 2005 and 2015.

For most countries, tertiary attainment is above 30 per cent, but it remains well below this in Italy, the Czech Republic and Slovakia. Countries with especially high proportions – above 45 per cent – of tertiary-educated workers are Ireland, Finland and Norway.

The proportion of tertiary-educated labour has grown everywhere from its 2005 level, though at varying speeds. Is growth likely to continue in the coming decade? An approximate indication of the future direction can be gleaned from the gaps between the tertiary education achievement ratios of younger and older cohorts. Where the gap is large, with the young being educated to a much higher level, we can expect a high growth rate of the overall education level of the workforce, as older cohorts retire and are replaced by the young (Green 2013: 167–9).

Figure 12.2 shows a positive gap in all countries, consistent with the expectation that the labour force as a whole is everywhere becoming more educated. Yet, there is substantive variation across countries in the young–old gap. The gap is smallest in Estonia, Finland and Germany, and especially large in Poland.

In sum, we can conclude that in every examined country the labour force is becoming more educated. It is often underestimated how far this represents a social revolution in the spread of education among working populations. Nevertheless, graduate labour forces are expanding at a widely varying pace. Signs of convergence are weak.

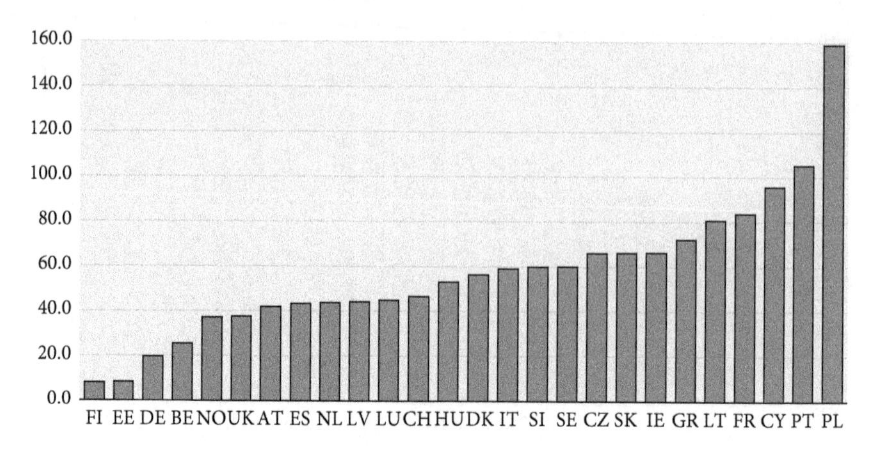

Figure 12.2 Tertiary attainment gap in Europe between ages 30–34 and 55–59, 2015.
Key: See Figure 12.1.
Source: European Union Labour Force Survey 2005 and 2015.

Trends in Graduate Jobs

If the graduate labour supply is universally growing, albeit at varying pace, what can be said about the labour market demand for workers educated to this level? Key to an understanding of the demand for highly skilled labour is the socio-economic environment (especially managerial cultures) in which decisions on labour deployment are made (Green 2013: Ch. 5). Whereas new technologies might expect to become universally adopted in similar ways, cross-country variations in industrial and labour market institutions[1] can lead to substantive variations in demand for high-level skills. The changing and internationally variable shape of product demand, and hence of industry demand, is also likely to be a major force driving the demand for skills. Demographic changes such as population ageing imply rising demands for caring and health services, and the relevant skills.

Technology is widely found to have been, for several decades, becoming more skills-intensive: economists' term for this is 'Skill-Biased-Technological-Change'; sociology's phrase is 'the knowledge economy', specifically the proposition that competition between economic regions is driven by skills (Green 2013: Ch. 1). There is also a growing relative demand for non-routine lower-level skills, albeit slower than the growth of high-level skills demand. This 'task-based' analysis of changing occupational skills demand predicts that middle-paid, middle-level skilled tasks have been most susceptible to displacement by automation (Autor,

Levy and Murnane 2003). Middle-level jobs have also been most easily offshored to well-educated labour forces in low-wage countries (e.g. Blinder and Krueger 2013).

Much of the demand for high-skilled labour is likely to be met by graduate labour, but the decision to deploy graduate labour, as opposed to alternative sources of skills from those trained to a high level through work-based routes, depends on the relative price and quality of those alternative sources of skills. In each country the relative quality of non-graduate skilled labour depends on the quality of institutions for vocational skills training, and on that of the higher education system. A 'graduate job' can be defined as one 'where a substantial portion of the skills used are normally acquired in the course of higher education, including many of the activities surrounding it, and of its aftermath – the years after higher education when skills are acquired in work through graduates' acquired faculty for learning them' (Green and Henseke 2016a: 3). The skills used in a graduate job may include professional skills, cognitive skills, knowledge creation, information-processing and management skills, as well as high-level communication skills (Allen and Van der Velden 2011; Barone and Ortiz 2011). This skills-oriented definition is quite distinct from the tautological concept of a graduate job as being 'what graduates do'.

The creation of an indicator for 'graduate job' with analytical value is a practical issue of some concern. Typically, a graduate job is taken to be one falling into the first three major occupational groups: managers, professionals and associate professionals. The European Commission, for example, deploys this indicator to assess the proportion of underemployed tertiary graduates (European Commission 2015). We use this approach below for looking at changes in graduate jobs over the years.

However, recent research has developed more satisfactory and discerning skills-based methods for distinguishing between graduate jobs and other jobs. In this approach, most jobs in the first three major groups are deemed to be graduate jobs, but not all (Green and Henseke 2016a, b); for example, managers of small retail outlets are typically not found to be graduate jobs in most countries. Our preferred, validated method uses direct indicators of the skills requirements of jobs as reported by workers doing the jobs. Using such skills-based data, we have traced the evolution of graduate jobs in Britain and Germany, and generated indicators for graduate jobs across several countries (Henseke and Green 2017).

The graduate job is, then, a viable tool for helping to understand the demand for graduate labour. It can be used to address some big questions about high-skilled work in the modern economy. How are graduate jobs distributed across countries, and do they exhibit similar, or predictably varying patterns of growth?

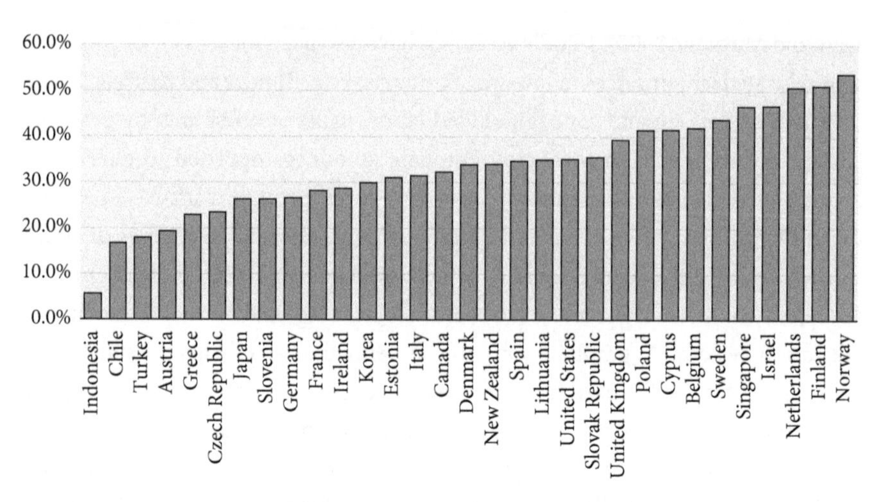

Figure 12.3 Proportion of labour in graduate jobs across countries.
Source: Survey of Adult Skills (PIAAC) Round-1 (2011/12) and Round-2 (2014/15).

Are graduate jobs inexorably and universally growing in prevalence, or is there evidence of saturation in the deployment of graduates' skills?

Figure 12.3 displays the prevalence of graduate jobs in several high and middle-income countries. In this operationalization, 'graduate-level' refers to skills taught at universities. What is most striking about this picture is the range – within Europe from 44 per cent in Norway to 19 per cent in Austria, and down to just 4 per cent in Indonesia.[2]

The variation bears no obvious relation to countries' levels of development: there are affluent countries both at the high end of spectrum, such as the Netherlands and Norway, and at the low end, like Germany and Austria. Yet, for many high-skilled jobs there are different educational pathways and qualifications that employers can choose from. In Austria and Germany, the renowned 'Dual System' offers pathways for upper secondary school leavers into business and public associate professional occupations, such as management assistants, or into occupations surrounding information and communication technologies (Henseke 2018). Thus some jobs which in other countries might require the deployment of university-educated labour are filled by highly skilled vocationally trained labour who are not classified as having had tertiary education. By contrast, the German higher education system has long struggled to adjust to new demands created by the drive towards mass global higher education (Baker and Lenhardt 2008). These national variations in the selectivity and quality of higher education systems account for a substantial fraction of the cross-national differences in the deployment of graduate jobs (Henseke and Green 2017).

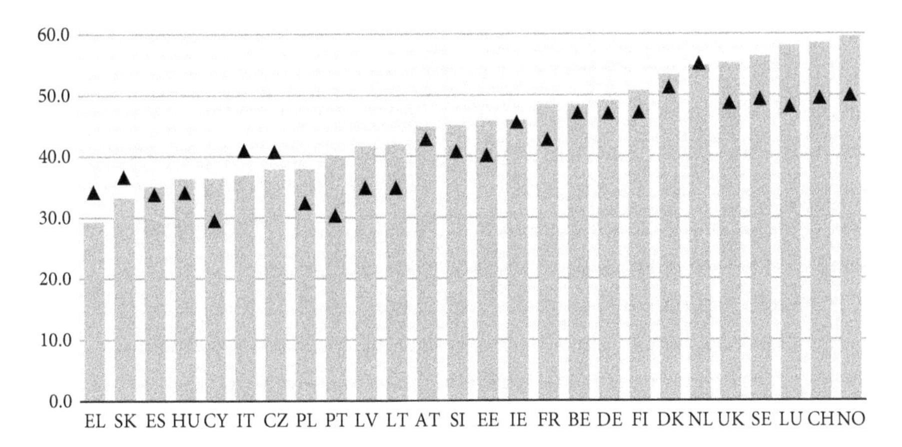

Figure 12.4 High-skill job growth in Europe, 2005 to 2015.
Key: see Figure 1.
Source: European Union Labour Force Survey, 2005 and 2015.

To trace the trend in graduate jobs across several countries, we deploy an occupation-based indicator of high-skilled jobs, defined for this purpose as workers in any of the first three major groups: managers, professionals and associate professions. As Figure 12.4 shows, in the majority of countries there has been a rise in the proportion of graduate jobs. Nevertheless, in contrast to the rising supply of graduates, there are a few countries where the proportion of graduate jobs has fallen, if only slightly: Greece, Italy, Slovakia and the Czech Republic. And in others the uplift of graduate jobs has been relatively small.[3]

Trends in Graduate Underemployment

Most markets have equilibrating mechanisms. Where incentives are strong, it is typically the price which brings supply and demand into line with each other as buyers and sellers respond. With graduate skills, however, any supply responses to the price incentive of graduate labour (in effect, the wage premium over less-educated labour) are both muted (the decision to go to college or university being overlaid with uncertainties and social norms) and played out on a very long timescale. (It being years before the decision is reflected in a change in graduate labour stocks.) With graduate labour demands subject to the economy's independent trends, it is easy to see how it is possible for supply and demand to become seriously out of kilter, and remain in mismatch for many years. A common concern is that graduate underemployment is becoming more widespread.[4] Occupations where underemployed tertiary-educated graduates are found include clerical support workers (e.g. general and keyboard clerks) and service and sales workers (e.g. models, salespersons and demonstrators): not the lowest paid but assuredly not graduate jobs. There is certain to be some graduate underemployment in an economy, but the extent is expected to vary, reflecting a combination of skill-match imperfections and macro-disequilibrium. If the prevalence of underemployment is rising it is likely to reflect a worsening macro-disequilibrium.

It should be noted that underemployment does not correlate perfectly with underutilization of skills, and that not all graduates are of similar skill. Unsurprisingly, graduates with lower skills are somewhat more likely to find themselves working in non-graduate employment (Green and McIntosh 2007; Chevalier and Lindley 2009). However, the causation may also be reversed: rather than being in a lowly job because they are low skilled, their skills may have atrophied as a consequence of their employment in jobs with less scope for learning. Whatever the reason for this, such skill differences account for only a fraction of the underemployment found in many countries. Those who airily dismiss the concept of underemployment, presuming that *all* graduate underemployment could be explained away by skills heterogeneity, are committing the common 'part to all' fallacy: just because *some* heterogeneity exists, that does not imply that all underemployment is illusory, or else the fault of universities.[5]

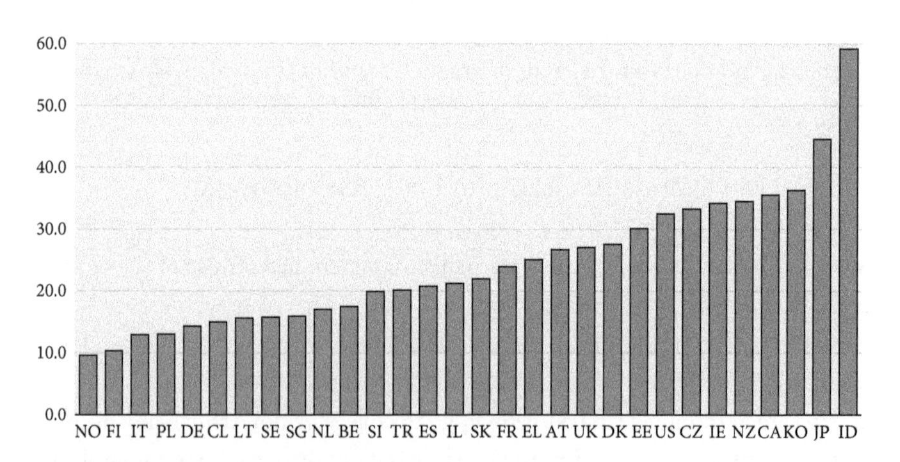

Figure 12.5 Underemployed higher education graduates.

Key: AT Austria, BE Belgium, CA Canada, CZ Czech Republic, DE Germany, DK Denmark, EE Estonia, EL Greece, ES Spain, FI Finland, FR France, ID Indonesia, IE Ireland, IL Israel, IT Italy, JP Japan, KO Korea, LT Lithuania, NL Netherlands, NO Norway, NZ New Zealand, PL Poland, SE Sweden, SG Singapore, SI Slovenia, SK Slovak Republic, TR Turkey, UK United Kingdom, US United States.

Source: Survey of Adult Skills (PIAAC) Round-1 (2011/12) and Round-2 (2014/15).

Do the graduates of different countries experience underemployment to a similar extent? Is there a varied pattern of change over time? Figure 12.5 shows the prevalence of graduate underemployment across some high- and middle-income countries. The computation is based on the graduate job classification described earlier, based on the PIAAC data (see Green and Henseke 2016b). There is an astonishingly large range, from just 10 per cent in Finland and Norway to nearly half in Japan.[6]

Country-specific studies have found a tendency for the extent of graduate underemployment to increase over various past intervals (Rohrbach-Schmidt and Tiemann 2011; Kiersztyn 2013; Korpi and Tåhlin 2009; Green and Henseke 2016b). To compute a picture of how underemployment among graduates is changing over the recent decade, we loosely proxy graduate employment by the notion of high-skilled employment, as defined by the first three major groups: managers, professionals, and technicians and associate professionals. Here, therefore, the definition of underemployment is taken to be a tertiary graduate employed in an occupation outside these three groups.

Among all graduates working in Europe, taken as a whole, the proportion underemployed edged up from 19 per cent in 2005 to 21 per cent in 2015 (Figure 12.6). The predominant picture is one of growing graduate underemployment within most countries. The tendency is strongest in two Eastern European countries (Slovenia and the Slovak Republic) and Greece,

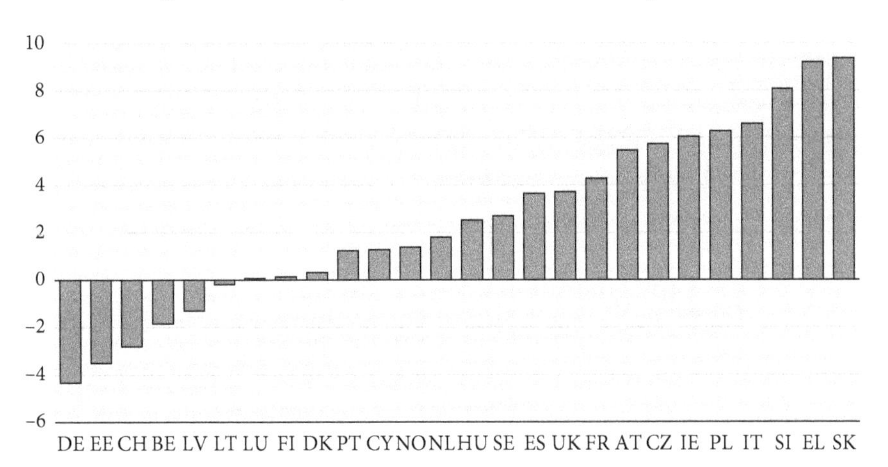

Figure 12.6 Changes in graduate underemployment, 2005–15, aged thirty to fifty-nine.

Changing proportion of economically active graduates in ISCO major groups: Clerks, Service Workers, Skilled Agricultural Workers, Skilled Trades and Crafts Workers, Plant & Machine operators, Elementary Occupations.

Key: see Figure 1.

Source: Survey of Adult Skills (PIAAC) Round-1 (2011/12) and Round-2 (2014/15).

but there has also been growing underemployment in thirteen other countries. In five countries, there has been negligible change, while in some countries, notably Estonia, Germany and Switzerland, underemployment has decreased significantly.

What might account for the cross-country variation in the level and growth of graduate underemployment? A proximate factor is the country-level gap between the prevalence of graduate jobs and the supply of graduates – what might be termed the 'relative demand' for graduates. In Green and Henseke (2016b) we found some evidence for this explanation: countries where the relative demand had fallen more were those where the prevalence of underemployment among graduates had risen more. Verhaest and van der Velden (2012), using a different measurement protocol and earlier data, also found evidence in favour of this proximate explanation. However, there are no simple explanations as to how the relative demand for graduates varies. Ultimately, it comes down to each country's constellation of labour market and educational institutions and how they interact with its macroeconomic orientation (fiscally expansive or conservative). While no simple classification of countries accounts for the range of underemployment, we see from Figure 12.5 that Anglophone countries Canada, Ireland, the United Kingdom and the United States are concentrated at the upper end of the spectrum, while most Nordic countries, except for Denmark, are in the lower half.

In sum, the prevalence of graduate underemployment varies widely across countries. It has risen over the last decade, but not everywhere. Increases have been located primarily in Southern and Eastern Europe, and in general were greatest where the aggregate imbalance between the share of graduate jobs and the share of graduates declined the most.

Optimism, Pessimism and the Future for Graduate Labour Markets

Given that a substantive rise in the share of graduates in the labour force can be expected everywhere for the foreseeable future, whether graduate underemployment will continue to rise in the next decade will depend on the future pace of growth of graduate jobs.

At the risk of oversimplifying, one can distinguish two broad understandings of recent graduate labour markets: one hopeful, the other pessimistic. The optimistic approach looks primarily to the earnings premiums (sometimes loosely referred to as the 'returns') associated with achieving a higher education qualification, taking this to be the key signal. The fact that in many countries the premium has been mainly stable or slightly increasing, despite the mass expansion of tertiary education, is seen as evidence that the demand for graduates' skills has been increasing alongside the supply of graduates. Analysts extrapolate this past trend, and the optimistic argument is then bolstered by forecasts that there will be increases in the demands for cognitive and creative skills that graduates are thought to possess (e.g. Bakhshi and Yang 2015). Moreover, where higher education participation entails high debt, the optimistic approach expects this to be sustainable. With a dearth of evidence about trends in the social returns to higher education, this evidence on the private returns has underpinned the case for policies that support the ongoing expansion of higher education.

Optimism is less common in countries where the average returns have declined, such as Italy, Portugal or Taiwan (Crivellaro 2016; Almeida et al. 2017; Huang and Huang 2015). A pessimistic understanding of graduate labour markets in many countries comes from studies that put an explicit focus on indicators of the demand for high-skilled labour. Such studies often contend that it is not credible to presume the demand for high skills has risen as fast as the stocks of graduate labour in past decades (e.g. Holmes and Mayhew 2014, 2016). It is questioned whether modern technology really does require increasing skills, with the impact of IT in particular seen as encouraging 'digital Taylorism' (i.e. jobs with more employer control and requiring more intensive effort, rather than higher skill) (Brown, Lauder and Ashton 2010). The assumption of human capital theory that an increased supply of graduate skills would induce employers to adopt different product strategies and forms of work organization that would utilize those skills is questioned. Evidence that the same occupation is populated by increasing proportions of graduates is taken as implying, either that an increasing proportion of graduates are underutilizing their skills in the workplace or that the average graduate's skills have been decreasing as college grades are inflated. If employers continue to demand more graduate qualifications, this is interpreted as reflecting increased credentialism and the 'positional' character of education.

This spectrum from pessimism to optimism has a direct parallel in discourse about the future effects of new technology on work and jobs (British Academy,2018). Beaudry et al. (2016) present evidence that since about 2000 in the United States computer use has become less skill-biased. Looking to the future, other writers (e.g. Ford 2015) fear the impact on jobs of artificial intelligence, machine learning and robots, the so-called 'fourth industrial revolution'. Yet the widely cited forecast of Frey and Osborne (2013) – to the effect that roughly half of jobs are at risk of displacement in the foreseeable future – has been met by several others that have suggested that the true figure is very much less. Arntz, Gregory and Zierahn (2017), for example, calculates the automation risk of American jobs at 9 per cent of jobs, while Nedelkoska and Quintini (2018) find that only 14 per cent of jobs across OECD countries are at high risk of automation. In any case new jobs are expected, as yet unidentified, that will replace those destroyed. As in the past, automation is likely to continue to substitute for labour in certain tasks but to complement the performance of other tasks and thus raise productivity and the demand for labour (Autor 2015). The policy challenge, then, is not to prepare for a world of precious few jobs but to ensure a smooth transition to the new technologies and to address the distributional consequences if the ownership of robots becomes ever more skewed (Freeman 2015).

Our perspective embraces neither the optimistic nor the pessimistic perspectives entirely. For the coming decades the balance of argument suggests a continued increase in the demand for graduate skills. Yet, there is considerably uncertainty over the pace of change, and hence over whether it will exceed or fall short of the rising shares of graduates that are much easier to anticipate. The increases (or decreases) in graduate jobs will vary substantially across countries, as will the trend in graduate underemployment.

How much should governments be concerned, if an increasing proportion of graduates come to be working in non-graduate jobs? Graduate underemployment assuredly matters for those concerned because they receive lower pay and tend to be dissatisfied with their work. Underemployment is for some graduates highly persistent. Studies show that non-graduate employment spells can result in dead-end jobs with limited career prospects (e.g. Mavromaras and McGuinness 2012; Nunley et al. 2016). Underemployment embodies part of the risk for all when they invest in tertiary education: there may be an adequate return for the average student, but the downside possibility of underemployment has to be considered, especially when the investment entails substantial debts. Underemployment should also be a concern for governments concerned with the fiscal costs of tertiary education. There is an ongoing need, then, for governments to monitor the utilization of graduates in each country. The proportion of graduates in graduate jobs should be a standard reported statistic, alongside graduate unemployment rates, in each country's ongoing understanding of its labour market.

As for the social returns, however, the picture is more rosy. A good tertiary education is valuable in non-work spheres of life and brings benefits for others, not just the students concerned. The public good aspects of higher education have been well documented (e.g. Marginson 2011), and external benefits from tertiary education have been found in several countries (Huang, van den Brink and Groot 2011; Green and Henseke 2016b). Should graduate underemployment continue to increase, attention is likely to be drawn, increasingly, to purposes of higher education other than the purely instrumental ones of raising students' chances of profitable employment.

Notes

1 'Institution' is here used in its broadest, Veblenian, sense to include norms and habits of thought, as well as legal and regulatory structures.
2 Note that the UK figure applies only to England and Northern Ireland, because Wales and Scotland did not participate in the Survey of Adult Skills in 2011. The figure is also not directly comparable with the analysis of graduate jobs based on EU-LFS data, because the here-deployed classifier defines adequate employment more narrowly for higher education graduates (ISCED5A and ISCED6) only, thus leaving out high-level tertiary qualifications (ISCED5B).
3 In qualification to this observation, it should be noted that it is possible that there has been some skill upgrading within occupations in these countries; in which case, the figure would understate somewhat the extent of any rise in the demand for the skills of graduates.
4 Underemployment is sometimes referred to as 'overeducation', but the problem with that term is that it assumes that the *only* purpose of education is employment, and can be pejorative.
5 Several writers have focused their analyses on subjective indicators of skills mismatch, or utilized indicators combining subjective mismatch with test scores across occupations. While this approach has some potential appeal, there is no scientific consensus on an adequate indicator for skills underutilization.
6 Graduate underemployment may also come on top of other forms of graduate underutilization – especially, unemployment. Unsurprisingly, underemployment tends to be higher in countries where graduate unemployment is higher.

References

Allen, J. and Van der Velden, R. (eds) (2011), *The Flexible Professional in the Knowledge Society: New Challenges for Higher Education* . Dordrecht: Springer Science & Business Media.
Almeida, A., Figueiredo, H., Portela, J. M., Sá, C. and Teixeira, P. (2017), 'Returns to Postgraduate Education in Portugal: Holding on to a Higher Ground?', IZA Discussion Paper, No. 10676, Bonn: IZA – Institute of Labor Economics.

Arntz, M., Gregory, T. and Zierahn, U. (2017), 'Revisiting the Risk of Automation', *Economics Letters*, 159: 157–60.

Autor, D. (2015), 'Why Are There Still So Many Jobs? The History and Future of Workplace Automation', *Journal of Economic Perspectives*, 29 (3): 3–30.

Autor, D. H., Levy, F. and Murnane, R. J. (2003), 'The Skill Content of Recent Technological Change: An Empirical Exploration', *The Quarterly Journal of Economics*, 118 (4): 1279–333.

Bakhshi, H. and Yang, L. (2015), *Creativity and the Future of Work*, London, UK: NESTA.

Baker, D. P. and Lenhardt, G. (2008), 'The Institutional Crisis of the German Research University', *Higher Education Policy*, 21 (1): 49–64.

Barone, C. and Ortiz, L. (2011), 'Overeducation Among European University Graduates: A Comparative Analysis of Its Incidence and the Importance of Higher Education Differentiation', *Higher Education*, 61(3): 325–37.

Beaudry, P., Green, D. A. and Sand, B. M. (2016), 'The Great Reversal in the Demand for Skill and Cognitive Tasks', *Journal of Labor Economics*, 34 (1): pt. 2, S199–S247.

Blinder, A. S. and Krueger, A. B. (2013), 'Alternative Measures of Offshorability: A Survey Approach', *Journal of Labor Economics*, 31 (S1): S97–S128.

British Academy (2018), *The Impact of Artificial Intelligence on Work*, London: British Academy.

Brown, P., Lauder, H. and Ashton, D. (2010), *The Global Auction: The Broken Promises of Education, Jobs, and Incomes*, Oxford: University Press.

Chevalier, A. and Lindley, J. (2009), 'Overeducation and the Skills of UK Graduates', *Journal of the Royal Statistical Society: Series A (Statistics in Society)*, 172(2): 307–37.

Crivellaro, E. (2016), 'The College Wage Premium over Time: Trends in Europe in the Last 15 Years', *In Inequality: Causes and Consequences*, 287–328. Bingley, UK: Emerald Group Publishing Limited.

European Commission (2015), *Education and Training Monitor 2015*, Luxembourg: Publications Office of the European Union.

Ford, M. (2015), *The Rise of the Robots: Technology and the Threat of Mass Unemployment*, New York: Basic Books.

Freeman, R. (2015), 'Who Owns the Robots Rules the World', *IZA World of Labor*, 2015: 5. doi: 10.15185/izawol.5

Frey, C. and Osborne, M. (2013), *The Future of Employment: How Susceptible Are Jobs to Computerisation?* Oxford, UK: Oxford Martin School Working Paper.

Goldin, C. and L. F. Katz (2008), *The Race Between Education and Technology*, Cambridge: Harvard University Press.

Green, F. (2013), *Skills and Skilled Work: An Economic and Social Analysis*, Oxford: Oxford University Press.

Green, F. and Henseke, G. (2016a), 'The Changing Graduate Labour Market: Analysis Using a New Indicator of Graduate Jobs', *IZA Journal of Labor Policy*, 5 (1): 14.

Green, F. and Henseke, G. (2016b), 'Should Governments of OECD Countries Worry About Graduate Underemployment?', *Oxford Review of Economic Policy*, 32 (4): 514–37.

Green, F. and McIntosh, S. (2007), 'Is There a Genuine Under-Utilization of Skills Amongst the Over-Qualified?', *Applied Economics*, 39 (4): 427–39.
Henseke, G. (2018), 'Against the Grain? Assessing Graduate Labour Market Trends in Germany Through a Task-Based Indicator of Graduate Jobs', *Social Indicators Research*, 141: 809–40.
Henseke, G. and Green, F. (2017), 'Cross-National Deployment of "Graduate Jobs": Analysis Using a New Indicator Based on High Skills Use', *Skill Mismatch in Labor Markets* (Research in Labor Economics, Vol. 45) (pp. 41–79), Bingley, UK: Emerald Publishing Limited .
Holmes, C. and Mayhew, K. (2014), 'The Winners and Losers in the "hourglass" Labour Market', *Understanding Employer Engagement in Education: Theories and Evidence* (pp. 110–31), London: Routledge.
Holmes, C. and Mayhew, K. (2016), 'The Economics of Higher Education', *Oxford Review of Economic Policy*, 32 (4): 475–96.
Huang, J., van den Brink, H. M. and Groot, W. (2011), 'College Education and Social Trust: An Evidence-Based Study on the Causal Mechanisms', *Social Indicators Research*, 104 (2): 287–310.
Huang, L. H. and Huang, H. Y. (2015), 'Rigid Low College Premiums and the Expansion of Higher Education in Taiwan', *The Singapore Economic Review*, 60(4), 228–35.
Kiersztyn, A. (2013), 'Stuck in a Mismatch? The Persistence of Overeducation During Twenty Years of the Post-Communist Transition in Poland', *Economics of Education Review*, 32: 78–91.
Korpi, T. and M. Tahlin (2009), 'Educational Mismatch, Wages, and Wage Growth: Overeducation in Sweden, 1974–2000', *Labour Economics*, 16 (2): 183–93.
Marginson, S. (2011), 'Higher Education and Public Good', *Higher Education Quarterly*, 65 (4): 411–33.
Marginson, S. (2016), 'High Participation Systems of Higher Education', *Journal of Higher Education*, 87 (2), 243–71.
Mavromaras, K. and McGuinness, S. (2012), 'Overskilling Dynamics and Education Pathways', *Economics of Education Review*, 31 (5): 619–28.
Nedelkoska, L. and Quintini, G. (2018), *Automation, Skills Use and Training*. OECD Social, Employment and Migration Working Papers No. 202. Paris: OECD
Nunley, J. M., Pugh, A., Romero, N. and Seals Jr., R. A. (2016), 'College Major, Internship Experience, and Employment Opportunities: Estimates from a Résumé Audit', *Labour Economics*, 38 (1): 37–46.
Powell, J. J. and Solga, H. (2010), 'Analyzing the Nexus of Higher Education and Vocational Training in Europe: A Comparative-Institutional Framework', *Studies in Higher Education*, 35 (6): 705–21.
Rohrbach-Schmidt, D. and Tiemann, M. (2011), 'Mismatching and Job Tasks in Germany–Rising Over-Qualification Through Polarization?', *Empirical Research in Vocational Education and Training*, 3 (1): 39–53.
Verhaest, D. and Van der Velden, R. (2012), 'Cross-Country Differences in Graduate Overeducation', *European Sociological Review*, 29 (3): 642–53.

Part VI

Institutions and Markets

13

Commodifying Higher Education

The Proliferation of Devices for Making Markets

Janja Komljenovic

Introduction

This chapter focuses on the higher education (HE) industry. Scholars have been studying processes such as marketization, commodification and privatization in HE for decades and have created a wealth of knowledge. However, the HE industry and its fast growth are not yet conceptualized in their entirety. While some useful conceptualizations have been made, such as that on internal and external privatization by Ball and Youdell (2007), they cannot satisfactorily cover the recent and ever-changing market-making processes in higher education.

Furthermore, we have only started to analyse the processes of market-making. In other words, how do markets come to life; how are they imagined, made, implemented and maintained. While some authors have argued that HE could never be enclosed as a 'real' capitalist market due to knowledge being a public good and universities subject to status competition (Marginson 2013), other authors identify the struggles over doing just that (Jessop 2017). There is still much to be learnt about the microwork of making markets in the HE industry in their various forms and shapes. Therefore, the essential questions to ask are as follows: How can we better think through HE industry? And which are the theoretical tools that we could use to analyse market-making processes? Instead of discussing the abstract traits of the HE market had it ever existed, we ought to investigate the market-making on the ground and see what that could tell us about the reality of the HE industry and its future.

Higher Education Industry and Its Markets

The literature on HE as a market is often limited in thinking of HE as a homogeneous group consisting of universities selling teaching services to students for a fee. Although there seems to be a shift in the literature from discussing whether HE is or could ever be a 'real' market towards discussing various types of governing it as a market (e.g. Jungblut and Vukasovic 2018; Marginson 2018), the majority of the literature still stays within the framework of HE as homogenous and bounded in one country. Instead, conceptualizing HE not as 'the university' but as a sector involving different actors operating at various scales (Robertson et al. 2012) helps us to see that there are HE *markets* in the plural, which constitute the HE industry. In other words, opening up the black box of the HE industry allows us to illuminate the various markets that are being imagined and made, actors that move in and around the sector and all the commodities that are being created and exchanged.

With Robertson, I have developed a heuristic to conceptualize the HE industry along two dimensions (Komljenovic and Robertson 2016): First, whether market transactions are immediately for-profit or not. Second, whether universities are sellers or buyers of commodities. This way it is possible to group the various markets, their institutions, actors and commodities into four quadrants. First, *inside-out and not-for-profit* is where the university generates income, but not explicitly to create a surplus; and the financing of activities are mostly supplemented with public sources. Examples of such commodities in the UK are study programmes for local students, non-commercial research, services for other public bodies and the like. Second, *inside-out and making a profit* are markets where the university is selling things and services and makes a surplus (which in case of charities or public institutions needs to be reinvested back into the institution). Example commodities in the UK are study programmes to non-UK and non-EU students, commercial research, consultancy services, intellectual property, patents, services of catering, conferences and so on. Third, *outside-in and for-profit* is where the university acts as a buyer and pays for goods and services for the profit of other companies. Examples are commodities such as computer software, consultancy, data and research, student recruitment agents, brand recognition research and representation in foreign countries. Finally, *outside-in and not-for-profit* is where the university is using services but is not immediately paying for them. Examples in the UK include universities using Facebook groups, Twitter accounts, LinkedIn services, collegial relations with local solicitors and accounts at the Home Office for visa advice. Markets, institutions, actors and commodities in these groups are in constant dynamic and motion, and so are various market forms that might be positioned on the boundaries of this heuristic. For example, public–private partnerships such as joint ventures between universities and private companies can sit in the boundary between the inside-out and making a profit and outside-in and for-profit.

These four groups allow us to think about the various kinds of markets and quasi-markets, as well as numerous commodities that are exchanged at different prices and under different rules. They also make visible the variety of actors that move in and around these markets, the power relations between them, and scales of their operation. We can be attentive towards how these variations of markets and their combinations impact each other and change the fundamental nature of HE actors and services. It thus includes the complexity and variety of different actors, rules, institutions, scales and relations among them.

All of these markets need to be made, negotiated and maintained and do not merely emerge by policy fiat. The making of markets is a never-ending set of social processes that are as much cultural and political as they are economic (Beckert 2009). These processes contain making and unmaking, framing and reframing, stabilizing and destabilizing in struggles between various actors and their power relations (Çalışkan and Callon 2010). The crucial question is, How can this be done? Callon's work on market-making and market devices is particularly useful, to which I turn next.

Market Devices

Market devices are 'material and discursive assemblages that intervene in the construction of markets' (Muniesa, Millo and Callon 2007: 2). They vary in type and form and span from price tags to shopping carts, computer screens, accounting reports, data analytics, rankings and many others. The commonality among these different devices is that they *perform* the economy by equipping market actors with prostheses, which help them in their calculations (Callon 1998). They are technologies of the market that expand possibilities for calculation and proliferate calculative agencies. As Fourcade (2017) reminds us, this is not always about rational calculation as profitability is often feeding on human irrationality, emotion and failure. An important caveat is, therefore, to understand that market devices make market actors calculate, but in different ways and not always rationally, albeit aligned with economic relations and rationalities.

An essential aspect of market devices is that they shape particular markets and articulate actions by acting or making others act (Berndt 2015). In the process of market-making, they reconfigure specific social relations into market relations (Muniesa, Millo and Callon 2007). Market devices seem neutral, but they never are as they are always constructed by specific agents in a particular way, in line with the constellation of power relations, which are continuously subject to challenge and change. Besides asking what market devices include, we should also ask what they exclude.

In this chapter, I will focus on market information tools as market devices. By describing four different vignettes corresponding to four different groups of markets in the HE industry elaborated earlier, I will investigate what kind of calculative agencies these market information tools produce by being constructed as they are, what sort of logic they motivate and what kind of HE they enclose and promote. Focusing our analysis on market devices and how they are produced, employed, legitimated and circulated helps us to understand how local markets and their particularities are constitutive of globally interrelated economies (Peck 2012). Following this argument, a study of various market devices within different HE markets could help us to understand not only the workings of the particular cases but also the relationality of variegated HE markets in the global HE industry.

Vignettes

Out of the University and Not-For-Profit: The Case of the Student Consumer in England

Higher education undergraduate provision market in England has been consistently built over the past two decades including its essential element of the student as a consumer (Komljenovic, Ashwin, McArthur and Rosewell 2018; Tomlinson 2017b). Of the many market information tools available, Unistats is the 'official website for comparing UK HE course data' launched in 2007. It gained momentum in 2012 with the rise in tuition fees cap and became an interactive tool for comparing course-specific data. Unistats is also one of the key instruments of the newly established Office for Students (OfS), which aims to bring transparency into the HE market. It should, therefore, be seen as one of the chief devices to make, institute and order the undergraduate HE market in the UK.

Unistats offers a wealth of information on every study course and draws from information provided by universities as well as nationally administered datasets

(Destinations of Leavers from Higher Education (DLHE) survey introduced in 2003, the National Student Survey (NSS) launched in 2005, and the Longitudinal Education Outcomes (LEO) issued in 2018). It focuses on students and other decision-makers such as parents or school advisers and aims to equip them with data to make informed choices about what and where to study. It is invoking particular kinds of calculation by offering specific information and omitting others, as well as foregrounding certain information. By doing so, it is framing the student as a consumer, albeit it is a comparative tool that does not rank universities or study courses. Unistats also has a potential to frame a seller in a university and a calculative agent that not only provides data for Unistats but also uses the data for their strategic actions in HE markets.

The information that is foregrounded is student satisfaction (from the NSS), information on employment and salary (from LEO), career or study paths of graduates (from DLHE), entry criteria and course accreditation. The most dominant information is on the NSS, and employment and salary data. Effectively, this market device is framing a new valuation of the university (Tomlinson 2017a), which becomes utilitarian and captured by labour market statistic. What is omitted is the public role of universities, the transformative potential of HE through engaging with knowledge, the intangible experience of being a student and learning about the diversity of opinion, critical thinking and democracy, among other dimensions of HE.

Unistats invokes the future of the HE market as involving more competition and the opening of the HE undergraduate provision market while basing it on what is encouraged to be rigorous and reliable market information. While Unistats claims to offer objective and reliable information, it is also complex and opaque. Moreover, it is an assemblage of various data including compound information such as the awarded category in the Teaching Excellence Framework (TEF), a national exercise to assess quality of teaching at universities and colleges. Through this complexity and opaqueness, Unistats classifies and categorizes universities, student experience, value and the future.

Out of the University and Making a Profit: The Case of MOOCs

There is by now a big offer of a variety of massive open online courses (MOOCs), but there is no consistency in their types, duration, price or end certificates as well as no information about their 'value' in the labour market or otherwise. Robertson (2019) wrote about the political economy of MOOCs and teased out their expansion, differentiation and monetization, and what is ultimately market-making in the HE sector. Market information tools available for the MOOCs market are based on two main sources – that is, marketing of MOOC platforms themselves, and various commercial reviews providers such as reviews.com.[1] I will illustrate the case of market information offered by 'Coursera for Business' targeted at the corporate e-learning market. Albeit this case is positioned as 'out of the university and making a profit', it is a form of a public–private partnership and thus sits on the boundary between this group of markets and the outside-in and for-profit.

The target audience is companies that are interested in providing training and learning opportunities for their employees. The website is promising quality and credibility of courses, the flexibility of provision, help and support with developing tailored courses, and importantly, measuring the 'returns on investment'. The issue of quality is fully based on the reputation of the universities and academics offering the modules or courses. Since universities have legal and legitimate authority to issue credentials for the achieved level of knowledge and competence, a new market actor – MOOC, builds on a traditional authority – universities, to be part of making its market. The value and credibility of the whole MOOC system rely on universities and its brands dating back to their start in 2012 and the involvement of prestigious US universities such as Stanford, Harvard and MIT (Robertson 2019).

The second essential element of the market information is the flexibility of training in that employees can learn anytime, anywhere, with any pace, in various languages and any combination of content. Such flexibility feeds into the discourse of globalization and speeding temporality of competition between firms and job seekers, as well as life cycles of individuals' skills and knowledge. 'Coursera for Business' is portrayed as a solution for the fast-paced fast-changing competencies of labour.

Finally and importantly, Coursera promises employers to monitor the returns on investment and tracking the progress of their staff in learning, as well as calculating the economic benefits. Coursera states that it 'correlates your learners' course progress with market data on the economic value of the skills they're learning'.[2] Coursera's algorithms in this case already *make* calculations and equip responsible individuals at companies to think about training through immediate economic returns on skills in abstract calculations of possible value.

The future that this market information tool is framing is a dynamic, fast, competitive environment in which skills are an asset. While this market device frames students as ideal lifelong learners (see Robertson 2019), it frames universities as flexible and adaptable providers of a variety of skills and knowledge for global audiences. It lifts them from the constraints of local and national boundaries, as well as from rigid quality assurance and accreditation rules. They are also unbundled from their roles as providers of full study courses that end in university degrees into providers of short modules that can be re-bundled into courses together with modules provided by other universities.

Into the University and For-Profit: The Case of International Student Recruitment Agents

International student recruitment agents are relatively new phenomena in HE, but they represent an expanding market (Robinson-Pant and Magyar 2018). Despite evidence for agents benefitting students and universities, the practice is uneven around the world, and there have been concerns about it tarnishing academic values (Altbach and Reisberg 2013) as well as reports on agents' misconduct and mis-selling (Huang, Raimo and Humfrey 2016). Thus market information tools are particularly important in ordering this relatively new market. They can be grouped in three main types: first, marketing material from agents themselves; second, lists of agents that are identified as legitimate by state agencies such as the British Council; and finally, lists of agents that are identified as legitimate by private companies in the business of brokering agents. I will illustrate the third of these.

There are a few private companies that act as agents' brokers around the world, such as the Study World from the UK, BMI and FPP EduMedia from Brazil, ICEF from Germany and Weba from Switzerland. These companies organize meeting sessions between what they define as trustworthy student recruitment agents and education providers including HE institutions. These events act as market information on the agents' market in their own right as the brokers guarantee agents' quality by bringing them to their events (Komljenovic 2017). Through bringing order into the agents' industry, building alliances with government agencies around the world and investing in its agents' screening, it develops a mechanism of trust through its brand.

ICEF's information on agents acts as a market device that works through trust in screening and training procedures. While it attempts to bring transparency into the system and it does to some extent, the opaqueness is rather high. Universities and students are meant to trust that the agents' training programmes or screenings are working. The market is by far from ordered, and in the case of high ambiguity, actors tend to turn to conventions (Beckert 2009). Agents' brokers (and state agencies) target these conventions with the market information tools that they have developed and by doing so are normalizing and legitimizing the use of agents.

The market device frames the services of agents as a commodity that is legitimate if regulated. It is expanding HE markets into new domains and scales in that universities are not the only ones selling services in the growing HE international student market. It is now also intermediaries between universities and students – that is, agents; and intermediaries between universities and agents – that is, agent brokers.

Into the University and Not-For-Profit: The Case of LinkedIn

Launched in 2003, LinkedIn is the biggest social media platform for professional networking. It is heavily involved in the HE sector as it comprises an assemblage of individuals, skills, universities, employers, content, metrics and numbers (Komljenovic 2019). Albeit LinkedIn coordinates multisided markets, I will illustrate the case of market information on labour.

The target audience is companies in their capacity as employers. LinkedIn serves many functions in the recruitment process, and providing information on possible candidates is one of them. This information tool marries what is called the 'network effects' of social media platforms (Langley and Leyshon 2017) with self-reported information. An individual reports information on their professional experience, education and qualification, skills that they have, accomplishments and interests. This is supplemented with endorsements of skills by the person's network in a numerical form and recommendations by the network more generally. The primary drive behind these digital profiles of individuals is that self-reporting can be verified by the social network, which becomes a new form of valuation of skills, experience and personalities.

This market information tool already calculates the value of skills (what kind of skills are most in demand or in need for particular jobs) and of individuals (to what extent a person possesses all of the skills demanded by a job, where they got those skills and who vouches for them). It then equips the responsible individuals for recruitment at companies with this information and makes them calculate with the focus on the offered information. Moreover, the network and algorithms enable new scales and scope of valuation.

The future of the labour market is framed as a constant comparison of people and skills; and always adjusting depending on the calculated insights. The platform is classifying and categorizing people, skills, jobs, universities and employers. The metrics that are offered are mostly in the form of compound information based on the underlying classification and categorization.

Market Devices and Future Framing in the Higher Education Industry

There is much to be gained from examining market devices involved in the processes of market-making in the HE industry. Not least, the chapter illustrates how market devices frame market actors into new subjectivities; how students and universities are equipped to become calculative agents in their roles of buyers and sellers; how HE activities are reframed into economic value of markets and its commodities; how new actors become part of the HE markets and thus the governance of the HE sector; and how the future is portrayed, framed and captured. The four vignettes show how market information tools can act as market devices and come in different forms, are constructed by different actors, show different means of enforcement and frame different aspects of what is valued in HE (see Table 13.1).

All described market devices share the following trends. First, market devices distribute the cognitive and calculative processes in that a given task is not performed by an unaided individual, but by an assemblage of people, things and sociotechnical devices (Berndt 2015). In other words, the market devices themselves are calculating and comparing (such as the LinkedIn data on skills and people based on its algorithms) and thus equip individuals with decision-making possibilities and particular framings of the solutions. The individual's rationalities, decision-making possibilities and meanings that are engraved into the logic and nature of devices become crucial in defining these different HE markets. This way devices *perform* and stabilize markets. Market information tools are not a simple representation of available possibilities in the market, but they change the conditions of the world that they are supposed to represent by calculating and equipping individuals with calculations (Berndt and Boeckler 2010).

Second, while the presented market devices are predicted to bring transparency into the system, and they do to some extent, they are at the same time opaque due to the complexity of data and the compound, multifaceted measures. It also seems that a certain level of opaqueness is in the nature of these devices so that they can frame commodities, actors and value in a particular way. While, on the one hand, these market information tools are serving the function to inform

Table 13.1 Market Devices and the Higher Education Industry

Vignette	Market Information Tool as a Market Device	Data Generation	Governance and Enforcement	Value of Higher Education
Framing students as consumers in the UK	State created search engines applied on the web	Students, universities, state agencies and state databases	State: State generated or supported population surveying, merging of official state databases and state regulation like TEF and OfS	A combination of hedonistic experience of pleasure and comfort (student experience) and utilitarianism (employability and salary)
MOOCs	Marketing material by MOOC platforms	MOOCs users, marketing and sales departments of MOOCs, basic statistics from platforms' analytics	Provider: Marketing, number of enrolled students; brand and reputation of university / academic delivering the course	Unbundled and fast-achievable skills, flexibility, globalization
LinkedIn	Individual education credentials, skills, experience and achievements; institutional information and connections	LinkedIn platform; Individual posting via principles of Web 2.0; and LinkedIn algorithms	Third party: Likes; skill recommendations and endorsements; number of individual and institutional user accounts, profiles; metrics such as top skills and top employers	Skills, experience and credentials suggested and valuated by social network
International student recruitment agents	Listing, accreditation or other form of recognition by companies, state agencies or partnerships between the two	Companies or state agencies	Third party: Trust in agents generated by trainings, lists backed by reputation of the company or legitimacy of the state agency	Future framing for students (value of international degree); cultural and economic benefits for universities

Source: Author.

market actors and enable their calculative choice, they are, on the other hand, also devices for scoring and classifying individuals and institutions.

Market devices that were presented are in most cases compound devices. They all rely on multiple steps of classifications that are done along the way to publish particular market information finally. The classification goes all the way down from the system level through institutional to the individual and classifies on every step. They are also dependent on the categorical work of third parties, which may hide more than it reveals. They are promoted as being objective and reliable in representing the world, but they are instead interpreting, classifying and structuring the world (Fourcade 2017).

Third, these devices each in their way determine and structure new criteria for value. They seem to interact to some extent and some are shared across markets' settings and by so doing relate and interact in reframing HE as a sector. Zgaga (2005) argues that it is the precise nature of HE that it is constituted by the totality of its multifaceted roles spanning from economic or technological development to personal growth and nourishing democratic cultures. However, the market devices presented in this chapter attempt to unbundle this totality of university roles and re-frame them in a more individualized, flexible, unbundled, measurable and utilitarian way.

Finally, the described market devices frame a particular kind of future, which seems to be increasingly competitive, digital, quantified and relational. The four vignettes not only predict but also enable their respective market expansion through ordering markets with information. Moreover, all of the examined tools are themselves expanding in size, scope, span and temporality. The future is portrayed and performed through the digital and the quantified. Most of the devices are based on some sort of counting and metrics to collect data, on the one hand, and to communicate it, on the other, in an analysed and framed form. By using the devices, individuals use and produce data that measure and frame activities, services, actors and markets. Finally, it seems the devices are interacting in full or in part across data that they generate and draw from, actors that use them, markets that they help construct and scales that they operate on. Thus the future of HE seems to be increasingly networked.

Conclusions

Albeit this chapter was only a short experiment in thinking through market-making and market devices, it proved to be productive in analysing not only how particular 'real' markets are imagined, framed, constructed and maintained but also how the various markets at different scales are connected in the global HE industry without losing sight of heterogeneity and differentiation of practices.

There is a need for more research that aims to understand the details of how markets are put to work through market devices. This would enable us to unmask market-making processes as a deeply ambivalent endeavour, which is never finished and always challenged. Moreover, it would unveil the classification criteria that are enmeshed in the market information tools and not let them fade into the background as if they are representing the world itself with natural categories that we are predicted to believe in, use and act upon. It would also bring into focus the role of technology in market-making. Finally, it would illuminate the different possibilities of the kinds of market actors and market relations that are being constructed in HE through different devices. As different devices have different consequences, critically scrutinizing their nature and effects enables us to discuss how HE industry can promote or worsen social equality and social justice more generally.

Notes

1 https://www.reviews.com/mooc-platforms/ (last accessed 10 August 2018).
2 https://www.coursera.org/business/products/ (last accessed 17 August 2018).

References

Altbach, P. G. and Reisberg, L. (2013), *Agents and the Ethics of International Higher Education*. Retrieved 9 August 2016, from http://www.universityworldnews.com/article.php?story=20130911143830201

Ball, S. J. and Youdell, D. (2007), *Hidden Privatisation in Public Education*. Preliminary Report, prepared by Stephen J. Ball and Deborah Youdell, Institute of Education, University of London for Education International 5th World Congress, July 2007. London.

Beckert, J. (2009), 'The Social Order of Markets', *Theory and Society*, 38 (3): 245–69.

Berndt, C. (2015), 'Ruling Markets: The Marketization of Social and Economic Policy', *Environment and Planning A*, 47: 1866–72.

Berndt, C. and Boeckler, M. (2010), 'Geographies of Markets: Materials, Morals and Monsters in Motion', *Progress in Human Geography*, 35 (4), 559–67.

Çalışkan, K. and Callon, M. (2010), 'Economization, Part 2: A Research Programme for the Study of Markets', *Economy and Society*, 39 (1): 1–32.

Callon, M. (1998), 'The Embeddedness of Economic Markets in Economics', in M. Callon (ed.), *The Laws of the Markets*, 1–57, Oxford: Blackwell Publishers.

Fourcade, M. (2017), 'The Fly and the Cookie: Alignment and Unhingement in 21st-Century Capitalism', *Socio-Economic Review*, 15 (3): 661–78.

Huang, I. Y., Raimo, V. and Humfrey, C. (2016), 'Power and Control: Managing Agents for International Student Recruitment in Higher Education', *Studies in Higher Education*, 41 (8): 1333–54.

Jessop, B. (2017), 'Varieties of Academic Capitalism and Entrepreneurial Universities', *Higher Education*, 73 (6): 853–70.

Jungblut, J. and Vukasovic, M. (2018), Not all Markets Are Created Equal: Re-Conceptualizing Market Elements in Higher Education', *Higher Education*, 75 (5): 855–70. https://doi.org/10.1007/s10734-017-0174-5

Komljenovic, J. (2017), 'Market Ordering as a Device for Market-Making: The Case of the Emerging Students' Recruitment Industry', *Globalisation, Societies and Education*, 15 (3): 367–80.

Komljenovic, J. (2019), 'Linkedin, Platforming Labour, and the New Employability Mandate for Universities', *Globalisation, Societies and Education*, 17: 28.43

Komljenovic, J., Ashwin, P., Mcarthur, J. and Rosewell, K. (2018), 'To Be Or Not To Be Consumers: The Imperfect Alignment of English Higher Education Marketization Policy and the Narratives of First Year University Students'. In CGHE 2018 Annual Conference: The New Geopolitics of Higher Education, Centre for Global Higher Education. Retrieved from http://www.researchcghe.org/perch/resources/uk-sa-cg-paper-22.3.18.pdf

Komljenovic, J. and Robertson, S. L. (2016), 'The Dynamics of "Market-Making" in Higher Education', *Journal of Education Policy*, 31 (5): 622–36.

Langley, P. and Leyshon, A. (2017), 'Platform Capitalism: The Intermediation and Capitalisation of Digital Economic Circulation', *Finance and Society*, 3 (1): 11–31.

Marginson, S. (2013), 'The Impossibility of Capitalist Markets in Higher Education', *Journal of Education Policy*, 28 (3): 353–70.

Marginson, S. (2018), 'Public/Private in Higher Education: A Synthesis of Economic and political Approaches', *Studies in Higher Education*, 43 (2): 322–37.

Muniesa, F., Millo, Y. and Callon, M. (2007), 'An Introduction to Market Devices', *The Sociological Review*, 55 (s2): 1–12.

Peck, J. (2012), 'Economic Geography: Island Life', *Dialogues in Human Geography*, 2 (2): 113–33.

Robertson, S. L. (2019), 'Comparing Platforms and the New Value Economy in the Academy', in R. Gorur, S. Sellar and G. Steiner-Khamsi (eds), *World Yearbook of Education 2019: Methodology in the Era of Big Data and Global Networks*, London and New York: Routledge.

Robertson, S. L., Dale, R., Moutsios, S., Nielsen, G., Shore, C. and Wright, S. (2012), *Globalisation and Regionalisation in Higher Education: Toward a New Conceptual Framework*. Working Papers on University Reform No. 20, Department of

Education, University of Aarhus. Retrieved from http://edu.au.dk/fileadmin/www.dpu.dk/forskningsprogrammer/epoke/WP_20_-_final.pdf

Robinson-Pant, A. and Magyar, A. (2018), 'The Recruitment Agent in Internationalized Higher Education: Commercial Broker and Cultural Mediator', *Journal of Studies in International Education*, 22 (3): 225–41.

Tomlinson, M. (2017a), 'Conceptions of the Value of Higher Education in a Measured Market', *Higher Education*, 75: 711–27.

Tomlinson, M. (2017b), 'Student Perceptions of Themselves as "Consumers" of Higher Education', *British Journal of Sociology of Education*, 38 (4): 450–67.

Zgaga, P. (2005), 'Higher Education for a Democratic Culture – The Public Responsibility', in L. Weber and S. Bergan (eds), *The Public Responsibility for Higher Education and Research*, 107–15, Strasbourg Cedex: Council of Europe Publishing.

14

The New Private Sector in England

Can Subsidized Colleges Break Into the Mainstream?

Stephen A. Hunt and Vikki Boliver

Introduction

The twenty-first century has seen repeated government efforts to increase the presence of private or 'alternative' providers in the UK higher education system. Encompassing both for-profit and not-for-profit organizations, private providers are defined by the Higher Education Funding Council for England (HEFCE) as

> any provider of higher education courses which: is not in direct receipt of recurrent funding from HEFCE or from equivalent bodies in the Devolved Administrations; or does not receive direct recurrent public funding (for example, from a local authority, or from the Secretary of State for Education); and is not a further education college. (HEFCE 2014)

Historically, most private providers have been small scale with narrow curricula, often concentrating on sub-bachelor qualifications such as higher national certificates and diplomas (HNC/HND) or professional development. For decades there was only one private university in the UK: the University of Buckingham. Recently, however, the UK government has sought to encourage the growth of private higher education provision.

The latest expression of the government's ambitions regarding private providers was embodied in the 2017 Higher Education and Research Act which restructured England's higher education regulatory framework and established a new authority – the Office for Students (OfS) (H.M. Government 2017). The White Paper that preceded the act, *Success as a Knowledge Economy* (BIS 2016a), mapped the proposed changes and provided the rationale for more private provision, much of which was predicated on re-positioning students as customers. The White Paper argued that the quality and standards of teaching were falling, and that provision was 'inflexible, based on the traditional three-year undergraduate model, with insufficient innovation and provision of two-year degrees and degree apprenticeships' (BIS 2016a para 5: 8). These deficiencies in the higher education system could, it was asserted, be addressed by increased competition between providers (BIS 2016a para 7: 8).

The competition envisaged was not between existing providers but between existing incumbents and 'new and innovative providers' (BIS 2016a).

Government efforts to stimulate the private sector have included uncapping the number of publicly funded places for some private providers, and removing barriers to entry. Opportunities for market entry and expansion were to be enhanced by allowing private providers immediate access to degree-awarding powers (DAPs), at least under certain conditions, and an accelerated route to acquiring the title of 'University': 'high quality providers could complete the journey from starting as new providers with probationary DAPs to university title after 6 years' (BIS 2016a, Box 1.2: 30). Additionally, private institutions were to have greater access to public funds.

In this chapter, we consider how likely it is that private providers will be propelled into mainstream higher education, operating as an alternative to established publicly funded providers, taking into account some historical precedents.

The Increase in Demand for Higher Education

Mainstream UK higher education remains largely composed of publicly funded institutions: universities, further education colleges and specialist institutions in areas such as art, nursing and veterinary science. To date, increased demand for higher education from prospective students and graduate employers has been met by expanding public-sector provision.

The UK is likely to experience a rise in demand for higher education in the third decade of the twenty-first century because of national demographic changes. The number of eighteen-year-olds (who make up the vast majority of undergraduate entrants) is expected to rise every year between 2020 and 2030, leading to a projected demand for 50,000 additional places by 2030 (Bekhradnia and Beech 2018). However, Bekhradnia and Beech (2018) estimate that the rise in demand will far exceed this demographic increase, with as many as 350,000 extra places being sought by 2030.

It is possible the British government will turn to the private higher education sector to meet at least some of this increasing demand, simply as an expedient. Governments across the globe have often used the private sector as a demand absorbing resource; examples exist in post-war Japan, post-coup Chile and post-communist Poland (Hunt, Callender and Parry 2016). However, between 2013 and 2015 the government phased out the cap on the number of students public-sector institutions could recruit. These institutions, in theory, could then absorb some or all of the growth in demand. The expansion of the private higher education sector, therefore, is not guaranteed by a simple rise in demand for higher education, and is likely to require active promotion by the government.

The Increase in the Supply of Higher Education

Since 2011, the government has encouraged private higher education sector growth by extending the right to enrol publicly funded students (i.e. those eligible to government-funded student loans and financial support) to about 140 designated alternative providers, and by lifting restrictions on the number of such students these providers could recruit. However, this approach had mixed results and exposed flaws in the relationship between publicly funded enrolments and alternative providers (National Audit Office 2014).

The growth in student recruitment at private providers initiated in 2010/11 exceeded expectations. Students claiming government-funded financial support for courses at designated private providers rose from 7,000 to 53,000 between 2010/11 and 2013/14. Over the same period, the amount paid to students at alternative providers in grants and loans rose from £50 million to £675 million (The Committee of Public Accounts 2015), or possibly by as much as £724 million, according to the National Audit Office (2017).

The increase in student numbers did not shift demand for undergraduate bachelor's degree courses at established providers to the alternative sector (McGettigan 2016; Shury et al. 2016; Hunt & Boliver 2019). The growth in private provider student numbers and the associated increase in students claiming financial support were largely concentrated among students taking sub-degree level Higher National Certificate and Diploma (HNC and HND) courses (National Audit Office 2014). A heavy skew in the subjects these students studied was also evident: some 45 per cent of the designated private providers' students were studying for qualifications in business and administration; 16 per cent law; and 18 per cent creative arts and design. Across all levels and providers in England, the figure for business and administration was 14 per cent; law, 4 per cent; and creative art and design, 8 per cent (HESA 2018a; HESA 2018b).

The Department for Business Innovation and Skills (BIS), the government department then responsible for the sector, was warned at the time that any expansion would take place in the absence of a 'robust legislative framework to protect public money' (The Committee of Public Accounts 2015: 4). BIS lacked, for example, the right of access to private providers, as they were not directly publicly funded.

The National Audit Office (2014) identified four problematic issues associated with alternative providers during this period of expansion. First, a significant proportion of students claiming student loans were not entitled to them. Secondly, some students in receipt of publicly funded student support were being recruited onto courses that were not approved by the relevant authority, resulting in seven providers having payments suspended between 2012 and 2014, and one provider having all course approvals revoked. Thirdly, under qualified or poorly motivated students were being recruited to courses leading to dropout rates of more than 20 per cent at nine alternative providers, compared to just 6 per cent across UK higher education as a whole (HESA 2018b). Finally, some providers were failing to supply accurate information to BIS, leading to three providers having payments suspended because they supplied inaccurate information about student attendance.

The growth in the number of students studying at private providers had a particular character: 50 per cent of it was accounted for by just five institutions. These providers were among those with high rates of ineligible student loan applications, or high dropout rates, possibly related to inappropriate recruitment practices (National Audit Office 2014). In the words of a Downing Street policy adviser, dropout rates are considered 'one of the few proxies we have of bad provision' (quoted in McGettigan 2016).

The government's response, mediated through BIS, was to instruct the twenty-three fastest growing alternative providers to stop recruiting publicly funded students, and in 2014/15 student number controls were introduced. Total student support paid in 2014/15 fell to £417 million. Between 2012/13 and 2014/15, non-continuation rates dropped from 38 per cent to 25 per cent, 15 percentage points higher than publicly funded providers in England, although only three percentage points above the alternative sector's benchmark figure,[1] which is designed to reflect a student population more at risk of non-completion. A revised system of oversight was also imposed on the sector (National Audit Office 2017).

Removing Barriers to Entry

The reintroduction in 2014 of a cap on the number of students private providers in receipt of public funds could recruit, clearly restricted growth. However, attempts to expand the alternative higher education sector have involved increasing access not only to income streams but also to social or cultural signifiers under state control.

The titles 'University' and 'University College' are legally protected: granted by royal charter prior to 1992, and by the Privy Council between 1992 and April 2018 (Privy Council 2017). The University of Buckingham, founded in 1973 as a University College and incorporated as a University ten years later, was the first private university in the UK. It has grown steadily in recent years: between 2007 and 2017 its student population doubled to 2,603, much of growth put down to the establishment of two new schools: Education and Medicine. Buckingham also introduced two-year accelerated degree programmes, and multiple course entry points staggered throughout the academic year (QAA 2012, 2017).

A series of educational reforms implemented from 2004 onwards aimed to increase the presence of new providers in the higher education system. These saw the removal of several requirements necessary for the award of the title 'University'. The long-standing identification of a university with research – as an institution undertaking research – was decoupled: staff would no longer be required to undertake research, nor were institutions required to offer research degrees in order to award taught degrees, effectively extending degree-awarding powers to private higher education institutions. Institutions are no longer required to be active in a wide range of disciplines either, opening up the possibility for specialist universities (Bekhradnia 2003; Middlehurst 2016).

A secondary route for awarding the titles 'University' and 'University College' was uncovered. The only recognized route had been through royal charter or latterly the Privy Council. However, these titles are also protected terms under company law, and it transpired they could, legally, be awarded through Companies House legislation as trade names, under the Companies Act, 2006 (Evans 2016a). The College of Law became the University of Law through this route (Willetts 2017).

The ongoing effect of the changes in the regulations led to the establishment of four private universities and four private university colleges: these were pre-existing colleges elevated to the status of a university. One of the long-standing features of the private higher education sector has been the delivery of either subjects or aspects of subjects, which due to their vocational emphasis were not, historically, provided in the traditional university sector. These established colleges were largely concerned with professional or vocational qualifications, such as law, chartered accountancy, business, land management and finance. Private providers were, in this respect, mainstream providers: institutions offering tuition for the qualifications required by regulatory bodies for entrance to specific professions.

The Higher Education and Research Act 2017 marked a renewed attempt to advance the cause of alternative providers, principally by addressing perceived barriers to entry for 'more innovative and flexible institutions'. The intent being to 'streamline the process so that they can get up and running as quickly as possible' (BIS 2016c).

> New and innovative providers offering high quality higher education continue to face significant and disproportionate challenges to establishing themselves in the sector. (BIS 2016a: 9, para 11)

The Competition and Markets Authority, a government agency promoting competition for the benefit of consumers both within and outside the UK, and quoted in *Success as a Knowledge Economy* (BIS 2016a: para 15), identified the restrictions on degree-awarding powers as a significant potential barrier to new entrants. The government also identified an opportunity, founded on a faith in the ineluctable effects of competition rather than any evidence, to realize a series of positive outcomes.

> Making it easier for these providers to enter and expand will help drive up teaching standards overall; enhance the life chances of students; drive economic growth; and be a catalyst for social mobility. (BIS 2016a: para 11)

The prospective legislation was also a means of addressing a series of purported deficiencies or failings identified in the public higher education sector including the under-presentation of disadvantaged young people; inflexible courses; poor innovation; skill shortages in the wider economy; and student dissatisfaction (Fielden and Middlehurst 2017; BIS 2016a:7, para 5).

The government pledged to introduce a more flexible use of degree-awarding powers. New providers would be able to award foundation or taught degrees when they first started operating, albeit on an initial three-year probationary basis, rather than after four years of successfully delivering higher education programmes.

The White Paper was also concerned to grant swifter access to the title 'University', and allow 'smaller and niche providers the prestige that comes from a "University" title' by removing the 'artificial' student numbers barrier completely, and allowing the title to be available to any institution with bachelor's degree-awarding powers (BIS 2016a:10, para 14). Theoretically, six years after an institution was founded it could be awarded the title 'University', or opt for the title 'University College' (BIS 2016a:28/29, Box 1.2; p. 30, para 19).

To realize these changes, the authority to grant and remove degree-awarding powers and 'University' titles, including those bestowed by royal charter, were relocated from the Privy Council to the OfS, which under the Higher Education and Research Act, 2017 replaced HEFCE.

In April 2018, in the opening weeks of the OfS's existence, a private 'University Campus' and a private 'University Academy' were established. The first title was granted to UCFB: it is now known as the University Campus of Football Business; the second to a prospective provider, not due to begin teaching until September 2019, but also in the business of football – Academy 92 (UA92).

The precise status of these titles and the institutions that hold them is not entirely clear. Neither institution held or was granted degree-awarding powers, and retention of the title University, whatever its suffix, depends on a continued relation with a validating authority. A Department for Education spokesperson stated: 'The term "university" is protected by law and strictly controlled. Higher education providers may apply to use a term such as university centre or campus in their name if they are in partnership with a university and are delivering degree-level courses' (DfE, quoted in Morgan 2018a).

Criticism has been levelled at this approach. Gordon Marsden, Labour's then shadow minister (Education), said that the government was showing 'contempt for the long-established requirements for university title' and risked 'damaging the reputation of our higher education sector' (Marsden, quoted in Morgan 2018a).

Removing Barriers to Entry: Consequences for the Private Sector

There have been hints that the changes to higher education will open the way for an infusion of foreign based capital into the alternative sector.

> Briefings to the press have indicated that large US institutions and corporations, such as Google and Facebook, may be enticed into the English sector by opportunities that are not available in the States, or Middle and Far East branch campuses. (The press release though concentrated on the much less disruptive University Campus Suffolk and a new HEI in Hereford.) (McGettigan 2016)

Rendering the title 'University' more accessible may also have been intended to promote investment in the sector. There is some evidence that this has occurred, but perhaps not in the way anticipated: large-scale investment has been concentrated on buying and selling existing institutions, rather than establishing new ones. BPP University, for example, originally a school specializing in accountancy, has been owned, through BPP Holdings Ltd, by a US-based for-profit education service provider, Apollo Global, since in 2009, which acquired it for 'over £303 million' (Connelly, 2016). Apollo Global is a segment of Apollo Education Group, Inc., itself now owned by a group of private equity investors bought at a cost of $1.14 billion (Smith 2017).

The College of Law, following a Byzantine restructuring, was flipped from not for-profit to a for-profit institution in 2012; later the same year, it was awarded university status, becoming the University of Law. It has since been bought – for £200 million – and sold – for an undisclosed sum – by Montagu Private Equity. It is now owned by the Netherlands-based Global University Systems (GUS); so too are a further nine UK private educational institutions. These include Arden University, which had previously been known as Resource Development International Ltd (RDI) and specializes in online delivery (Ames 2015). It was bought for £9.3 million becoming a subsidiary of the US-based Capella Education Company in 2011, then sold to GUS in 2016 for £11.5 million (Business Wire 2011; Education Investor Global 2016).

The New College of the Humanities (NCH), a private provider incorporated in 2010 and vying for degree-awarding powers but struggling financially, has been the subject of a planned acquisition by the private non-profit US-based college Northeastern (fee undisclosed) (Morgan 2018b; Redden 2018). NCH, effectively a small-scale liberal arts college with an Oxbridge style one-to-one tuition system, is credited with being a prime exemplar of the kind of alternative provider the government wanted to see thrive. However, it continues to be dependent on a shareholder loan, and its student numbers – around 200 – are insufficient to meet its operating costs. Critically, NCH had been seeking either new investment or a buyer since 2014 (Morgan 2018b). The implication is that the private sector may well be dependent on international investment if it is to expand, or even, in some cases, remain viable.

The importance of international investment may have unintended consequences. Large-scale investment originating largely from beyond the UK could concentrate provision in the hands of a few multi-provider owners, and effectively dilute the competition the government is keen to have course through the higher education sector. Concerns that this is occurring in the private sector have already been raised: GUS now has a concentration of private creative media providers after recently acquiring the failing London College of Creative Media (Boyd and Kernohan 2018).

The ambition to infuse private providers with prestige, stemming from the acquisition of the title 'University', marks a point where the supposed positive attributes of even a highly competitive new provider may dissolve.

> Higher education operates as a 'positional good' in which some student places offer better social status and lifetime opportunities than others. … The acid test is that when faced by choice between a prestigious university with known indifference to undergraduate teaching and a lesser institution offering better classroom support nearly everyone opts for prestige. (Marginson 2006: 3)

The issues of institutional prestige and reputation are as live in the private sector as in the public. A survey of students in UK private higher education institutions found the reputation of the provider was the most significant factor in students' choice of institution, rated as important by 87 per cent of respondents (Hughes et al. 2013; Middlehurst 2016). Marginson's observations, applied to new providers, is that even where they do offer beneficial and innovative schemes, or higher quality teaching, they will confront a relative deficit in prestige compared to at least some established providers. Acquiring the title of 'University' will only partly address this lack of prestige, if at all. Providers are often abandoned by students for more prestigious counterparts when there is an opportunity to do so: as a consequence, efficiencies and innovations tend to go unnoticed (Quiggin 2014).

The government has claimed that increasing alternative provision will 'lead to high-quality teaching, and staff earning promotion for teaching ability rather than research alone' (BIS 2011 quoted in Evans 2016b, p. 11). This assertion is partly based on an assumption that teaching is subordinated to the demands of research in traditional public institutions. Yet there are doubts about the likelihood of alternative providers delivering the innovation and greater value educational programmes that would challenge incumbent providers.

> There appears currently to be a policy discourse favouring disruption innovation and 'challenger institutions' in the UK HE field. This literature suggests challengers may provide acceptable rather than outstanding levels of quality but operate with lower costs and may be attractive to traditionally under-served populations that cannot afford elite products. (Ferlie and Trenholm 2018: 232)

The outcomes for graduates of private higher education institutions show little evidence of students having experienced 'high quality teaching'. A 2013 survey of students enrolled in privately funded higher education providers found in a third of providers half their students had failed to find graduate level jobs, and for three-quarters of providers less than half of their students went on to further study. The lowest figure with respect to either of these measures in the public sector was 78 per cent, with a sector wide figure of over 90 per cent, although the two populations may not be directly comparable (Hughes et al. 2013; Middlehurst 2016).

Restructuring of Official Oversight of Higher Education

Impending changes to the sector's regulation in England will, for the first time, impose a common framework on both public and private providers. Providers that register with the OfS gain access to public funding; can recruit and get visas for international students; and apply for degree-awarding powers and the university title. Registered providers are assigned to one of two categories: approved (fee cap) and approved (Office for Students 2018).

It is estimated that of the likely 390 approved (fee cap) providers, 57 will be private (BIS 2016b). These private providers will have their fees (and loans) capped at the same level as public providers, currently £9,250 per annum, and be eligible for public grants for teaching and research. The increased access to public funds and identical regulatory oversight is likely to bring at least some of the 57 private providers closer to mainstream higher education. For-profit institutions in particular are likely to attract greater investment while demonstrating direct comparability in terms of quality standards and performance indicators with more established mainstream providers.

The second regulatory category, approved providers, is projected to be composed entirely of 88 private providers. These providers will have uncapped fees but no entitlement to direct public funding for teaching or research, while their students will have restricted access to student finance: they will only be eligible for tuition fee loans worth up to £6,125 per annum (DfE 2017).

Most private providers active in England, some 600, will not be registered at all with the OfS: they will continue to remain an unknown quantity, and, essentially, unregulated (Fielden and Middlehurst 2017; Hillman 2017). A proposed 'basic category' that could have included many of these was abandoned by the OfS due to concerns that mere registration could be interpreted by students as conferring a degree of quality the OfS could not guarantee (Boyd 2018; Kernohan 2017).

The new regulatory system for higher education is likely to propel a small proportion of private providers towards the mainstream, while effectively distancing the vast majority.

Conclusion

The recent history of private, particularly for-profit, providers indicates they may occupy a position of increasing significance in mainstream UK higher education as a destination for non-traditional students, as has long been the case in the United States. This trend was already evident during the period of uncapped recruitment.

There have been a series of policy initiative designed to capitalize on the competitive nature of for-profit enterprises, along with a systematic removal of barriers to entry for new providers to help clear some obstacles to entry. However, it remains unclear how many potential private providers will emerge to take advantage of the reordered landscape and compete with public providers in a densely populated market place. A winnowing out of public providers through underfunding may create space. But, private providers are likely to be interested in the provision of low-cost and popular courses, such as business and management and social sciences, or specialist courses, and hence may continue to occupy only part of mainstream higher education. Consequently, they are likely to find they are competing with each other as much as with public providers, due to similar curricula and levels of prestige, hence raising the probability of market exit.

Private providers that take advantage of the removal of barriers but ultimately prove to be under resourced might provide the building blocks for a more consolidated presence in mainstream higher education. Buying and incorporating failing private and even public providers, and then forming an integrated conglomerate may prove to be a means of establishing a presence in mainstream higher education or maintaining one.

Note

1 Reported by the NAO as a benchmark, this figure is in fact an average, not to be confused with the benchmark rates produced by HESA in the UK Performance Indicators.

References

Ames, J. (2015), *The University of Law Has Been Sold for the Second Time in Three Years*. Retrieved 19 March 2018, from https://www.legalcheek.com/2015/06/the-university-of-law-has-been-sold-for-the-second-time-in-three-years/

Bekhradnia, B. (2003), *Implications of the Government's Proposals for University Title: Or What Is a University?* (No. 5), London: HEPI. Retrieved from http://www.hepi.ac.uk/2003/11/01/implications-of-the-governments-proposals-for-university-title-or-what-is-a-university/

Bekhradnia, B. and Beech, D. (2018), *Demand for Higher Education to 2030* (No. 105), HEPI. Retrieved from https://www.hepi.ac.uk/2018/03/15/demand-higher-education-2030/

BIS (2011), *Higher Education: Students at the Heart of the System*, London: TSO.

BIS (2016a), *Success as a Knowledge Economy: Teaching Excellence, Social Mobility and Student Choice*, London: BIS. Retrieved from https://www.gov.uk/government/publications/higher-education-success-as-a-knowledge-economy-white-paper

BIS (2016b), *Impact Assessment: Higher Education and Research Bill* (No. BIS/16/264), London: BIS. Retrieved from https://www.gov.uk/government/uploads/system/uploads/attachment_data/file/524517/bis-16-264-he-research-bill-impact-assessment.pdf

BIS (2016c), *New Universities to Deliver Choice and Opportunity for Students*: Press release. Retrieved 31 May 2018, from https://www.gov.uk/government/news/new-universities-to-deliver-choice-and-opportunity-for-students

Boyd, C. (2018), 'Regulatory Framework 2.0 - What You Need to Know'. Retrieved October 5, 2018, from Wonkhe website: https://wonkhe.com/blogs/regulatory-framework-2-0-what-you-need-to-know/

Boyd, C. and Kernohan, D. (2018), *What Happens When an Alternative Provider Falls into Administration?* Retrieved 14 August 2018, from https://wonkhe.com/blogs/what-happens-when-an-alternative-provider-falls-into-administration/

Business Wire (2011), *Capella Education Company Acquires Resource Development International Ltd*. Retrieved 2 August 2018, from https://www.businesswire.com/news/home/20110715005369/en/Capella-Education-Company-Acquires-Resource-Development-International

Connelly, T. (2016), *BPP Law School Owner Apollo Education to Be Sold for £760 Million*. Retrieved 19 March 2018, from https://www.legalcheek.com/2016/02/bpp-owner-apollo-education-sold-for-760-million/

DfE (2017), *Accelerated Degree Courses: Consultation Assessment of Impact* (No. DFE-00319-2017). Retrieved from DfE website: https://www.google.com/search?q=Accelerated+Degree+Courses%3A+Consultation&ie=utf-8&oe=utf-8&client=firefox-b-e

Education Investor Global (2016), *Global University Systems Acquires Arden University for £11.5m*. Retrieved 2 August 2018, from http://www.educationinvestor.co.uk/showarticle.aspx?ID=5599&AspxAutoDetectCookieSupport=1

Evans, G. R. (2016a), 'Alternative Providers of Higher Education: What Are the Risks?' *Higher Education Review*, 49 (1): 5–25.

Evans, G. R. (2016b), 'Speedy Entrances and Sharp Exits: Letting in More Alternative Providers'. Retrieved 13 August 2018, from http://cdbu.org.uk/speedy-entrances-and-sharp-exits-letting-in-more-alternative-providers/

Ferlie, E. and Trenholm, S. (2018), 'Exploring New Organisational Forms in English Higher Education: A Think Piece', *Higher Education*, 1–17. https://doi.org/10.1007/s10734-018-0269-7

Fielden, J. and Middlehurst, R. (2017), *Alternative Providers of Higher Education: Issues for Policymakers* (No. 90), HEPI. Retrieved from http://www.hepi.ac.uk/wp-content/uploads/2017/01/Hepi_The-alternative-providers-of-higher-education-Report-90-04_01_17-Screen2.pdf

HEFCE (2014), *England Higher Education System*. Retrieved 20 August 2018, from http://www.euroeducation.net/prof/ukco.htm

HESA (2018a), *Higher Education Student Statistics: UK, 2016/17 – Subjects Studied*. Retrieved 11 July 2018, from https://www.hesa.ac.uk/news/11-01-2018/sfr247-higher-education-student-statistics/subjects

HESA (2018b), *Non-continuation Summary: UK Performance Indicators 2016/17*. Retrieved 28 November 2018, from https://www.hesa.ac.uk/news/08-03-2018/non-continuation-summary

Hillman, N. (2017), *Four Reasons Why the Higher Education and Research Act (2017) Needs Supplementing*. Retrieved 20 August 2018, from https://www.hepi.ac.uk/2017/11/28/four-reasons-higher-education-research-act-2017-will-need-followed-legislation/

H.M. Government (2017), *Higher Education and Research Act 2017*. Retrieved 19 July 2017, from http://www.legislation.gov.uk/ukpga/2017/29/contents/enacted/data.htm

Hughes, T., Porter, A., Jones, S. and Sheen, J. (2013), *Privately Funded Providers of Higher Education in the UK*, London. Retrieved from https://www.gov.uk/government/uploads/system/uploads/attachment_data/file/207128/bis-13-900-privately-funded-providers-of-higher-education-in-the-UK.pdf

Hunt, S. A. and Boliver, V. (2019), *Private Providers of Higher Education in the UK: Mapping the Terrain*. CGHE Working Papers, London: CGHE.

Hunt, S. A., Callender, C. and Parry, G. (2016), *The Entry and Experience of Private Providers of Higher Education in Six Countries*, London: UCL IOE CGHE. Retrieved from http://www.researchcghe.org/publications/the-entry-and-experience-of-private-providers-of-higher-education-in-six-countries/

Kernohan, D. (2017), *A Game of Risk*. Retrieved October 5, 2018, from Wonkhe website: https://wonkhe.com/blogs/a-game-of-risk/

Marginson, S. (2006), *Dynamics of National and Global Competition in Higher Education* (Vol. 52). Retrieved from http://link.springer.com/10.1007/s10734-004-7649-x

McGettigan, A. (2016), *The Challengers (and Challenges) in Higher Education Market Reform*. Retrieved 29 May 2018, from https://wonkhe.com/blogs/analysis-the-challengers-and-challenges-market/

Middlehurst, R. (2016), 'Privately Funded Higher Education Providers in the UK: The Changing Dynamic of the Higher Education Sector', in M. Shah and C. S. Nair (eds), *A Global Perspective on Private Higher Education*, 81–95, London: Chandos Publishing.

Morgan, J. (2018a), *DfE Accused of 'Contempt' for Rules in 'Football University' Move*. Retrieved 23 May 2018, from https://www.timeshighereducation.com/fr/news/dfe-accused-contempt-rules-football-university-move

Morgan, J. (2018b), *Northeastern Set to Take over New College of the Humanities*. Retrieved 27 November 2018, from https://www.timeshighereducation.com/news/northeastern-set-take-over-new-college-humanities

National Audit Office (2014), *Investigation into Financial Support for Students at Alternative Higher Education Providers*, London: The National Audit Office. Retrieved from https://www.nao.org.uk/report/investigation-financial-support-students-alternative-higher-education-providers-2/

National Audit Office (2017), *Follow-Up on Alternative Higher Education Providers* (No. 411), Department of Education.

Office for Students (2018), *Securing Student Success: Regulatory Framework for Higher Education in England*. Retrieved from https://www.officeforstudents.org.uk/publications/securing-student-success-regulatory-framework-for-higher-education-in-england/

Privy Council (2017), *Higher Education*. Retrieved 25 April 2017, from https://privycouncil.independent.gov.uk/work-of-the-privy-council-office/higher-education/

QAA (2012), *University of Buckingham: Institutional Review by the Quality Assurance Agency for Higher Education* (No. RG 1041 11/12), Gloucester, UK: QAA. Retrieved from http://www.qaa.ac.uk/en/ReviewsAndReports/Documents/University%20of%20Buckingham/University-of-Buckingham-IRENI-12.pdf

QAA (2017), *Higher Education Review (Alternative Providers) of the University of Buckingham* (No. QAA2052-R8335). Retrieved from http://www.qaa.ac.uk/en/ReviewsAndReports/Documents/University%20of%20Buckingham/University-of-Buckingham-HER-AP-17.pdf

Quiggin, J. (2014), *Post-School Education in Australia: The Case Against Deregulation*. Submission to: Senate Education and Employment Legislation Committee Inquiry into the Higher Education and Research Reform Amendment Bill 2014.

Redden, E. (2018), *Northeastern Plans to Acquire Humanities College in London*. Retrieved 11 December 2018, from https://www.insidehighered.com/news/2018/11/14/northeastern-plans-acquire-humanities-college-london

Shury, J., Adams, L., Barnes, M., Huntley Hewitt, J. and Oozeerally, T. (2016), *Understanding the Market of Alternative Higher Education Providers and their Students in 2014*, London: BIS. Retrieved from https://www.gov.uk/government/publications/alternative-providers-of-higher-education-the-market-and-students-in-2014

Smith, B. (2017), *Apollo Education Group Acquired for $1.14bn*. Retrieved 19 March 2018, from https://thepienews.com/news/apollo-education-group-acquired-apollo-global-management/

The Committee of Public Accounts (2015), *Financial Support for Students at Alternative Higher Education Providers: Forty-First Report of Session 2014-15 Report, Together with the Formal Minutes Relating to the Report* (No. 811), London: House of Commons.

Willetts, D. (2017), *A University Education*, Oxford and New York: Oxford University Press.

Part VII

Public and Social Benefit

15

Undergraduate Education in South Africa

To What Extent Does It Support Personal and Public Good?

Paul Ashwin and Jennifer M. Case

Introduction

Examining the contribution that undergraduate education makes to South African society involves engaging in debates about the anticipated and actual relations between higher education and society. These debates often focus on the contribution that higher education makes to the public good. Marginson (2011) helpfully distinguishes between public goods, which are non-rivalrous and non-excludable, and the more normative notion of the (singular) public good which highlights collective endeavours and higher education's role in developing and democratizing societies, moving beyond the aggregative impacts on individual personal goods. It is the latter notion of public good that we use in this chapter, with our focus on the impact of undergraduate education on society.

Many writers on this topic note that the concept of 'public' has meanings related to time and place, which means that how higher education relates to the public good will need to be reinvented in new times and new places. Key writers have noted while the concept of the public might seem somewhat diminished in present times, contemporary political and social challenges make it more, not less, important that this idea be resuscitated, especially in relation to higher education. Nixon (2011) points to core aspects of the nature of higher education which signal this role – its focus on the development of individual capability, of collective reasoning, and a broad fostering of a sense of purpose among its participants. Mbembe (2015), writing in an African context, calls for the urgent rehabilitation of the public space, especially in universities. He rejects the contemporary fixation with the market and questions of efficiency, and argues for a centring on belonging and participation to advance social inclusion.

In this chapter, we seek to understand how higher education supports both the public and personal good. This dual focus is important because the personal benefits of engaging with higher education should not be overlooked, including the intrinsic personal good of participating in higher education in terms of the impact on the individual in terms of knowledge and personal growth, as well as the material benefits. To capture both the public and personal good requires a focus on the relations between higher education, the economy and society. In conceptualizing these relations Allais (2018), drawing on Halliday (2016), makes the distinction between the (frequently conflated) *developmental* and *screening* (signalling) roles of education. While educational perspectives tend to focus on higher education's intrinsic, developmental role, in giving individuals access to knowledge and skills, this can lead to the implicit assumption that individuals' chances in the labour market are determined by these acquisitions – that is, the more skilled individuals in society, the more highly paid jobs there will be. However, this is not typically the case because the labour market does not necessarily grow in proportion to available skills (Brown, Lauder and Ashton 2010). An expansion in education can increase the competition for limited jobs, and here the screening function of higher education comes into play in terms of sorting individuals in order to support the making of employment decisions.

The focus on the developmental role of higher education also informs the view that higher education can play a role in transforming society and in decreasing inequality. However, there is evidence that, while higher education might provide better opportunities for some individuals, overall it can be shown mostly to *reproduce* patterns of inequality in society (Cantwell, Marginson and Smolentseva 2018). Recognizing this is important in order to resist the temptation to overstate the impacts of higher education on society and to take seriously Clark's (2008) framing of universities as 'multi-purpose organizations' (p. 217). Mamdani (1993), in a speech to South African academics on the eve of the democratic transition, signalled clearly the risks of subverting the role of higher education fully to that of the African state, noting the lessons from universities in newly independent African states some decades earlier. This became framed in South Africa as the tension between equity and development in higher education (cf. Cloete and Moja 2005).

We therefore need to develop better responses to the difficult questions that arise from the tension between the reproductive and transformative potential of higher education. In this chapter, we first introduce the South African higher education context and then outline the project that has shaped our thinking and argument in this chapter. We then present the understandings the project has generated about the relations between higher education and society in South Africa.

The South African Higher Education Context

South Africa is a country defined by extreme inequality, which is seen throughout its society, including higher education. Its history of colonialism and apartheid continues to play a key role in structuring its present. Higher education is situated within a broader socio-economic context which includes significantly high levels of unemployment (most recently recorded as 29.0 per cent), particularly youth unemployment, with 32.3 per cent of young people not in education, employment or training – the NEETs (Statistics South Africa 2019). For the majority of young people, schooling outcomes are poor, and this is arguably the major impediment for access to higher education. In terms of post-schooling options, the vocational sector is weak, and thus for many young people higher education is considered the only route to social mobility. There has been a dramatic growth of enrolments in higher education since the early 1990s, with the undergraduate population doubling from that point to a total of just over a million students at present. However, concern has been raised over the academic performance outcomes that have been recorded in terms of graduate rates: only 55 per cent of students who register for three-year degrees at contact institutions have graduated five years after starting (Council on Higher Education 2018). Participation rates, in terms of the proportion of twenty- to twenty-four-year-olds attending higher education, has increased slightly for black African youth and now approaches 20 per cent, but still is starkly different to the 50 per cent participation rate for white youth (even though this has slightly declined).

The public higher education sector currently comprises twenty-six public universities, classified by the Department of Higher Education and Training as twelve 'traditional' universities, eight universities of technology and six comprehensive universities. The latter two categories of institution offer both diplomas and degrees.

Recently significant student protests have rocked the South African higher education system. The two core cries of the 2015/16 student protest movement – #RhodesMust Fall (RMF) and #FeesMustFall (FMF) – exposed a disconnect between the policy-based (and widely perceived) core role of higher education in facilitating social mobility and redress, and the realities facing many young people across the country (Mathebula and Calitz 2018). The protests highlighted barriers both at the point of access and within higher education, for those who were successful in gaining a place at university. This raised afresh questions about the ways in which higher education can transform society and the extent to which it has a role in reproducing existing inequalities. Two key challenges highlighted by Walker (2018a) illustrate the importance of this task. First, there is the challenge of the difference between the aspirations of South African school leavers and the current provision of places in undergraduate higher education, the issue of 'availability'. Wangenge-Ouma and Carpentier (2018) place the tuition fee debates in an international context with an increasing shift to cost-sharing, and note that the recent decision by the South African government to reverse aspects of cost-sharing was done in order to alleviate political pressure, and might well have unintended consequences for the sustainability of the overall system. A second challenge is that South Africa has a highly stratified higher education system, which limits its capacity to be an engine for social mobility. There are disparities in who has access to the most prestigious universities, which are seen to offer the highest economic and social returns. As such, even for students who gain an undergraduate degree, their possibilities for engaging in further higher education and entering the world of work are significantly structured by social background and geographical location.

These challenges have contributed to new patterns of inequality. The black middle class has grown substantially and thus scholars point to the increased salience of class (and socio-economic status) in structuring life opportunities, in addition to the enduring legacy of race (Southall 2016). The debate has thus expanded beyond that of access, by drawing attention to the way in which the experiences and academic success of students in higher education differ by their social and schooling background, as well as questions about the kinds of knowledge that universities offer students access to. At their core, these debates centre on questions around the purpose and focus of the university in a democratic society, as well as perceived uncertainties about employment prospects for graduates. They also raise the difficult question of whether we might be overestimating the power of higher education to change society.

The 'Pathways to Personal and Public Good' Project

This chapter is based on the Economic Social Research Council, UK, and National Research Foundation, SA, funded collaborative project 'Pathways to Personal and Public Good': understanding access to, student experiences of and outcomes from South African undergraduate higher education.[1] It was a collaboration between the Centre for Global Higher Education and a cluster of NRF projects in South Africa located at the University of Cape Town, Rhodes University and the University of the Free State.

This project examined the pathways from an undergraduate education to personal and public goods in South Africa through three interlinked themes: access to higher education, students' experiences while studying and the economic and social contributions made by university graduates. Although questions of access are crucially important in their own right, any examination of the transformative potential of higher education must also consider the *experiences* of students within higher education. There is a pressing need to understand the forms of curriculum, pedagogy and social experiences that support 'epistemological access' for all students who enter higher education. In terms of *graduate outcomes*; there remain concerns about the availability of graduate employment, particularly for certain groups, as outlined in the reviews by Case, Marshall and Fongwa (2018) and Fongwa, Marshall and Case (2018). Race continues to structure graduate access to the workplace, even though overall the outcomes are strong.

The project outcomes are discussed in depth in the edited book *Higher Education Pathways: South African Undergraduate Education and the Public Good* published by open-access publishers African Minds (Ashwin and Case 2018).

The approach of the project was informed by the need to move beyond any individual research project to consider what the collective body of literature as a whole could tell us about South African undergraduate education and its role in creating pathways to the personal and public good. The tendency for literatures to exist in silos is a major barrier to developing a shared sense of what we know about higher education in South Africa and internationally.

As we worked together as a project team, it became clear that, while there was a rich literature on higher education in South Africa, this literature is partial. In particular, it tends to focus on the pathways through access, student experience and graduate outcomes in historically advantaged institutions rather than in other institutions (Ashwin et al. 2018). There was also a tendency to treat the experiences of poor, black and rural students as a single set of experiences rather than exploring the diversity of experiences that are brought together under these descriptors (Masehela 2018). These challenges were further exacerbated by the lack of publicly available data on higher education in South Africa, especially in relation to the limited statistical data presently available for economic or sociological analyses of South African society. As it stands, the literature is dominated by single institution studies, as there is currently limited access to publicly managed and available data across the system.

The project also highlighted the importance of comparative research in developing a better understanding of higher education systems both in South Africa and internationally. Some of the researchers developed useful illustrative comparisons: Carpentier, Lebeau and Välimaa (2018) looked at access across the UK, Finnish, French, Nigerian and Senagalese systems, to form a backdrop for South African debates on the issue; Pedrosa and Kloot (2018) compared the engineering education systems in Brazil and South Africa; and Oanda and Ngcwangu (2018) consider graduate employment across Sub-Saharan Africa. Comparisons can operate at different scales (e.g. comparing institutions or comparing higher education systems) and comparisons can focus on different dimensions of higher education. The problem with a lack of comparative research is that it tends to limit thinking to a particular context and so makes it more difficult to discern how things might be different than they are. It can also lead to a tendency to compare what is currently happening with an ideal rather than understanding how similar challenges are managed in different settings. It seems possible that the tendency for South African research to see the South African higher education context as unique ('South African exceptionalism') is more a product of this lack of comparative studies rather than the uniqueness of the challenges faced in South African higher education.

Relations between Undergraduate Education and Society in South Africa

In the rest of this chapter, we will focus on what the project illuminated about the relations between undergraduate education and society in South Africa. Most evident from our collaborative work was the diversity and complexity of students' pathways through higher education. This complexity stemmed from differences in socio-economic background, institutional context, curriculum choice, student aspirations, teaching and learning, and, following graduation, opportunities for employment. We identified not only multiple barriers experienced by students but also opportunities for personal and societal transformation. In thinking about what our work highlighted about the relations between undergraduate education and society, we present our findings regarding the meaning of the notion of the public good in South Africa, ways of thinking about the South

African higher education system and the relations between the transformative and reproductive functions of higher education in South Africa.

The Meaning of Public Good in South Africa

Given its centrality in the underlying thinking of the project, it was unsurprising that we spent a considerable amount of time discussing the particular meaning of the notion of 'public good' in relation to South African higher education. The public good was a concept developed in the Global North and a question driving the explorations in the project was the extent to which the concept needed to be adapted to fit with contexts in the Global South and how much needed to remain the same in order for the concept to be recognizable. Deem and McCowan (2018) show how much of this conceptualization stems from the work of Habermas in relation to his notion of the public sphere – and the possibilities for universities to be an arena for the discussion of public problems.

Walker (2018b) argues for a capability approach for conceptualizing the public good of higher education in South African universities, based on its humanizing ethic and its focus on whether opportunities are fairly distributed. It foregrounds participation by considering what students are able to do and become through their engagement with higher education.

In thinking about how the notion of the public good applied in the South African context, the project also discussed the importance of recognizing the relative openness of South African society and the value that it assigns to academic freedom, compared to many developing country contexts. The importance of these conditions in underpinning a productive notion of the relation between higher education and the public good might be seen to push in the direction of a universal concept of the public good; the project rather aimed to identify underpinning conditions that are required for higher education institutions to play a role in supporting the public good. To develop this further, however, will require comparative research examining how higher education contributes to the public good in a range of national settings, including its international impact.

In addition to the work on interrogating the meaning of the notion of 'public good', the project carried out allied work on related concepts in the higher education literature. Ashwin and Komljenovic (2018) consider how the South African literature conceptualizes the transformation of student identity through the experience of higher education, and how this relates to the international literature on the topic. What these researchers find is that while the broad concepts are relevant, in the South African context identity transformation cannot be seen separately from students' broader lives and societies outside of higher education. In similar work, Schendel (2018) looks at the research that has been conducted on the relationship between institutional cultures and pedagogical change in South Africa, and finds that this literature has useful contributions in showing both the inherent sluggishness of change and the possibilities for dynamic impacts in contexts of dramatic broader social change. Finally, on this topic, Hlengwa, McKenna and Njovane (2018) analyse the South African literature on student experiences, and find that conceptually this has been rather limited.

Understanding the Higher Education System

In thinking about the relations between higher education and society, there is a tendency to consider the higher education system as somehow homogenous. As we discussed earlier, the South African system is highly differentiated, comprising institutions with very different histories and access to material resources. However, in shifting from a system that was differentiated by race, there has been an understandable avoidance of conceptualizing other forms of differentiation in the system because of the fear that it would simply entrench the low status and poor resource levels in many historically black institutions.

However, with the attempt to move past inherited inequalities in South Africa with a homogenized policy, there is the risk of overlooking institutions' distinct institutional histories, cultures and values, and resources and needs. The tendency to think of a single undifferentiated system in South Africa obscures the fact that, as we discussed earlier, we know far more about higher education in historically advantaged institutions than we do about historically disadvantaged institutions.

While there is something inclusive about positioning higher education as a single system, the danger of this is that it underplays the inequalities between institutions; moreover, it does not allow for the potential strengths inherent in systems that are differentiated deliberately according to mission. Naidoo and Ranchod (2018) trace the policy trajectory across the full democratic period and note that what is needed for social and economic development, but has not even been properly conceptualized, is a system comprising a range of institutions with high quality but different academic and vocational choices. Institutions have different identities and material resources which are 'flattened' (and even ignored) by homogenizing discourses of institutional excellence. The work in this project highlighted the need to find a more inclusive 'both/and' way of discussing the higher education system in South Africa so that the common mission of making transformative knowledge accessible to as many people as possible is recognized but so too is the value of distinctive institutional missions, with appropriate allocations of public funding.

The Entwined Nature of the Reproductive and Transformative Functions of Higher Education

As we discussed earlier, there is an explicit expectation in government policy that higher education will transform society in South Africa. However, it is also important to be clear that much of the attraction of higher education for students and their families is the 'graduate premium' that they expect to receive from engaging with higher education. Thus the reproductive and educative functions of higher education are deeply entwined. The experience of studying at university and the subsequent access it can provide to a graduate career can clearly be hugely personally transformative for individuals and their families. However, graduate premiums are also a clear indicator of inequality because they signal the differences in income between graduates and non-graduates (Marginson 2016). Thus, much of the popular support for higher education, in South Africa and globally, is related to its role in reproducing existing inequalities in society because the support stems from its role in personal rather than societal transformation. Indeed, if higher education was successful in supporting the transformation of society in the way envisaged in policy, then it is likely that graduate premiums would fall, especially in the context of an economy that is not substantially growing. For this not to lead to a sense of disillusionment with higher education, it would appear to be crucial that the societal transformation is underpinned by a personal transformation in students that ensures a commitment to a transformed society.

Therefore, if higher education is expected to play a role in transforming society then this needs to be explicitly considered in the design of university programmes and through additional structures, beyond higher education, that are designed to support this transformation. Here the potentials for transformation are identified at the level of curriculum (Shay and Mkhize 2018), academic staff development (Clarence 2018) and extracurricular activities (Kerr and Leuscher 2018).

Overall the entwined nature of the reproductive and transformative functions of higher education mean that developing a higher education system so that it can play a deliberate role in transforming society is extremely difficult. There are no straightforward or obvious paths to developing a system in this way. Our explorations of the South African higher education system suggest a situation in which many students are personally transformed by their experiences. However, we lack knowledge about students in the least privileged part of the system, and there are currently few signs that higher education has played a central role in systematically transforming South African society.

Conclusion

In conclusion, the Pathways to Personal and Public Good project suggests that there needs to be more extensive and detailed public debate, within and beyond higher education institutions, about the nature of the public good role that higher education is intended to play in South African society. Such debates need to be predicated on a clear understanding of the current higher education system in South Africa and the institutions that make it up. As part of this, far more needs to be known about students' experiences and institutional practices at historically disadvantaged universities. Finally, there is a need to develop a deeper understanding of the entwined nature of the reproductive and transformative impacts of higher education. However, it should be equally clear that such considerations are important not just to South Africa but to any society that seeks its higher education system to play an active role in supporting the development of a fairer society.

Note

1 ESRC project reference: ES/N009894/1; NRF project reference: UID 98365.

References

Allais, S. (2018), 'South African Higher Education, Society and Economy: What Do We Know About the Relationships?', in P. Ashwin and J. M. Case (eds), *Pathways to Personal and Public Good: Access, Experiences and Outcomes of South African Undergraduate Education*, 10–26, Cape Town: African Minds.

Ashwin, P. and Case, J. M. (eds) (2018), *Pathways to Personal and Public Good: Access, Experiences and Outcomes of South African Undergraduate Education*, Cape Town: African Minds.

Ashwin, P. and Komljenovic, J. (2018), 'The Conceptualisation of Students' Personal Transformation Through Their Engagement in South African Undergraduate Education', in P. Ashwin and J. M. Case (eds), *Pathways to Personal and Public Good: Access, Experiences and Outcomes of South African Undergraduate Education*, 125–35, Cape Town: African Minds.

Ashwin, P., Carpentier, V., Case, J. M., Marshall, D., McCowan, T., McKenna, S., Naidoo, R., Schendel, R. and Walker, M. (2018), 'What Have We Learned About Pathways to the Public Good from South African Undergraduate Education?', in P. Ashwin and J. M. Case (eds), *Pathways to Personal and Public Good: Access, Experiences and Outcomes of South African Undergraduate Education*, 291–8, Cape Town: African Minds.

Brown, P., Lauder, H. and Ashton, D. (2010), *The Global Auction: The Broken Promises of Education, Jobs, and Incomes*, Oxford: Oxford University Press.

Cantwell, B., Marginson, S. and Smolentseva, A. (eds) (2018), *High Participation Systems of Higher Education*, Oxford: Oxford University Press.

Carpentier, V., Lebeau, Y. and Välimaa, J. (2018), 'International Perspectives on Equality of Higher Education Opportunities: Models and Strategies for Accessibility and Availability', in P. Ashwin and J. M. Case (eds), *Pathways to Personal and Public Good: Access, Experiences and Outcomes of South African Undergraduate Education*, 95–111, Cape Town: African Minds.

Case, J. M. , Marshall, D. and Fongwa, S. (2018), 'Post-graduation Trajectories of Young South Africans', in P. Ashwin and J. M. Case (eds), *Pathways to Personal and Public Good: Access, Experiences and Outcomes of South African Undergraduate Education*, 232–44, Cape Town: African Minds.

Clarence, S. (2018), 'Understanding Student Experiences Through the Lens of Academic Staff Development Practice and Research', in P. Ashwin and J. M. Case (eds), *Pathways to Personal and Public Good: Access, Experiences and Outcomes of South African Undergraduate Education*, 204–15, Cape Town: African Minds.

Clark, B. R. (2008), *On Higher Education, Selected Writings, 1956–2006*, Baltimore, MD: Johns Hopkins University Press.

Cloete, N. and Moja, T. (2005), 'Transformation Tensions in Higher Education: Equity, Efficiency and Development', *Social Research*, 72 (3): 693–722.

Council on Higher Education (2018), *VitalStats: Public Higher Education, 2016*, Pretoria: Council on Higher Education.

Deem, R. and McCowan, T. (2018), 'Understanding the Role of University Graduates in Society: Which Conception of Public Good?', in P. Ashwin and J. M. Case (eds), *Pathways to Personal and Public Good: Access, Experiences and Outcomes of South African Undergraduate Education*, 61–8, Cape Town: African Minds.

Fongwa, S., Marshall, D. and Case, J. M. (2018), 'Exploring Differences in South African Graduate Outcomes', in P. Ashwin and J. M. Case (eds), *Pathways to Personal and*

Public Good: Access, Experiences and Outcomes of South African Undergraduate Education, 245–59, Cape Town: African Minds.

Halliday, D. (2016), 'Private Education, Positional Goods, and the Arms Race Problem', *Politics, Philosophy & Economics*, 15 (2): 150–69.

Hlengwa, A., McKenna, S. and Njovane, T. (2018), 'The Lenses We Use to Research Student Experiences', in P. Ashwin and J. M. Case (eds), *Pathways to Personal and Public Good: Access, Experiences and Outcomes of South African Undergraduate Education*, 149–62, Cape Town: African Minds.

Kerr, P. and Luescher, T. (2018), 'Students' Experiences of University Life Beyond the Curriculum', in P. Ashwin and J. M. Case (eds), *Pathways to Personal and Public Good: Access, Experiences and Outcomes of South African Undergraduate Education*, 216–31, Cape Town: African Minds.

Masehela, L. (2018), 'The rising Challenge of University Access for Students from Low-Income Families', in P. Ashwin and J. M. Case (eds), *Pathways to Personal and Public Good: Access, Experiences and Outcomes of South African Undergraduate Education*, 165–76, Cape Town: African Minds.

Mamdani, M. (1993), 'University Crisis and Reform: A Reflection on the African Experience', *Review of African Political Economy*, 20 (58): 7–19.

Marginson, S. (2011), 'Higher Education and Public Good', *Higher Education Quarterly*, 65 (4): 411–33.

Marginson, S. (2016), *The Dream Is Over: The Crisis of Clark Kerr's California Idea of Higher Education*, Oakland, CA: University of California Press.

Mathebula, M. and Calitz, T. (2018), '#Feesmustfall: A Media Analysis of Students' Voices on Access to Universities in South Africa', in P. Ashwin and J. M. Case (eds), *Pathways to Personal and Public Good: Access, Experiences and Outcomes of South African Undergraduate Education*, 177–91, Cape Town: African Minds.

Mbembe, A. (2015), 'Decolonizing Knowledge and the Question of the Archive', *Aula magistral proferida*. Unpublished paper available at: https://wiser.wits.ac.za/sites/default/files/private/Achille%20Mbembe%20-%20Decolonizing%20Knowledge%20and%20the%20Question%20of%20the%20Archive.pdf

Naidoo, R. and Ranchod, R. (2018), 'Transformation, the State and Higher Education: Towards a Developmental System of Higher Education in South Africa', in P. Ashwin and J. M. Case (eds), *Pathways to Personal and Public Good: Access, Experiences and Outcomes of South African Undergraduate Education*, 10–26, Cape Town: African Minds.

Nixon, J. (2011), *Higher Education and the Public Good*, London: Continuum.

Oanda, I. and Ngcwangu, S. (2018), 'Destination and Outcome Trends for Graduates from Sub-Saharan African Countries: Implications for South Africa', in P. Ashwin and J. M. Case (eds), *Pathways to Personal and Public Good: Access, Experiences and Outcomes of South African Undergraduate Education*, 260–73, Cape Town: African Minds.

Pedrosa, R. and Kloot, B. (2018), 'Engineering Graduates in South Africa and Brazil: A Common Good Perspective', in P. Ashwin and J. M. Case (eds), *Pathways to Personal and Public Good: Access, Experiences and Outcomes of South African Undergraduate Education*, 274–88, Cape Town: African Minds.

Schendel, R. (2018), 'Understanding the Relationship Between Institutional Cultures and Pedagogical Change', in P. Ashwin and J. M. Case (eds), *Pathways to Personal and Public Good: Access, Experiences and Outcomes of South African Undergraduate Education*, 136–48, Cape Town: African Minds.

Shay, S. and Mkhize, T. (2018), 'Curriculum Transformation: Looking Back and Planning Forward', in P. Ashwin and J. M. Case (eds), *Pathways to Personal and Public Good: Access, Experiences and Outcomes of South African Undergraduate Education*, 192–203, Cape Town: African Minds

Smith, S. and Bauling, A. (2013), 'Aiming for Transformation: Exploring Graduateness in South Africa', *Stellenbosch Law Review*, 24: 601–17.

Southall, R. (2016), '*The New Black Middle Class in South Africa*', Suffolk, UK, Boydell & Brewer.

Statistics South Africa. (2019), *Quarterly Labour Force Survey* , 2: 2019, http://www.statssa.gov.za/publications/P0211/P02112ndQuarter2019.pdf.

Walker, M. (2018a), 'A Multi-Dimensional Approach to Fair Access', in P. Ashwin and J. M. Case (eds), *Pathways to Personal and Public Good: Access, Experiences and Outcomes of South African Undergraduate Education*, 81–94, Cape Town: African Minds.

Walker, M. (2018b), 'Dimensions of Higher Education and the Public Good in South Africa', *Higher Education*, 76 (3): 555–69.

Wangenge-Ouma, G. and Carpentier, V. (2018), 'Subsidy, Tuition Fees and the Challenge of Financing Higher Education in South Africa', in P. Ashwin and J. M. Case (eds), *Pathways to Personal and Public Good: Access, Experiences and Outcomes of South African Undergraduate Education*, 27–43, Cape Town: African Minds.

16

Higher Education in China

Rethinking It as a Common Good

Lin Tian and Nian Cai Liu

Introduction

In 1949 to 1978, the era of planned economy in China, higher education was integrated closely with government. Fully funded without tuition fees, it was considered a pure public good, but resources were limited and the sector developed slowly (Mi and Li 2009). From the 1980s onwards China built a socialist market economy. Governance in higher education began to incorporate social needs and market factors (Wang 2007). Following China's accession to the WTO in 2001, the view of higher education as a service commodity gained ground. Privately funded colleges open to student choice expanded; all institutions, public and private, charged some tuition fees; and there was fierce competition among students for the best places.

This chapter reviews the ideas about higher education and public and common good in China from two sources: academic literature in China, and semi-structured interviews conducted in two universities and government as part of a ten-country research project on higher education as a public good. It also considers the UNESCO idea of education as a common good.

Scholarly Literature

Studies on higher education and public good(s) in China fall into three phases: Between 1998 and 2002, scholars started exploring the issue (Ke 1999). From 2003 to 2008, there was a growing number of studies, centring on issues raised by the profitability, marketization and industrialization of the sector (Lao 2002;

Guo 2005). From 2009 onwards, topics such as the relations between market, government and education, and the public good of private higher education were added (Li 2009a; Mi and Li 2009).

The issues are explored in China through the differing lenses of Western terminology and Chinese concepts. Both discussions have encountered ambiguities generated by China's social transition, which is an incomplete hybrid of state determination and market determination.

Western Concepts

Chinese scholars have focused on the meanings, classifications and externalities of public goods. Most draw on Samuelson's (1954) economic schema to demarcate pure public goods, entailing non-rivalry and non-excludability, from private goods (Li 2002, 2009b). In real life, goods with clear-cut public features are rare, and some scholars, citing Buchanan (1965) and Barzel (1969), identify three groups: pure public goods, quasi-public goods/mixed goods and private goods (Huang 2014; Zhou 2005). Following Buchanan (1965) and Ostrom (1990) others divide quasi-public goods into club goods and common-pool resources (Shen and Xie 2009).

In response to the effects of competition, process and selection in higher education, Chinese scholars fall into three groups. Some maintain higher education is a pure public good (Cheng 2006; Su 2009). Others define public higher education as a public good and private education as a private good (Yang 2007, 2009). A third group see higher education as a quasi-public good with attributes of both (Wang 2007; Li and Guan 2009). In this perspective, prevalent in recent years, higher education has a distinctive public character or responsibility to society and contributes various public goods, while it also produces private benefits such as academic certificates and individual professional skills (Yang and Zhang 2000). Because higher education charges tuition and students compete for places it is more or less excludable and rivalrous. It can be provided by both government in public universities and the market in private and for-profit educational institutions. Most scholars contend that while a limited market element is acceptable, regulation should be primarily by government (Lao 2002; Wang 2007).

The classifications described earlier are based on the natural attributes of goods, excludability and rivalry. Some scholars disagree. Zang and Qu (2002) refer to Marmolo's (1999) constitutional theory of public goods, whereby the nature of goods is determined by whether supply is public or private. For example, a free health-emergency service is a pure public good, up to a point. Congestion occurs when an overwhelming number of people use this service. At that point the service becomes a quasi-public good (non-excludable while somewhat rivalrous). Nevertheless, the government could consciously adjust the elements of excludability and rivalry by providing more hospital services, returning to a pure public good. This suggests that, when classifying goods as public or private, it is impossible to have objective criteria that provide a strict and clear boundary, free from all external influences (Marginson 2018). From this perspective, public goods are essentially determined by politics, and political decisions reflect social, cultural and ideological patterns (Zang and Qu 2002; Ma 2012). Some scholars argue that the appropriate medium is participative public decision-making.

Chinese Concepts

There is a wide array of Chinese translations for the concept of public good(s), including *gong gong wu pin*, *gong gong chan pin* and *gong yong pin*. The first is the most widely known. These translations fail to fully cover the Western meaning of public good(s). Working the other way, from Chinese, when defining the categories to which higher education belongs, *zhun gong gong wu pin* (a quasi-public good) is often used. However, when describing the nature of education and higher education, *gong yi xing* or *gong gong li yi* is often used. The latter represent the long-lasting and intrinsic attributes of higher education, often expressed as contributions to the public good. Additionally, in relation to the contributions of higher education, *gong yi wu pin* is often used. This appears as public goods, public welfare and public benefits in English-language abstracts of the Chinese literature. Chinese scholars can use these expressions interchangeably. Their meaning can be summarized as beneficial products enjoyed by the majority of citizens (Guo 2005; Yang 2004).

In the Chinese context there is a difference between 'a' public good, or public 'goods' in economics, and the more generalized notion of 'the public good', or common good or public interest. The latter refers to the philosophical or political idea of shared benefit at societal level (Morrell 2009). This suggests ambiguity. The overwhelmingly bulk of the literature – including policy documents, laws and decrees – emphasizes higher education's contributions to the public good by virtue of its positive externalities and non-profit nature. On one hand, higher education in China is selective and fee-charging. Also, higher education produces other public goods, such as knowledge. Does this mean that a quasi-public good can contribute to the generalized public good, and also generate specific public goods, under political and cultural influence?

Common Good(s)

In China, 'public goods' includes all mandatory collective activities based on solely common interests, including 'goods (services) of common consumption' (Ma 2012: 6). Public goods are goods for public benefit, produced to public demand and relying on public power realized via consensus and cooperation (Zhang and Qi 2016). This approach coincides with UNESCO's notion of common goods. Both notions suggest goods shared by and beneficial for all or most members of a community, generated by collective and shared participation (Locatelli 2016; Zhang 2015; see chapter 17).

UNESCO states that 'irrespective of any public or private origin', common goods 'are characterised by a binding destination and necessary for the realization of the fundamental rights of all people'. It notes that 'goods of this kind are therefore inherently common in their "production" as well as in their benefits' and 'inherent to the relationships that exist among the members of a society tied together in a collective endeavor' (UNESCO 2015: 77). This approach to common goods steps away from the long-disputed topic of public or private. Further, the notion of common goods may complement that of public goods. A public good is open to free-riding, whereas a common good highlights the collective endeavour of all participants.

Few Chinese scholars have considered this concept of common good(s). Discussion in China in the wake of the 2015 UNESCO report has not dealt with higher education. Some scholars argue that future educational reforms should incorporate the inclusive notion of the global common good (Huang and Tang 2017), moving beyond the implied conflict between private and public education, as policies and regulations based on the notion of public good restrict legitimate contributions made by the growing number of private institutions. Song and Rao (2018) propose that viewing education and knowledge as global common goods, surpassing short-term benefit, helps to form learners in global perspectives and responsibility. Yi (2018) discusses this in relation to moral education in elementary and secondary schools. He suggests that when using the concept of the global common good it is important to strike a balance between global perspective and national identity, cultural diversity and cultural uniqueness.

The Research in China

The semi-structured interviews concerning public and common goods in higher education in China are described more fully elsewhere (Tian and Liu 2019). The three principal research questions were the following:

1. What is the relation between government and higher education in China?
2. How does higher education in China relate to (global) public good(s)?
3. How does higher education in China relate to (global) common good(s)?

Three government people, nine university leaders and twelve academics were interviewed. University interviewees were divided into leaders (L) and academics (A). Interviews were conducted in a top research university (S) and a local university (N), with academic participants from engineering, economics and history. Government interviewees are designated G. Interviews were conducted in Chinese and parts translated into English.

Findings

Government and Higher Education

Interviewees from all three groups saw government as dominant in higher education. There were many references to its role in funding. Government personnel and university leaders saw government in similar terms, describing its role in terms of comprehensive responsibility, and overview functions such as system-level design, strategic planning, development and evaluation focused on quality improvement. 'The government's first function is to have macro control … the second is to give an overall plan for higher education in response to the national strategy', stated a leader at the local university (NL1). 'It acts like a director in a broad way', said one government person, while noting that government also had certain priority policies (G1).

Both government and university leaders also emphasized that universities must exercise autonomy when carrying out their responsibilities. Government personnel noted that university leaders managed human resources inside universities, including promotion and salaries. The tasks of universities in 'talent cultivation' included part determination of student selection, teaching and curriculum design. Universities should apply their 'own philosophy' based on 'what kind of people they hope to educate' (G3). University leaders used almost identical terms and examples when defining university responsibilities. To the government list, university leaders added the organization of fields of knowledge in degree programmes and research, arguing that universities should control the evolution of research.

In many other nations, public authorities, not universities, select students, set academic salaries or specify curricula. How then was the broad mandate of government in China, and its control, reconciled with generous operational university autonomy? The answer is that for both sides in China, university autonomy meant freedom to manage the university while following laws, government policies and national goals. Universities had their own positioning and development strategies, but state and universities shared a common governance culture and were aligned in intent and outcomes. University strategies were closely integrated with state programmes. Relations were sealed by funding, which determined the obligation of public universities to serve country and society.

> The autonomy of a university must conform to the country's social needs … under the country's macro-control. … The degree of autonomy of the university should be compatible with the stage of development of the society and also the ideas of the university administrators. (G1)

> The government has played a dominant role in higher education. China has a powerful government. … There will be a general education plan, and the university's plan must be in accordance with and responsive to this plan. (SL3)

The fact that the government and university leaders expressed such similar views, with no expressed university-government tensions, demonstrates the point about alignment.

Academic interviewees were less concerned about relations between government and higher education. Seven of the nine spoke in general terms of the public mission of universities to serve country, society and higher education and to promote economic and social development. A division of labour was evident. Academics from the leading research university took responsibility for serving the whole country. Those from the local university often attached more importance to strengthening the economy of the city and the province.

Higher Education and Public Goods

In discussion of higher education and public good(s), the role of government in funding and regulation readily led interviewees to tag the outcomes of higher education as 'public'. All nine university leaders placed higher education in 'the public service sector'. 'The word "public" ... emphasizes public use or sharing, not only for individuals, but also for the benefit of all people' (SL3). Yet market-like elements like tuition and non-state revenues, and competition, led some to modify this universal publicness. In the hybrid higher education space, interviewees found abstract notions of 'public' and 'private' to be somewhat elusive but they grappled with the problem.

Two of the three government interviewees argued that tuition fees were relatively low, government was still the largest sponsor and fee-charging alone did not make higher education into a private good. Higher education was not focused solely on profit. It was true that government wanted universities to seek funding from diversified sources. One interviewee emphasized the need to step up alumni donations. Matching funds were available. 'If you get 50 million RMB from your alumni, the government will provide you with the same amount of money' (G2). However, diversified funding in itself did not mean higher education had become a private good (G3).

For all three government interviewees, public and private goods were not necessarily zero-sum. The two types of goods could develop together. One suggested that the accumulation of private goods through higher education could lead to public goods. Private goods were 'individuality' while public goods were 'generality' (G2). Another stated that diversified funding was an indication that higher education was developing its social contribution (G3).

Government interviewees identified many contributions to public goods, mostly derived from the education and research functions. 'The talents we educate in higher education, I think they are the public goods, though we'd better not describe people as "goods"' said one official (G3). Cultivating talents had ongoing constructive effects with open potential: 'When they enter society they have their roles, and these positive roles are beneficial for social development.' Research solved problems and made 'our lives more beautiful' (G3). University leaders agreed, and also emphasized knowledge dissemination and transmission, including books and theses, new knowledge via research; and universities' role in passing on the cultural inheritance (NL1). Knowledge-related functions benefitted the whole society, partly because they had practical public spinoffs, such as technological innovations and academic advice to policy-makers.

> Our most important non-profit products are the new discoveries of knowledge and tools of knowledge dissemination, such as curriculum, textbooks, papers. These are completely non-profit things. ... Once produced they are shared. (SL3)

Most academic interviewees saw higher education as a quasi-public good. Though it was not a pure public good, it had a public nature and should insist on that (SA5). Academic interviewees saw charging tuition fees as defensible. Higher education had costs and China's national conditions made it unrealistic to provide free higher education. Further, three interviewees argued that student selection was essential to ensure the right students were enrolled and public resources were not wasted. At the same time, four interviewees mentioned that educating students from disadvantaged social groups was part of the public mission, and seven noted higher education's contribution to social mobility, for example when students from Western China move to more developed cities in the East: 'knowledge changes destiny' (NA6).

Higher Education and Common Goods

The questions about higher education and common goods often evoked similar responses to those about public goods but without funding as a defining element. For two of the government interviewees, common goods were beneficial to all people, defined collectively as 'society':

> Our fundamental direction of China's higher education is to serve the people, serve the society, and make efforts for China's modernisation … no matter who invests or trains talent, the final product serves the society. I think this is a common good. What higher education cultivates is to serve the society, not to nurture the development of a family, an enterprise, or an interest group. (G3)

Another government interviewee saw common good as being about 'core values' including 'equality, unity and dedication … higher education certainly contributes to the formation and optimization of such values'. However, it was necessary to identify the boundary of those included in the common good. 'Core values with Chinese characteristics promoted by Chinese universities might be applicable largely to Chinese people', whereas values related to 'the research spirit and scientific literacy … were applicable to people all over the world.' (G2)

Academic interviewees provided little about common goods additional to what was said about public goods. However, university leaders engaged, though their understandings of common goods varied slightly. Some explored notions of commonness, collective sharing. One university leader saw common goods as the collective property of a community with common interest. Interestingly, this interviewee suggested that both government and market may be ineffective in generating and distributing common goods but the university, as a community of people with common interest, was itself a common good (NL1). Another leader described this institutional commonness in the sense of shared resources, activities and outcomes:

> Higher education itself is a common good. You provide teaching resources, including laboratories, for many students to share in their use, and these students continue to deepen the process of a project. (NL3)

Global Public and Common Goods

Interviewees often saw global public goods and global common goods in similar terms. Global good(s) were understood in terms of values and defined by scope, by a world-level community of interest and/or by global perspective:

> The so-called local public good is related to the country, to the city. … There are also some goods, the so-called global goods, they are for all people. (SL3)

> Higher education … creates and maintains the basic things in human society, and promotes harmony, civilization and progress of mankind as a whole … higher education may not directly impact on these aspects, it creates and improves these things by exerting its functions. (SL2)

> You are cultivating talents who will be internationally-oriented, not only focusing on a region, but having a global perspective and vision, they will enter the international world and then serve the world. (G3)

One government interviewee and three university leaders mentioned China's president Xi Jinping's idea of 'a community of shared future for mankind' (*ren lei ming yun gong tong ti*), which extended beyond the nation or region and was of benefit for all. 'It represents the development of humans. In fact, we must take into account the ecological' (NL3).

Conclusions

The vast majority of interviewees saw government as still at the helm of higher education in China and the market as relatively marginal, as noted also by Lao (2002) and Wang (2007). Higher education tended towards a quasi-public good, as it was fee-charging and selective, but contributed to the local and global public or common good in many ways and embraced human well-being and the quality of life. People agreed that the public nature of higher education should be maintained. Some thought that higher education was better discussed in terms of common rather than public good(s), as it was deeply affected by collective culture as well as government.

These comments are consistent with most of the literature. As many scholars argue, higher education in China is not a pure public good but retains a public nature, serves the public good and produces public goods (Yuan 2009; Su 2009). It is shaped, controlled and largely financed by government. Article 24 of the Higher Education Law of the People's Republic specifies that higher education institutions must synchronize with national and social public interests (Ministry of Education 1998). Given the complex situation in China, including unbalanced development between Eastern and Western regions and the diversified student body, government needs to take into account equity, efficiency, reform, development and stability. These also define the priorities in different stages of system development.

It is true that higher education is a hybrid quasi-public good in that it is partly provided by the private sector, the market logic has a legal presence, and sector development and improvement requires diversified financing, as noted by Mi and Li (2009). In terms of Marginson's (2018: 331) analytical heuristic China's higher education is a combination of Quadrant 2 (social democracy) and Quadrant 3 (state quasi-market). This is typical of many countries. Yet in China's political culture, the public-as-government is ultimately decisive.

The public good (*gong yi xing*) of higher education is not just for individuals but for the overall public. Private goods, benefits confined to individual students or graduates, can grow at the same time as public goods. This finding may eliminate some scholarly concerns that higher education has narrowed its purpose by focusing on enhancement of individual earnings and employability (Lao 2003; Li 2010). Local public goods (*gong yi wu pin*) refer to specific outputs and activities produced on a non-profit basis. Global public goods are more generalized and refer to benefits for people throughout the world, such as knowledge, culture, global awareness and global mobility. This coincides with some Western scholarship (Kaul, Grunberg and Stern 1999).

Higher education's contributions to global public or common good(s) are manifest in talents with global perspectives who serve local, national and world development; research that solves challenging problems and improves human well-being; public services including outreach/engagement activities and policy advice; and international cultural inheritance and innovation. Higher education in China contributes to social mobility, as specified in UNESCO's interpretation of education as a global common good. It also expands tolerance, equity and inclusion. It helps to develop mutual cultural understanding among young people of different countries. These contributions will increase along with the growing power and influence of higher education.

Though higher education in China is largely government-led and regulated, its contributions to people, society and the whole nation receive wide attention. Culturally, higher education is seen as a collective endeavour. Politically, it is common to all people. In this sense, describing it in terms of 'common' good(s) may be more comprehensible than the term 'public'. Moreover, given that higher education in China is neither a pure public good nor a pure private good, describing it as a common good(s) may be more reasonable for that reason.

Common good(s) are defined in terms of a given group/community, socially embedded with a common interest, and require collective participation. Global common good(s) relate to all people worldwide. The Chinese concept of 'a community of shared future for mankind' (*ren lei ming yun gong tong ti*) implies that all humans live on the same planet and they shoulder the same responsibility to make their lives better. In other words, members of global society share a community of interest, underlining the growing interdependence and convergence between countries and regions. Everyone has unshakeable responsibility for making a better world and for the care of the earth, consistent with ideas of intrinsic value and shared participation in the common good Deneulin and Townsend 2007; UNESCO 2015; Zhang 2015).

The concept of 'the global common good' is similar to the Chinese concept of 'a community of shared future for mankind' (*ren lei ming yun gong tong ti*). If higher education is a global common good, universities need to cooperate extensively with an open mind, breaking down the barriers erected by self-interest, and constructing a community with a shared future.

References

Barzel, Y. (1969), 'The Market for a Semipublic Good: The Case of the American Economic Review', *The American Economic Review*, 61 (4): 665–74.

Buchanan, J. M. (1965), 'An Economic Theory of Clubs', *Economica*, 32 (125): 1–14.

Cheng, H. Q. (2006), 'A Discussion on the Responsibility of the Government: A Perspective of Public Good', *Jiangsu gao jiao*, (3), 47–9. In Chinese.

Deneulin, S. and Townsend, N. (2007), 'Public Goods, Global Public Goods and the Common Good', *International Journal of Social Economics*, 34 (1/2): 19–36.

Guo, L. (2005), 'A Public Good or a Private Good? A Theoretic Dilemma and Analysis of Higher Education's Social Positioning', *Guo jia jiao yu xing zheng xue yuan xue bao*, (2): 43–8. In Chinese.

Huang, J. X. and Tang, X. M. (2017), 'From Public Good to Common Good: Start with the Transition of Education Concepts from UNESCO', *Jiao yu fa zhan yan jiu*, (9): 78–84. In Chinese.

Huang, X. H. (2014), 'From Public Good to Public Service—The Change of Disciplinary Research Perspective in the Conceptual Evolution', *Xue xi lun tan*, (12): 44–9. In Chinese.

Kaul, I., Grunberg, I. and Stern, M. (1999), *Global Public Goods: International Cooperation in the 21st Century*, New York: Oxford University Press.

Ke, Y. X. (1999), 'The Contradiction and Coordination Between Industrialisation and the Public Good of Higher Education', *You se jin shu gao jiao yan jiu*, (4): 7–9. In Chinese.

Lao, K. S. (2002), 'Social Transformation and the Reorientation of Education', *Jiao yu yan jiu*, (2): 3–7. In Chinese.

Lao, K. S. (2003), 'Challenges to the Public Good of Higher Education', *Jiao yu yan jiu*, (2): 3–9. In Chinese.

Li, C. (2002), 'The Ownership and Supply Arrangement of Public Goods', *Jing ji ti zhi gai ge*, (4): 41–4. In Chinese.

Li, J. and Guan, L. X. (2009), 'Higher Education Supply: An Analysis Based on the Perspective of Economics', *Hei long jiang gao jiao yan jiu*, (4): 14–17. In Chinese.

Li, W. G. (2010), 'Profit-Seeking of Capital and the Public Good of Education: Discussion on the "Non-profit" Aspects of Private Institutions', *Zhong guo gao jiao yan jiu*, (10): 46–8. In Chinese.

Li, Z. (2009a), 'A Discussion on the Realization of the Public Good in Private Higher Education', *Gao deng jiao yu yan jiu*, 30 (9): 49–54. In Chinese.

Li, Z. J. (2009b), 'The Nature and Logical Implication of Samuelson's Public Goods', *Nanjing shi da xue bao (she hui ke xue ban)*, (5): 45–51. In Chinese.

Locatelli, R. (2016), 'Education as a Public and Common Good: Revisiting the Role of the State in a Context of Growing Marketization', PhD diss., University of Bergamo.

Ma, J. (2012), 'Issues of Public Goods: A Literature Review', *Zhong hua nv zi xue yuan xue bao*, (1): 5–17. In Chinese.

Marginson, S. (2018), 'Public/Private in Higher Education: A Synthesis of Economic and Political Approaches', *Studies in Higher Education*, 43 (2): 322–37.

Marmolo, E. (1999), 'A Constitutional Theory of Public Goods', *Journal of Economic Behavior and Organization*, 38 (1): 27–42.

Mi, H. and Li, X. W. (2009), 'Public Welfare: A Realistic Choice of Private University Development—Concurrently Discussing the Industrial Attributes of Private Higher Education', *Shanxi da xue xue bao (zhe xue she hui ke xue ban)*, 32 (3): 95–100. In Chinese.

Ministry of Education, China (1998), *Higher Education Law of the People's Republic of China*. Available online: http://en.moe.gov.cn/Resources/Laws_and_Policies/201506/t20150626_191386.html [accessed 5 August 2017].

Morrell, K. (2009), 'Governance and the Public Good', *Public Administration*, 87 (3): 538–56.

Ostrom, E. (1990), *Governing the Commons: The Evolution of Institutions for Collective Action*, Cambridge: Cambridge University Press.

Samuelson, P. A. (1954), 'The Pure Theory of Public Expenditure', *The Review of Economics and Statistics*, 36 (4): 387–9.

Shen, M. H. and Xie, H. M. (2009), 'Public Goods Issues and Their Solutions—A Literature Review Public Goods Theory', *Zhejiang da xue xue bao (ren wen she hui ke xue ban)*, 39 (6): 133–44. In Chinese.

Song, Q. and Rao, C. M. (2018), 'Focus on Global Common Good: The New International Research Trend on World Citizenship Education', *Xian dai jiao yu guan li*, (2): 106–11. In Chinese.

Su, L. Q. (2009), 'Public Goods: The Basic Attribute of Higher Education', *Xian dai jiao yu ke xue*, (3): 71–2. In Chinese.

Tian, L. and Liu, N. (2019), 'Rethinking Higher Education in China as a Common Good', *Higher Education*, 77 (4): 623–40.

UNESCO (2015), *Rethinking Education. Towards a Global Common Good?*, Paris: UNESCO. Available online: http://unesdoc.unesco.org/images/0023/002325/232555e.pdf [accessed 28 January 2017].

Wang, H. Y. (2007), '"Private Good", "Public Good" and "Quasi-public Good" —The Evolution of Educational Attributes Under the Interaction of State Concept and Market Logic', *Jiao yu li lun yu shi jian*, 27 (8): 3–7. In Chinese.

Yang, D. G. and Zhang, X. (2000), 'Public Goods and the Industrialisation of Education', *Jiangsu gao jiao*, (5): 3–8. In Chinese.

Yang, M. (2007), 'An Analysis of the Current Situation of China's Educational Products Delivery and Policy Options', *Zhe jiang da xue xue bao (ren wen she hui ke xue ban)*, (6): 99–107. In Chinese.

Yang, R. T. (2009), 'An Analysis of the Provision of Higher Education Based on the Nature of Higher Education Products', *Gao xiao jiao yu guan li*, 3 (3): 21–5. In Chinese.

Yang, X. X. (2004), 'The Dislocation of Government's Educational Function from a Perspective of Public Goods and Industrialisation', *Dang dai jiao yu lun tan*, (4): 12–14. In Chinese.

Yi, L. Y. (2018), 'Some Thoughts on Moral Education Reform in Elementary and Secondary Schools from the Perspective of the Global Common Good', *Jiao yu xue bao*, 14 (1): 45–50. In Chinese.

Yuan, Q. L. (2009), 'On the Public Welfare and Private Good of Higher Education', *Gao deng jiao yu yan jiu*, 30 (8): 43–8. In Chinese.

Zang, X. H. and Qu, C. (2002), 'From Objective Attributes to Constitutional Choice—The Development and Evolution of the Concept of "Public goods"', *Shan dong da xue xue bao (ren wen she hui ke xue ban)*, (2), 37–44. In Chinese.

Zhang, J. W. and Qi, S. Y. (2016), 'Defects of the Concept of Public Goods and its Reconstruction', *Cai zheng yan jiu*, (8): 2–13. In Chinese.

Zhang, P. G. (2015), *The Commons, Welfare and the State*, Guilin: Guangxi Normal University Press. In Chinese.

Zhou, Z. Q. (2005), 'The Extension of the Concept of Public Good and Its Policy Implications', *Jing ji xue dong tai*, (9): 25–8. In Chinese.

17

Public and Common Goods

Key Concepts in Mapping the Contributions of Higher Education

Simon Marginson

Introduction: The Gap in Social Science

Higher education develops persons by providing conditions and resources that facilitate their self-formation (Marginson 2018a). It also shapes their lifeworlds. John Dewey (1927) remarks that ultimately, it is meaningless to separate individuals from the society which sustains them and is sustained by them. We might as well try to separate the single letters of the alphabet from the alphabet itself, he says. Nevertheless, the contributions of higher education to single persons – or at least, its association with graduate salaries and employment rates – are better understood than what it does for the collective.

This is a frontier problem of social science. Universities, colleges and other institutions connect to societies, economies and polities at many points via their functions in teaching, research and service. These connections are local, national and global. What can be summed as the 'social' role of higher education is large and many-sided but it is difficult to define, observe and measure. There is no comprehensive theory of higher education as social formation. Economics has a narrower focus on its effects in economic value, which fail to cover those contributions of higher education to society that do not appear as monetary transactions. This gap in understanding the full contributions of higher education is more than an academic problem. Take the *Review of Post-18 Education and Funding*, the Augur report, released in the UK on 30 May 2019. The report's overall position was that both the social and individual value of higher education were measured by average graduate salaries. It referred to the 'wider value' of higher education once:

> We have used the available data to consider the economic value for students and the economy of different higher educational routes, for different people. However, we are clear that successful outcomes for both students and society are about more than pay. Higher levels of education are associated with wider participation in politics and civic affairs, and better physical and mental health. We also understand the social value of some lower-earning professions such as nursing and social care, and the cultural value of studying the Arts and Humanities. The earnings data enable us to make economically defined value calculations, not value judgements. Assessing this wider value is very difficult but government should continue to work to ensure that wider considerations are taken into account in its policy and funding decisions. (Augur 2019: 87)

Assessing the 'wider value' of higher education 'is very difficult', stated the Augar committee, effectively passing the problem to the British Treasury. However, Treasury was more likely to be influenced by the report's nomination of 'low value courses' on the basis of low salaries, than the report's tentative suggestion that 'government' should sort out the value of social benefits. Because the collective goods produced by higher education are under-recognized in social science, they are likely to be under-recognized in policy and hence are almost certainly underfunded. Further, if students and their families are constantly told that the main (if not the sole) purpose of higher education is individual jobs, earnings and social status, then all else being equal, graduates will be less committed to the common good than they would be if they believed that higher education should and does benefit the whole society.

One way forward is to review existing definitions and measures of the 'social', 'public' or 'common' work of higher education. As no one intellectual and policy tradition is likely to have all the answers, while many traditions have some answers, there are gains to be made from using a broad comparative approach. CGHE is investigating concepts and measures of higher education and 'national and global public goods', in ten countries – China, Japan, South Korea, France, Finland, Poland, UK, United States, Canada and Chile. It is hoped that this research will identify useful national ideas with relevance to other countries. More ambitiously, it is hoped that comparison between the countries will enable the research team to identify contributions of higher education that appear common to all countries, helping to establish generic social benefits in higher education. Data collection in most countries is now complete and some country studies have been prepared (e.g. Chapter 16 of this book, on the case of China, by Tian and Liu), though at the time of writing the comparative work had yet to begin.

This chapter critically discusses frameworks and concepts for mapping the many contributions of higher education. Though the research team is yet to form joint conclusions the discussion here reflects ideas from within the group.[1] The chapter begins with a comprehensive description of higher education outcomes, both individualized and collective. The next section considers 'public goods' and 'common goods' and their relevance to higher education. The final section discusses two domains, central to the contributions of higher education, that vary across the world: the state and civil society.

Individualized and Collective Contributions

Any comprehensive account of the contributions of higher education must touch on six large formative social effects (Marginson 2016; Marginson 2018a, b). First, higher education forms people, or rather it helps people to form themselves. Second, it helps to build relational human society. Third, it provides conditions for economic activity, not just people with diverse occupational skills but with social capital, information and expertise. Fourth, it produces, organizes, disseminates and reproduces formal knowledge. Fifth, it fosters criticism and civil discussion. Sixth, it furthers global cooperation. However, this list is a guide, not an analytical framework. The categories are large and overlapping. They lack precision and while suggestive, they are inaccessible to empirical observation. A more grounded and disaggregated approach is needed.

Figure 17.1 summarizes the many contributions of higher education, using a matrix structure in which the vertical axis spans from individualized to collective benefits (in this chapter the term 'goods' is used) and the horizontal axis spans from the national-local to the global. This generates four cells or categories of the contributions of higher education.

In discussion of the outcomes of higher education, the main focus tends to fall on Cell 1, the individualized national-local goods. The cross-border individualized benefits in Cell 2 are mostly seen as marginal to the national benefits, as internationally mobile students are seen as outside the norm despite the continuing growth of mobility (e.g. in the UK one student in five is an international student: see Chapter 4). The collective benefits of higher education in Cells 3 and 4, which are more difficult to observe and measure, especially at global level, are even less well understood.

Individualized National-Local Goods

Many of the items in Cell 1, the individualized contributions of higher education to students and graduates (Figure 17.2), are open to empirical observation and

INDIVIDUALISED GOODS

1 INDIVIDUALZED NATIONAL
Greater agency freedom
Better social position
Augmented earnings and employment rates
Lifetime health and financial outcomes, and so on

2 INDIVIDUALIZED GLOBAL
Cross-border mobility and employability
Communications facility
Knowledge of diverse languages and cultures
Access to global science

national-local | *global*

3 COLLECTIVE NATIONAL
Ongoing development of professions/occupations
Shared social literacy, equal opportunity
Inputs to government
Stronger regions, cities

4 COLLECTIVE GLOBAL
Universal global science
Diverse knowledge fields
Common zone of free critical inquiry
Systems for exchange, collaboration, mobility

COLLECTIVE GOODS

Figure 17.1 Individualized and collective contributions of higher education.
Source: Author.

- **Augmented earnings associated with education**
- **Augmented employment rates**
- **Stable or improved social position**
- **Greater agency freedom, the capacity for confident autonomous action**
- **Augmented social-relational capabilities – e.g. capacity to communicate, use technology, understand and tolerate cultural difference, trust other people**
- **Capability in dealing with states, markets, institutions and organisations**
- **Augmented political participation**
- **Lifetime health outcomes**
- **Personal financial management**

Figure 17.2 Individualized national-local goods.
Source: Author.

measurement. In *Higher Learning, Greater Good* (2009) Walter McMahon summarizes the then existing research on the pecuniary and non-pecuniary returns to individual graduates, including the contribution of higher education to capabilities in personal financial management, and the health of graduates and their families. The pecuniary returns include the most researched of all of the outcomes of higher education, which is the market value of graduates as human capital, measured by the net rates of return associated with investments in degrees, based on lifetime earnings.

Capability in social relations can be partly assessed on an individualized basis. In *Education at a Glance* the OECD has provided data from its 2012 adult skills survey concerning the association between educational qualifications and such variables as level of skill in using information and communications technologies (ICTs), whether survey respondents feel they have a say in government (sense of political connectedness), and whether they feel that they can trust others. For example, the survey found that of twenty-five- to sixty-four-year-olds with tertiary qualifications, 52 per cent had 'good ICT and problem-solving skills', and only 7 per cent had 'no computer experience' or refused an ICT skill test. However, among those with lower secondary education or below, 7 per cent had good skills and 47 per cent had no experience or refused the test. These patterns held across the twenty-two countries that supplied survey data (OECD 2015: 46–7).

Individualized Global Goods

Individualized global goods (Figure 17.3) are those aspects of student self-formation (Marginson 2018a) associated with cross-border mobility. They include capability in mobility itself; augmented skills, knowledge and earnings;

- **Global employability and augmented earnings**
- **Facility in cross-border communications and cooperation**
- **Knowledge of diverse languages and cultures**
- **Other global competences including understanding, tolerance and negotiation of cultural difference**
- **Access to global science and other knowledges**
- **Greater agency freedom, the capacity for confident autonomous action, in global society**
- **Capacity for cross-border mobility, and negotiation of unfamiliar sites and institutions**

Figure 17.3 Individualized global goods.
Source: Author.

and facility in languages and cultural diversity, which is personally enriching and often also occupationally useful.

Research (e.g. Marginson 2014) suggests that prolonged mobility can quicken personal flexibility in the face of difference and change and heighten confidence, proactivity and reflexive self-determining agency. In *Perspectives on Global Development 2017: International Migration in a Shifting World*, the OECD compares migration among people with, and without, university degrees. For those without degrees the tendency to migrate is correlated to income: as income rises people are more likely to move. Among those with degrees the pattern is different. As income rises, once a modest threshold is reached there is little change in mobility: it is income inelastic. In helping graduates to greater personal agency vis-à-vis mobility, higher education weakens the effects of economic determinism on their imaginings, choices and decisions (OECD 2016: 32).

Collective National-Local Goods

Among the important collective national and local goods created by higher education (Figure 17.4) are the contributions of large comprehensive research universities to building cities and regions, and the contributions of academic faculty to government policy and regulation.

One very important contribution made by higher education is provision of a structured set of opportunities to participate in higher education itself on the basis of norms of social equity. These norms vary by national political culture.

- **Ongoing development of the professions/ occupations as cooperative social activity**
- **Graduate work that constitutes common social benefits (e.g. in health care, education)**
- **Shared social literacy**
- **Nationally-specific knowledges (e.g. in professional fields such as law)**
- **Higher education as an opportunity structure meant to deliver socially equitable outcomes**
- **Academic inputs to government policy and regulation**
- **Economic, social and cultural building of localities, cities, regions, including job creation, modernization, connectedness**

Figure 17.4 Collective national-local goods.
Source: Author.

Notwithstanding that diversity, there are numerous options for measuring equity, such as gender ratios of participation in specific disciplines; and comparative participation or completion on the basis of social or rural/urban background, which can be differentiated also on the basis of discipline or institutional type.

Collective Global Goods

The collective global goods (Figure 17.5) generated in higher education include research and codified knowledge, discussed in Chapter 3. There are extensive data on international research collaboration, including work on common global problems such as climate change. However, the global contribution is larger than such measures suggest. There is a culture of collaboration in almost every research university that fosters bottom-up disciplinary exchanges: joined together, the disciplines constitute not only a vast machine for intellectual production but an expanding global space for free critical thought, which might be termed a 'world mind'. Universities and researchers stimulate and support each other's research and scholarship. In this common zone violations of academic freedom are readily made visible. Repressive national governments can be called to account.

Another important contribution to collective global goods is the facilitation of people mobility. Networked higher education institutions and national administration form a common system that enables ease of movement across borders. This includes formal frameworks such as Erasmus in Europe, the evolving lattice of one-to-one and multilateral cooperative agreements; partnerships and university consortia; localized mobility schemes for students

- **Global knowledge, in diverse fields especially in science [but biases, omissions]**
- **Systems of universal global science, including publishing, certification protocols**
- **Fostering of global cooperation in research including work on common global problems**
- **Common global zone of free critical inquiry, with cross-border disciplinary networks**
- **Systems for international collaboration, exchange, mobility between universities (recognition protocols, Erasmus, and so on)**

Figure 17.5 Collective global goods.
Source: Author.

and faculty; and accreditation and recognition protocols, including interlocking quality assurance. The mobility system enables students and staff to acquire individualized global goods of mobility and facilitates cooperation in research.

This four-way matrix framework is useful because it aims to be comprehensive, because it highlights the under-studied collective contributions and global contributions, and because it helps in identifying possible metrics for development. However, it is merely descriptive. It tends to a miscellany in which, again, the categories overlap and do not form a unitary set with analytical purchase that can be internally differentiated. Nor do these categories, take together, enable a normative calibration. The next section reviews the concepts of 'public goods' and 'common goods' which have been developed to facilitate analysis and policy.

Public and Common Goods

The term 'public' has been used in several ways in relation to higher education. The idea of the 'public sphere' is discussed later under the heading 'Civil Society and the University as Public Sphere'. 'Public good' in the singular normally refers to the broad general welfare or condition of virtue of the public or society as a whole (Mansbridge 1998). It is sometimes equated with the European feudal metaphor of the commons, a shared resource that all can utilize, not subject to scarcity or contaminated by congestion, such as a river or a pasture where animals are grazed. Public good is also associated democratic and often communitarian forms, openness, transparency and popular sovereignty. 'Public goods', the plural form, has two different meanings: the economic definition and the political definition. Both meanings are widely used.

Two Kinds of Public Goods in Higher Education

In the political distinction between public and private, public goods are outcomes produced by institutions owned or controlled by government. A transaction is a public matter when it is of broad concern, affecting persons other than those directly involved, and so must be resolved by the state. Dewey (1927) provides a justification for this use of 'public'. The state/non-state distinction is the most common understanding of the public–private divide in education and other sectors.

In the economic definition, originating in Paul Samuelson (1954) and influential in policy in the English-speaking world, public goods are goods that cannot be produced profitably in a market because they are non-rivalrous and/or non-excludable. Goods are non-excludable when the benefits cannot be confined to single buyers, such as clean air regulation. Goods are non-rivalrous when consumed by any number of people without being depleted, such as a mathematical theorem, which sustains its value as knowledge indefinitely and on a global basis. Private goods are neither non-rivalrous nor non-excludable and may be produced and sold in markets. Public goods and part-public goods require at least some state funding or philanthropic support. There are also variations on Samuelson's definition such as club goods, excludable but non-rivalrous inside the club; and common-pool goods, non-excludable but rivalrous because subject to congestion.

Samuelson's public–private distinction is a means of determining the minimum necessary government funding of higher education in a market economy. This is its primary importance in higher education policy. However, it assumes that all activity should be placed in markets unless there is market failure, suggesting that students should pay the full cost of tuition unless they are so poor as to be unable to take out tuition loans (at which point there is market failure and government steps in). Following the Samuelson logic, government should pay for basic research, which is a natural economic public good, but not teaching, which is normally a private good. Few governments support this position in pure form. One reason is that while Samuelson defines public goods in terms of natural qualities, goods such as education are policy determined, in that treating them as non-rivalrous or non-excludable is a policy decision that shapes their nature. Higher education can generate public goods, private goods, or a mix of the two, as suggested by the term 'quasi-public good' used in China (Chapter 16) – higher education that is competitive, partly selective and fee-charging but subject to government control and shaping, including access policy, and with fees below full cost, rather than operating as a fully developed economic market.

A second problem in Samuelson's formula is that of zero-sum, the idea that if a good is more public it is less private, and vice versa. Under some circumstances the expansion of private goods in higher education is also associated with the growth of public goods, and also vice versa. For example increased access (a collective public good) grows the number of private benefits in graduate labour markets. More graduates receiving private benefits adds to the number of persons with advanced literacy, which also advances collective public goods. This again underlines the mixed public–private character of higher education. Rather trying to settle whether higher education is naturally and holistically public or private, it is better to recognize that it is socially constructed (not natural) and heterogeneous and multiple (not holistic) – enabling focus on the public or private character of each *particular* good associated with it, and the conditions under which it is public or private in character.

In sum, there are two contrary ideas of the public–private distinction, based on the state–non-state divide and the non-market–market divide respectively. Both are useful. Using both public–private definitions together in one framework enables analysis of the different kinds of political economy found in higher education systems (Marginson 2018b). However, neither one of these public–private distinctions, nor both of them taken together, can fully explain the social contributions of higher education.

Common Goods

To state that a good is 'public' says nothing about its content or even whether it is broadly distributed. Public does not necessarily mean goods beneficial for all, or even for any one person. Not all public goods augment the general welfare. For example, when a nation conducts an aggressive war against a neighbouring nation, its military effort is technically a public good in both economic and political senses. Many public goods, in either sense, become captured by powerful social groups; for example, affluent families often dominate selection into elite public research universities.

The concept of 'common goods' addresses these issues. Its application to education has been popularized by UNESCO (Locatelli 2018). Common goods are broadly beneficial goods that contribute to sociable human agency, to shared social welfare and relations of solidarity, inclusion, tolerance, universal freedoms, equality, human rights, individual capability on a democratic basis. Equality of opportunity in education is one example. The Nordic countries, in which equal and solidaristic society is an end in itself, emphasize educational policies designed to secure common goods, including free and universal access to high-quality courses. The British National Health Service is another example of common goods provision. It provides universal care free of charge to all, while prioritizing people who are in greatest need because of serious illness or accident.

Common goods are collective non-market goods, public goods in the economic sense, but not always public goods in the political sense. Because 'common' is defined by the content of the activity, both government and non-government organizations, including voluntary local cooperation (Ostrom 1990), can contribute to common goods. However, 'some kinds of private participation are more defensible than others' (Locatelli 2018: 8); and state funding and regulation ('public') may be needed to ensure commonality (p. 13).

The idea of common goods also emphasizes the political process of participation whereby the community defines what it values, and joint production and democratic distribution.

Some common goods are global common goods. The 'global common good' refers to 'participation of all persons in a diverse and differentiated, yet solidaristic and collaborative, world society' (Deneulin and Townsend 2007: 29). International norms such as climate change accords, the Universal Declaration of Human Rights, and the Sustainable Development Goals, which include commitments on tertiary education, are global common goods. As noted, publicly accessible scientific knowledge is an important global common good fostered in higher education and the incubating chamber of many other common goods, global and national-local.

The State and Civil Society

Every concept that we used highlights some parts of reality and occludes other parts. The notion of 'public' in both senses is primarily categorical, technical and a matter of empirical observation: goods are or are not state-based and are or are not incapable of market production. In contrast the notion of 'common' is primarily relational not categorical and to be identified requires not just empirical observation but normative judgement. It also foregrounds agency – in higher education, the agency of the stakeholders who determine what is the common good. Unlike 'public' it highlights participatory processes and community.

Both 'common' and 'public' can be used when investigating the contributions of higher education, though arguably, the concept of 'common goods' enables richer insights into the social contribution of the sector (Marginson 2016). Economists have reached no consensus on the application of 'public'. Calculations of the public goods generated by higher education are assumption dependant. Social democrats value the public contribution more highly than neoliberals.

Nevertheless, neither term in itself is sufficient as a starting point for a universal theory of higher education. This is not only because each term can glimpse only part of the contributions of higher education but also because of worldwide variation in political cultures and especially in the role of the state in higher education. Though this variation especially affects usages of 'public' as state, both terms are rooted in particular political traditions not universal to higher education everywhere.

'Common good' is grounded in Western European participatory and communitarian ideas about democracy, which have spread also to other parts of the world. Dewey's (1927) idea of a participatory democratic 'public' resonates also with the common good idea (see also Chapter 15 on South Africa). Samuelson's 'public goods' also have their origin in Western liberalism. They are founded in a zero-sum relation between public and private goods, privileging the market economy, that derives from the Anglo-American liberal tradition. Liberalism imagines a division of powers between state, market economy and civil society; and within the state between executive, legislature and judiciary. Here freedom lies in minimizing the scope for government intervention. But the limited liberal state imaginary does not always fit the realities of modern Western higher education, which was primarily built in deliberate fashion by top-down state intervention rather than formed spontaneously by bottom-up markets – though it is true that once established, the modern systems became accessible to bottom-up social demand (Chapter 1).

The limited liberal state imaginary is still less appropriate to societies grounded in, say, the Chinese civilizational tradition of the comprehensive state. In this tradition, society is ordered on the basis of devolution not division of powers, and the state retains the option of intervening in any sector. In China everything is always 'public' in the sense of the state, and it is also non-market, for no market can exercise the political prerogatives of the state. At the same time, the contemporary Chinese state makes extensive use of markets as a tool of government.

In Chapter 16, Lin Tian and Niancai Liu conclude that the term 'common good' is more appropriate to higher education in China than the term 'public good'. Common good fits better with China's collective orientation as a society including the long tradition of self-managing local communities. Still, naming 'higher education for the common good' in China does not make the meaning of 'common good' the same as in, say, Scandinavia, or Northern Italy, especially when moving from the local to the macro scale.

Civil Society and the University as Public Sphere

The relation between higher education and civil society is also subject to national-cultural variation. In the US higher education is understood primarily as part of the fecund civil society not the state. In the French Republican tradition, in which the state provides for the civil order, the university is an autonomous branch of state. In Chinese tradition, where civil society has a lesser role and is more open to political regulation, higher education is unambiguously part of the state – though university leaders manage their institutions with autonomy, professors collaborate freely abroad and disciplinary networks regulate intellectual life as they do in the United States or France.

These differences have implications for higher education as a zone of critical civic and public discussion. In positioning higher education, Calhoun (1992) invokes Habermas's (1989) idea of the 'public sphere' in seventeenth-century London. The 'public sphere' was the networked discussion in salons and coffee houses and newspapers that sat between civil society and the state and provided critical reflexivity for the government of the day. Calhoun finds that universities operating in analogous fashion, as semi-independent adjuncts of government, providing constructive criticism and strategic options, and expert information that helps state and public to reach considered opinions. Pusser (2006) models the university as a zone of reasoned argument and contending values, noting that US higher education has been a medium for successive political and sociocultural transformations, such as the 1960s civil rights movement. While not all American or Western universities operate consistently in this manner, the role of public sphere, including scope to foster critical discussion in civil society, is within their reach.

Michael Ignatieff suggests that within a liberal division of powers the university is not just a habitual critic of society and government but a counter to majoritarian populism in the state:

> Academy freedom and university autonomy are under attack these days as the privileges of a professorial elite, but they should be understood as 'counter-majoritarian institutions' – like a free press and an independent judiciary – an essential counter-balance to majority rule. Across Europe, counter-majoritarian institutions are under pressure from populist movements and parties seeking to mobilise 'the people' against the press, the courts – and universities too. (Ignatieff 2018)

In China the state is a comprehensive state and the liberal division of powers does not apply, but the university shares with its Western counterparts the role of constructive critic on the edge of government – as well as (like the Western university) serving the state in the positive sense. The difference is that in China leading universities express their free and active criticism of policy within the state rather than outside. Frank discussion inside the universities does not meld with open criticism in civil society as in the West. In China from time to time universities have been incubators of social and political transformations. Peking University was the starting point for most of the twentieth-century political movements, from May the Fourth in 1921 to Tiananmen in 1989 (Hayhoe and Zha 2011). However, the legitimacy of this role is never clearly established and as happened in 1989 the party-state habitually moves to constrain the larger political potential of the universities when the stability of its rule is in question.

Nevertheless, in China as elsewhere, all else being equal the spread of participation in higher education fosters the joint capabilities of the population on an ever-growing scale, expanding the potential for civil association. This in turn has implications for the relation between higher education and the state. A population in which highly developed skills of sociability and dealing with institutions are more widely disseminated is better placed to foster the transparency and democratization of the state itself. In this, as in so many other ways, higher education everywhere can advance the common good.

Note

1 The research team is Simon Marginson, Vincent Carpentier, Lili Yang and Tom Brotherhood in the UK; Niancai Liu and Lin Tian in China; Futao Huang and Kiyomi Horiuchi in Japan; Krystian Szadkowski in Poland and Carolina Guzmán Valenzuela in Chile. Aline Courtois in relation to France and the UK and Olga Mun in South Korea and Finland have contributed to the field work. The case studies in Poland and Chile were self-funded and run collaboratively in parallel with the CGHE research rather than being managed within the core project.

References

Augur, P. (2019), *Post-18 Review of Education and Funding: Independent Panel Report*, Department of Education, United Kingdom. https://www.gov.uk/government/publications/post-18-review-of-education-and-funding-independent-panel-report

Calhoun, C. (1992), 'Introduction', in C. Calhoun (ed.), *Habermas and the Public Sphere*, 1–48, Cambridge, MA: The MIT Press.

Deneulin, S. and Townsend, N. (2007), 'Public Goods, Global Public Goods and the Common Good', *International Journal of Social Economics*, 34 (1–2): 19–36.

Dewey, J. (1927), *The Public and Its Problems*, New York, NY: H. Holt.

Habermas, J. (1989), *The Structural Transformation of the Public Sphere* (T. Burger, Trans.), Cambridge, MA: The MIT Press.

Hayhoe, R. and Zha, Q. (2011), 'Peking University – Icon of Cultural Leadership', in R. Hayhoe, J. Li, J. Lin and Q. Zha (eds), *Portraits of 21st Century Chinese Universities*, 95–130, Hong Kong: Springer/CERC, The University of Hong Kong.

Ignatieff, M. (2018), *Academic Freedom and the Future of Europe*. CGHE Working Paper 40, July. London: ESRC/HEFCE Centre for Global Higher Education. https://www.researchcghe.org/publications/working-paper/academic-freedom-and-the-future-of-europe/

Locatelli, R. (2018), 'Education as a Public and Common Good: Reframing the Governance of Education in a Changing Context', UNECSO *Education Research and Foresight Working Papers*, 22, February. http://unesdoc.unesco.org/images/0026/002616/261614E.pdf

Mansbridge, J. (1998), 'On the Contested Nature of the Public Good', in W. Powell and E. Clemens (eds), *Private Action and the Public Good*, 3–19, New Haven: Yale University Press.

Marginson, S. (2014), 'Student Self-Formation in International Education', *Journal of Studies in International Education*, 18 (1): 6–22.

Marginson, S. (2016), *Higher Education and the Common Good*, Melbourne: Melbourne University Publishing.

Marginson, S. (2018a), *Higher Education as Self-Formation*, Inaugural Professorial Lecture at the UCL Institute of Education. https://www.ucl-ioe-press.com/books/higher-education-and-lifelong-learning/higher-education-as-a-process-of-self-formation/

Marginson, S. (2018b), 'Private/Public in Higher Education: A Synthesis of Economic and Political Approaches', *Studies in Higher Education*, 43 (2): 322–37.

McMahon, W. (2009), *Higher Learning Greater Good*, Baltimore, MD: The Johns Hopkins University Press.

Organization for Economic Cooperation and Development, OECD. (2015), *Education at a Glance, 2015*, Paris: OECD.

Organization for Economic Cooperation and Development (OECD) (2016), *Perspectives on Global Development 2017: International Migration in a Shifting World*. http://www.keepeek.com/Digital-Asset-Management/oecd/development/perspectives-on-global-development-2017_persp_glob_dev-2017-en#page1

Ostrom, E. (1990), *Governing the Commons: The Evolution of Institutions for Collective Action*, Cambridge: Cambridge University Press.

Pusser, B. (2006), 'Reconsidering Higher Education and the Public Good', in W. Tierney (ed.), *Governance and the Public Good*, 11–28, Albany, NY: SUNY Press.

Samuelson, P. (1954), 'The Pure Theory of Public Expenditure', *Review of Economics and Statistics*, 36 (4): 387–9.

Index